D1264995

THE DEEP END OF
FLAVOR

THE DEEP END OF
FLAVOR

RECIPES AND STORIES FROM
NEW ORLEANS' PREMIER SEAFOOD CHEF

TENNEY FLYNN

WITH *SUSAN PUCKETT*

PHOTOGRAPHS BY DANNY LEE

GIBBS SMITH
TO ENRICH AND INSPIRE HUMANKIND

To the memory of my father, Tom Flynn,
and to all the unique and wonderful people in his
restaurant who shaped my cooking
and gave me a love for the lifestyle in this business.

To Mary Johnston, who talked me into going
out on a limb to open a seafood restaurant.

And to Gary Wollerman, my longtime
business partner, without whom
there would be no GW Fins, and hence no book.

First Edition
23 22 21 20 19 . . . 5 4 3 2 1

Text © 2019 Tenney Flynn
Photographs © 2019 Danny Lee

Published by
Gibbs Smith
P.O. Box 667
Layton, Utah 84041

1.800.835.4993 orders
www.gibbs-smith.com

Front Cover designed by Sky Hatter
Designed by Sheryl Dickert
Printed and bound in China

Gibbs Smith books are printed on either recycled, 100% post-consumer waste, FSC-certified papers or on paper produced from sustainable PEFC-certified forest/controlled wood source. Learn more at www.pefc.org.

Library of Congress Cataloging-in-Publication Data

Names: Flynn, Tenney, 1954- author. | Puckett, Susan, 1956-, author.
Title: Deep end of flavor : recipes and stories from New Orleans' premier seafood chef / Tenney Flynn with Susan Puckett.
Description: First edition. | Layton, Utah : Gibbs Smith, [2019] | Includes index.
Identifiers: LCCN 2018032231 | ISBN 9781423651000 (hardcover)
Subjects: LCSH: Seafood. | Cooking, American--Louisiana style. | LCGFT: Cookbooks.
Classification: LCC TX747 .F555 2019 | DDC 641.6/9209763--dc23
LC record available at https://lccn.loc.gov/2018032231

Tenney Flynn talked trash (fish) early on. He championed fresh Gulf seafood when most chefs crushed on frozen Atlantic salmon. Now, it's time to learn how smoked sizzling oysters came to be, how to do redfish on the half shell right, and how GW Fins helped lead the modern seafood revolution.

John T. Edge, author of The Potlikker Papers: A Food History of the Modern South

Tenney Flynn is the grand master of Gulf Coast seafood. This book, full of his delicious recipes and deep sea wisdom, can lead you to mastery as well.

Lolis Eric Elie, story editor of HBO's "Treme" and author of Treme: Stories and Recipes from the Heart of New Orleans

After more than 20 years behind a French Quarter stove, Tenney Flynn has not only absorbed the culinary history of New Orleans, he's taught us all a thing or two with his dazzling takes on the region's freshest fish and shellfish. From the day it opened, GW Fins has been one of my absolute favorite New Orleans "go-to" spots. The signature hot biscuits are perfection, the wine list is superb, and I'd walk a mile for the ethereal lobster dumplings alone. This book is an extension of the history and extraordinary hospitality of the restaurant and is a must for anyone who loves seafood even half as much as Tenney does.

Julia Reed, author of Julia Reed's South *and* Julia Reed's New Orleans
Contributing editor, Garden & Gun

I love that Chef Tenney shares so much how-to and comprehensive info on seafood selection. Recipes are clear and concise, photos excellent.

Frank Brigtsen, James Beard Award-winning chefowner of Brigtsen's in New Orleans

Technique, style, and finesse without losing touch of where Tenney's feet are on the ground! The flavor of NOLA and the exquisite photography of the city, sea, and landscape as well as the fine combination of dishes put this book as one of my favorites.

David Burke, New York chef/restaurateur, James Beard Foundation Who's Who of Food and Beverage in America

Tenney Flynn's really good with handling some stuff I don't trust anybody to cook. He's the best cook I know.

Mac Rebennack, aka Dr. John, Singer and songwriter

My friend, Tenney Flynn, has been a leading force in the seafood industry here in New Orleans for decades. In the last few years he has added deep sea diving to his already impressive skill set and he is using those skills to highlight the importance of including sustainable, underutilized, and invasive species on our menus. I always turn to Tenney when I have a seafood related question.

Susan Spicer, James Beard Award-winning chef/owner of Bayona and other New Orleans restaurants

Tenney Flynn's *The Deep End of Flavor* goes far beyond the classics that make New Orleans America's premier seafood city. A clean, modern, comprehensive and delicious approach to all that is seafood!

Paul Kahan, James Beard Award-winning Chicago chef/restaurateur, author of Cheers to the Publican: Repast and Present

CONTENTS

INTRODUCTION

WHERE I COOK

My restaurant, GW Fins, is sixty feet off Bourbon Street in New Orleans, across from Arnaud's and around the corner from Galatoire's—two dining institutions that are each about one hundred years old. I live seven blocks away in a quiet corner of the lower French Quarter, in a building that was once a livery stable. Behind the big wrought iron gate is a courtyard lush with banana trees and other tropical vegetation, about twenty condo units, and a rooftop garden where I can putter with the distant sounds of steamboat whistles and Dixieland jazz in the background. Fortunately, the calliope with its awful music selection doesn't crank up until after I leave for work.

Living so close to the water, I think it's cool to see those ships high above the riverfront as I walk or ride my bike to work. Along Royal Street, with its art galleries and antique stores, and through the section of Bourbon Street where day-shift strippers hang out of sleazy clubs beckoning passersby, I soak in the surroundings as if it's all new to me. It never gets old.

And the smell . . . the *smells*. No matter where you're standing in the Quarter, you're never far from the big river, which you can feel even if you don't see it. It adds more moisture to the omnipresent humidity. When the wind is right, you can smell coffee roasting in the Marigny, or bacon frying or crawfish boiling or aftershave or burnt toast as you're walking past kitchens and living rooms right on the sidewalk. All of the funky, earthy smells bloom in the steamy summer air.

Everything about this place—the history, the climate, the quirky characters, the decadence, the endless *joie de vivre*—impacts the way I cook and think about food. Mostly what it boils down to, though, is the seafood.

Seafood is my favorite thing in the world to cook, and to eat. As a chef for more than two decades in the most seafood-centric city in the country, I'm lucky enough to get to do that practically every day.

Seafood is the backbone of our cuisine—in restaurants, at home, and in big neighborhood gatherings centered around newspaper-covered picnic tables piled high with oysters ready for shucking or gas-fired pots full of boiled crawfish or fat blue crabs redolent of sea and spice. Fishing is a hugely popular pastime here, and even those who don't fish usually have friends and neighbors who share.

New Orleans' first public fish market dates back to 1790. The 1930s song "Hold Tight Hold Tight (Want Some Seafood Mama)" by the New Orleans jazzman Sidney Bechet has layered meanings, but the reference is because seafood so permeates the culture. Pompano en Papillote, Speckled Trout Amandine, and Oysters Rockefeller all hark to bygone times in a city big on ancestor worship. Many of the places that made those dishes famous closed decades ago, yet their merits are still debated relentlessly by the locals today.

I think all chefs here, whether locally born or transplants like myself, are influenced by the cooking culture that is such a vital part of New Orleans history. There are a lot of great fish dishes that originated in town and a couple of notable places that mostly tout seafood, but no one does it to the extent we do. We offer ten to fourteen fish varieties daily. With hundreds of diners a night, we are busy enough to buy a lot. We butcher our fillets and steaks on a custom-chilled cutting table from whole fish hauled into the nearby docks or sourced from oceans around the world.

For almost as long as we've been open, GW Fins has been the featured restaurant on the locally produced *Big Fish* show. For each episode, I demonstrate a dish starring the featured catch after the fishing segment. I have been fortunate to fish with expert captains and friends on C. T. Williams' boats offshore and in the marsh. Fishing boat captains often direct out-of-town customers to our restaurant with their day's catch. Several times a week guests bring fish they just caught to Fins, and we cook them in a variety of ways and serve them family style. The usual catch is marsh fish —speckled trout, redfish, sheepshead, and drum with the occasional flounder or channel mullet. We typically fry, sauté, grill, and blacken their fish, which in many cases is the absolutely freshest and best seafood they have ever tasted.

HOW I GOT HERE

I grew up in Stone Mountain, Georgia, a little town outside Atlanta that's now a suburb. In the 1960s and 1970s, my father owned a large family-style Southern restaurant there, and I spent a good part of my childhood in its kitchen learning about food from the African-American staff. I internalized the beauty of simple preparation with our fried chicken—we were known for it, and it had only a very few ingredients. The trick was the technique and that came from thousands of repetitions.

I liked the kitchen better than the dining room, which had its own cast of wonderful characters. I was assigned to the service bar when I was sixteen and pretty much thrown in with bad companions. It was also my first exposure to professional musicians in the lounge band. My dad was just as likely to hang out with a police captain as a professional gambler. He had a well-developed promotional bent and had fun with it. In the event of a death in the family of a customer, the goal was to arrive with food before the preacher got there.

After high school, I followed a girl to Boston University and did a couple of semesters there, flunked out, then boarded a Greyhound bus for Arizona with no clue of plans more than a week away. I bounced around aimlessly for the next few years, and finally settled down working at a bar making hot dogs. This was the start of eight years of bar and nightclub work. My lifestyle finally got the best of me and I sobered up, closed the rock club I was running at the time, and looked for a new opportunity.

I applied to the Culinary Institute of America in Hyde Park, New York, and within that structured environment, I applied myself and thrived. I have never looked back.

While there, I landed an internship at the Fish Market at Lenox back in Atlanta. The restaurant was owned by Pano Karatassos of the highly regarded Buckhead Life Restaurant Group, who had built a reputation for offering the widest selection of fresh fish in the Southeast. I was exposed to all kinds of amazing species of seafood from all over the world that I had never seen up close, and I became obsessed with learning everything I could about them and their preparation from the chefs there.

After graduating from the CIA, I came back to Buckhead Life's flagship French-continental restaurant, Pano's and Paul's, and worked my way up to daytime sous chef at the Fish Market, then to executive chef at Chops, a high-end steakhouse also within that restaurant group. I held that post for three years until 1992, when I moved to New Orleans to become director of culinary operations for Ruth's Chris Steak House. The eccentric vibe of the city quickly won me over. Here there is a real celebration of flavor and specific dishes that is totally removed from anything other than enjoyment. I love the unrushed, almost European way we eat—planning the next meal in the middle of the current one.

Even though Ruth's had no traditional Cajun-Creole dishes on the menu, by eating out I came to appreciate the city's best culinary traditions—both in restaurants and in the homes of friends. But much as I loved the muffulettas at Giorlando's—and all the food at Gabrielle, Brigtsen's, Bayona, and Uglesich's—it was those "alive five minutes ago" seafood flavors that captivated me most. So when Gary Wollerman, whom I'd gotten to know while he was chief operating officer of Ruth's Chris Corporate, and I started talking about opening our own restaurant, we decided that it would be a fish house on a classic steakhouse frame.

We opened GW Fins in 2001 (Gary is the "GW") in a historic building that had been the old warehouse for the D.H. Holmes department store. Gary and I didn't take a day off for six months. The four-bean review in the *Times-Picayune* by critic Brett Anderson that first summer was very welcome. We continued building strong relationships with local fishermen who knew these waters well. Gary and I also opened a barbecue joint, Zydeque, down the street from Fins.

In August of 2005, Hurricane Katrina hit. I took twelve feet of water into my house in the Lakeview community. But GW Fins suffered almost no damage. We had no employees, though, and didn't reopen until almost Thanksgiving. In the meantime, we refitted the smoker at Zydeque to burn propane, and with a skeleton staff we continued to serve barbecued pork sandwiches, dark gumbo with potato salad, skillet cornbread, and freshly baked mini pecan pies on paper plates to customers who'd been living on MREs for days on end.

After months of living in a trailer, I moved to a tiny apartment on Bourbon Street in the French Quarter. We sold the barbecue restaurant to concentrate on Fins. Fortunately, our new sous chef, who had arrived only a month before the hurricane, came back after the waters receded. Mike Nelson quickly proved his talent and has risen the ranks to executive chef, and is now a transplanted New Orleanian with a wife and two kids. He has fully embraced the "nose-to-tail" philosophy as applied to seafood cookery and has earned a national reputation for his state-of-the-art fish butchery techniques and dishes using fish parts often discarded for trash. I got more serious about incorporating overlooked and underused species from the Gulf on our menus.

Scuba diving was a gateway to that end.

A DEEPER DIVE

As a kid in the 60s, I watched as much TV (on three channels) as I was allowed to. One of the shows I never missed was *Sea Hunt* with Lloyd Bridges who played a scuba diver. My gear never progressed past a mask and fins in the local pool until the summer of 2011. That's when, at age fifty-five, I was asked to cook for a lionfish rodeo in Boynton Beach, Florida, and got my first exposure to the problem these predatory species cause.

Lionfish are actually native to the Pacific. They were introduced to the Gulf by an accidental release, either by pet owners or an aquarium, depending on what story you prefer. They eat six fish for breakfast and six fish for dinner, and with bodies covered in fourteen venomous spines, nothing eats them. They are good at depths we can't go and are fine with low-salinity water. The only thing keeping them out of our estuary is the temperature. They can't take anything under fifty degrees. So far.

Traps are being tested, but right now the only way to get them is by divers hand-spearing them. Local diving communities on the Gulf host "rodeos" where divers, anglers, and commercial harvesters compete in tournaments designed to raise awareness of the problem while paring down the predators. There are butchering and cooking demos and booths that sell lionfish-themed stuff.

Everyone loves free food, especially if fresh fish are involved. This is where I came in. I made lionfish ceviche and batter-fried lionfish soft tacos, and they were delicious. I wanted to explore more ways to cook with this versatile fish. But what I really wanted to do was put on a wetsuit and catch them myself.

I started with hogfish in Florida. They are curious and pretty cooperative as far as lining up a shot. My friend was instructing me underwater via pantomime in gun operation, but neglected recoil training. I learned this immediately on my first bent-elbow shot that knocked my diving regulator right out of my mouth. Got the fish, though.

Scuba diving and spearfishing have made me more aware of the conservation issues surrounding the harvesting of seafood and enhanced my appreciation of the diversity and beauty of the underwater world. I am convinced these experiences have also made me—and our entire staff—better chefs. We've gotten more serious about using all our catch, not just the fillets.

The menu at Fins is never set in stone. There's pompano, bluefin tuna, and swordfish on a full moon; flounder when a cold front blows through; stone crab claws when we're lucky. We print it daily in-house and sometimes supply issues are maddening. We literally don't know what will be on the finished menu until four in the afternoon.

The more you get to know and understand the abundance our oceans and rivers have to offer, the easier it is to plan a great dinner on the spot based on whatever looks good in the market seafood case, wherever that might be.

HOW TO USE THIS BOOK

Fish and other seafoods are, hands down, the quickest protein to prepare. A delicious dish can be minutes away. And there are other points in their favor: the sheer variety of choices to sample, the fact that this is the last wild food many people eat, that we support our coastal fishing community, and that fish is a healthy choice. As a chef, it's still all about the flavors.

I wrote this book as a resource for cooks who'd like to eat more fish at home, but need help figuring out what to do with any fish that's available to them, wherever they live and whatever their skill level. The New Orleans flavors I am surrounded with daily figure prominently into my cooking. Gulf species are naturally my focus, and I will introduce you to the ones that excite me the most—many that are widely available and others worth seeking out. I give alternatives in every recipe where applicable so that you can adapt with what's available to you.

I have organized the first eight recipe chapters according to my favorite techniques with seafood that, once mastered, can be applied to myriad recipes beyond this book. In the last three chapters, you'll find recipes for my favorite sauces and side dishes to pair with the fish dishes, as well as suggestions for drinks and desserts to round out your seafood feast.

At Fins, we pride ourselves on our award-winning wine program. Our staff is knowledgeable and passionate about making thoughtful recommendations from our extensive selection to complement every order, and I've turned to their expertise to help you find the perfect wine match for every recipe in this book that calls for one.

My hope is that once you understand the fish and the technique, you'll discover that cooking them can be as easy as frying an egg and perhaps the most sublime thing you'll ever put in your mouth.

A FISH AND
SEAFOOD
PRIMER

AN OCEAN OF CHOICES

The world of fish and seafood is vast, and varies greatly from one region to the next—and for that matter, one market to the next. In this cookbook, I focus on the types of fish I enjoy working with the most and give you some idea of the interchangeability of species in any given recipe. I can't emphasize enough the need for flexibility in menu planning

before shopping. If you catch the fish yourself or get a donation from a fishing neighbor (which happens a lot in New Orleans), you have a hard and fast supply, but if you're relying on the seafood selection of your local market, not so much. This is why I advise, above all else, to buy from a fishmonger you trust, learn how to use your senses to spot the best fish in the case, and look for the country of origin label. When in doubt, demand American.

THINK SUSTAINABLE, BUY DOMESTIC

I buy fish. I sell fish. I catch fish myself whenever I can, and I eat fish practically every day.

And I want to do my part to make sure that there will always be plenty of them. The health of the ocean mirrors the health of the planet, and there are so many huge man-made factors that can disrupt this fragile ecosystem: oil spills, coastal erosion, the fertilizer runoff flowing down the Mississippi that causes the dead zone in the Gulf. Add to that hurricanes, red tides, and invasive

species like the lionfish that eat every fish in sight, with no local predators.

I don't pretend to understand the complexity of a marine ecosystem with thousands of moving parts. But from the perspective of someone who deals with fresh fish daily, I believe that, for the most part, the fisheries in the US are managed well.

That's why I was excited to be asked to chair the Chef Council for the Audubon Nature Institute's Gulf United for Lasting Fisheries (G.U.L.F.) program, which works to ensure seafood sustainability in the Gulf of Mexico. A big part of its mission is also to support the livelihoods of those in south Louisiana communities who practice sustainable fishing methods.

The Audubon Nature Institute works with the National Oceanic and Atmospheric Administration in overseeing the stewardship of the nation's ocean resources and their habitat, ensuring that the only seafood harvested is that which can be replaced. To that end, GW Fins serves only seafood that is deemed acceptable by NOAA's annual quota, determined by science-based catch limits.

At Fins, we rely on boat captains and licensed wholesale fishermen we know by name, as well as purveyors who stay attuned to the comings and goings of the fishing fleets. Seafood from outside the region that has to be shipped requires a higher level of trust, since rejecting that product is more complicated than just turning a local truck around. We look to a few people we've been dealing with for many years to provide scallops, John Dory, Dover sole, and occasional exotics from far away.

It is hard to find anyone, fisherperson or no, who is happy with regulations. Yet I've gone on dives in Honduras, the British Virgin Islands, and Guam—all places with no regulations and, as a consequence, reefs with no fish. I would never want that to happen here.

Often, the best and tastiest choices are the most underutilized and unknown. We take great pride in promoting these species by their real names and not market terms—sheepshead and lionfish, for instance—in the hopes of encouraging folks to get out of their comfort zones and try something other than the factory-farmed tilapia and salmon they're used to.

Some fish populations need to be pared down, like the lionfish, and one way we can do that is with our knives and forks. Yes, you can eat fish to save fish if you choose the right kinds!

KNOW YOUR WATERS

The fish in your local fish market case may come from a variety of places. The vast majority will probably be from salt water—either caught wild by numerous methods in the ocean or farmed in ocean pens. If you're within shipping distance of an estuary (a transition zone between fresh and salt water, with somewhat salty or brackish water), your market may receive fish from there. Estuaries are the wild fish nurseries of the world, providing a rich breeding ground for many species.

Freshwater fish are more readily accessible in many parts of the country than are saltwater ones. In Louisiana, the line is a little blurred because the waters

from the Mississippi River and Lake Pontchartrain mix in the marshes to create one of the largest estuaries in the world, and that is the reason sportfishing here is unparalleled.

As you eat more varieties, I hope you will learn to appreciate different flavors that are determined not only by size and species, but also by water temperature, sex, diet, and season.

FINFISH

When I say finfish, I'm talking about what everyone commonly knows as fish—they have fins, first of all. And most of them have scales, live in water, and extract oxygen through their gills.

This excludes shellfish, crustaceans, mollusks, and cephalopods. To me, there is little difference between a "flatfish" like a flounder (even though I think the moving-eye thing is so creepy) and a "roundfish" like a salmon. The skeletal structure is pretty much the same, and I fillet them the same way.

FAT CONTENT

Generally speaking, in regard to fat content, fish are classified as lean, medium-fat, and fat. But even those broad classifications move around a bit depending on size, season, and diet. Unfortunately, there is no USDA grading system and, other than the size of the fish, you have to cook it to tell absolutely. The general rule is always to cook leaner fish less than fat ones, as they are much less forgiving. Also, some of the fish in the medium category can be cooked like lean fish, but probably not vice versa.

LEAN FISH These are typically good quickly sautéed or fried. They are harder to grill successfully, but many of the smaller ones can be roasted whole. A lot of the recipes here pair these with richer sauces and butter. A list of the ones we cook regularly include drum, halibut, speckled trout, triggerfish, lionfish, flounder, catfish, all the varieties of snapper, jolthead porgy, spadefish, and yellowfin tuna. Bar jack, amberjack, African pompano, and certainly wahoo are also in this category because they are so easy to overcook. Yellowedge and scamp groupers belong here.

WILD VERSUS FARM-RAISED

All wild-caught seafood isn't good, and all farmed seafood isn't bad. At Fins, seventy percent of our menu selections are caught wild from the Gulf of Mexico, and the remaining thirty percent is made up of scallops, halibut, Maine lobster, and farmed Atlantic salmon usually from Scotland or Ireland or sometimes Canada. We also occasionally put New Zealand Ora Kings on our menu.

Ocean farming is here to stay, like it or not. It can be done responsibly and cleanly, but it will seldom produce a fish that has the flavor of a wild fish. In the case of salmon, the debate is similar to the relative merits of grass-fed versus feedlot-fattened beef. I've eaten more prime feedlot beef than just about anybody I know, having spent ten years in the steakhouse business, and plenty of grass-fed as well. They are certainly different—feedlot beef being fatter and juicier than grass-fed. The same is true with good farmed salmon.

Yes, wild flavors can be better and are certainly different, and if I lived in the Pacific Northwest or Alaska, I would source local fish over a farmed Atlantic one. But in my experience, most of the wild Alaskan salmon I see in the East Coast or southern fish markets is doubled in price, but not doubled in flavor. The difference may not be worth the cost.

MEDIUM-FAT FISH This category is more flexible. Tripletail is great on the grill, but also good sautéed—as are black, Warsaw, and gag groupers, mahi mahi, and large redfish. Mangrove snapper can slide into this one if they're big. These fish can be bronzed or blackened.

FAT FISH The fish in this category are the most full-flavored and are my favorite. If I could pick only one fish it would probably be a juicy, fat pompano. Luckily I don't have to. Varieties to look for include cobia, most salmons (particularly the big, farmed ones readily available in markets in the eastern part of the country), Spanish mackerel, bluefin tuna, Chilean sea bass, Alaskan sablefish, escolar, bonito, mullet, bluefish, and most swordfish. All these fish are rich and benefit from acidic sauces and garnishes.

In every entrée recipe where applicable, I will give you a handful of suggested options to further guide you.

SHAPE AND FORM

At the market, fish are sold butchered and unbutchered, in various forms. Here is a quick glossary.

WHOLE OR ROUND—fish is completely intact, just as it came out of the water.

DRAWN— fish is gutted of entrails, but with skin, bones, and head intact.

DRESSED—fish is gutted with scales, head, and tail removed.

PAN-DRESSED—fish is gutted, with scales, head, and fins removed, with tail trimmed to fit a pan.

STEAKS—slices of fish, usually from one that's been drawn, perpendicular through the backbone.

FILLETS—skinless, boneless fish, usually the whole side.

BUTTERFLIED, BOOK-FILLETED, OR SPLIT—both sides of the fish are left joined together at the backbone when filleted, usually done for a small fish such as a rainbow trout.

HOW TO FILLET A WHOLE FISH

If you're lucky enough to come into possession of a quantity of whole fish, you may find yourself faced with the prospect of doing your own butchering.

Don't be afraid, and don't be too hard on yourself if your first attempt looks like you've filleted with a hammer. Practice makes perfect. You will need:

- a very sharp boning knife

- a cutting board

- two iced containers

- a pair of fish tweezers or needle-nose pliers for removing pin bones.

THE BEST FILLETING TECHNIQUE

- If you're right-handed, place the whole fish on the cutting board with the head to the right and make a deep slice just behind the gill plate. The knife will stop when it hits the backbone.

- Turn the knife completely parallel to the fish and, using only one inch of the tip, cut a slit just on top of the fins, the length of the fish from head to tail.

- Now open the slit you cut with your left thumb and again keeping the blade parallel to the backbone slice the fillet to the backbone resting the knife on the exposed bones. Turning the blade this way will make for a more intact fillet.

- When you get to the backbone, use the tip of the knife to cut just over it so you can get all the flesh on the bottom. At this point, I leave the side loosely attached by a little belly meat, so when I flip it to the other side, it's still rounded and easier to cut.

- Repeat this procedure in the opposite direction pressing down on the blade as you slice. Remove both fillets and place on ice.

HOW TO SKIN A FISH FILLET AND REMOVE THE PINBONES

- Lay a fillet flat on the board and make a small cut at the tail to loosen an inch of skin. Hold the skin tight in your left hand, place the knife between the skin and meat and, holding the knife at a slight angle, simultaneously pull the skin and slide the knife in a sawing motion to remove the meat from the skin.

- Place the fillet on an iced pan (not directly on the ice.) Sanitize the cutting board for the next operation of removing the pinbones.

- Place the fillet on the sanitized cutting board with the tail away from you and feel for the bones in the center with your left thumb. Slide the slightly opened needle-nose pliers or fish tweezers in the same direction as the bones run, slightly angled away from you, and grasp the bone.

- Pinch the surface around the pliers with thumb and forefinger (to keep extra meat from being removed) and smoothly pull out the bone. Return the side of fish to an iced pan for portioning.

HOW TO SCALE A FISH

If you're scaling the fish before butchering, which should be an entirely separate operation, I recommend newspapers or parchment paper to try to contain flying scales and doing this outside. Most of the recipes contained herein use skinned fillets but a few leave the skin on. Use a serrated steak knife if you don't have a scaler and go from tail to head being careful of the sharp fins. Doing this under running water helps but make sure you have a basket in the drain to avoid clogs. Place the whole fish back on ice awaiting the filleting process.

SHELLFISH

The Gulf supplies a huge percentage of the nation's shrimp, oysters, and crabmeat, which figure big into my menus and recipes. They're also widely available in many forms.

SHRIMP

In Louisiana, white shrimp are caught April through December, and brown shrimp, April through February. Pink shrimp, landed on the Florida side of the Gulf, are thinner-shelled and easier to peel. The taste of all three is indistinguishable to most palates. Royal Reds are a fragile, deep-water shrimp with a lobster-like flavor fished on special trawling gear primarily in Alabama. They cook in about half the time of regular shrimp and are great grilled in the shell because of their delicacy. All shrimp freeze extremely well and are available year-round.

I recommend buying shrimp in the shell and, if possible, with their heads intact, even for gumbos and soups. The quality is unquestionably better, and you can use those shells and heads to make stock. There are several ways to buy shrimp: headless shell on, IQF (individually frozen, shell on, sometimes including the head), and peeled block frozen. The most accurate measurement of shrimp is the number of shrimp per pound. The three most common sizes are 40–50 shrimp per pound, 21–25 shrimp per pound, and 16–20 shrimp per pound.

The lower the count, the larger each individual shrimp. The letter "U" in the description means the count is under that number. U-10 might mean 9 shrimp per pound and they will be quite big. Words like large, jumbo, colossal, and medium are misleading terms when it comes to the actual size of shrimp.

CRAWFISH

Crawfish in Louisiana are sold either live in forty-pound sacks or cooked and shelled tail meat. The peak season for crawfish is May through June, but you can find live crawfish in Louisiana from late fall to mid-summer. Crawfish tails freeze pretty well, but only for six months or less because of the fat content.

BLUE CRABS AND CRABMEAT

Hard-shelled Louisiana blue crabs have two claws as large as five inches wide, and in restaurants are often served boiled in the shell for communal cracking. They're most plentiful in the warmer months but are available year-round. Prices tend to be cheaper in the summer. Since I'm most interested in the meat out of the shell for my dishes, I personally don't think it's worth cooking and cracking crabs if I can buy the meat fresh (though I give you instructions on how to do that on page 54), which is how most of it's sold. Jumbo lump crab from the center is the sweetest and most expensive. Regular lump crab comes in smaller pieces and needs to be picked through more thoroughly. Meat from the blue male claws and dark orange female claws or "fingers" has a good flavor but a brown tinge, and is the cheapest of the three. For most recipes, I opt for already picked lump crab. Hands down, your first choice should be fresh (already steamed or boiled), chilled domestic meat from Louisiana, Alabama, or Mississippi.

LOBSTER

Here on the Gulf, we have spiny lobsters, also called rock lobsters—with long antennae and no edible claw meat. They're good when I can get them, but they're no comparison to the tender, sweet claw meat of the lobsters that arrive live at the restaurant from Maine.

Buy Maine lobsters live. They can be kept alive, covered in your refrigerator, for a day at least. Keep them in their container and cover them loosely with a moistened paper towel, as the fridge fan will dry them out and cut down their shelf life. Spiny lobster tails are sold frozen. They can be thawed the day before in your refrigerator (preferred) or under cold running water.

OYSTERS

Louisiana is home to the world's largest remaining oyster reefs and most of the oysters you see in local markets throughout the US come from the Gulf. We source from P&J Oyster Company, the oldest processor in the US. They're large and tender, though their saltiness will vary because they're harvested in brackish water—where freshwater meets seawater—and the salinity of the water varies. When I travel, I like to eat the saltier seawater oysters from the West Coast and from the Malpeque and Chesapeake bays on the East Coast, but in New Orleans, I try to source locally. Health considerations notwithstanding, oysters spawn in the summer and aren't as good to eat as in cooler months. We serve oysters late November through May. If you're buying them in the shell to shuck yourself, make sure the shells are tightly closed. They should have a lot of liquid in their shells. If you buy them already shucked and packed, check to see that the pack date is no more than a week from purchase—closer to the sell date the better. For instructions on shucking and serving on the half-shell, see page 33.

OTHER

Even though I've cooked and eaten plenty of snakes and turtles and alligator garfish and prehistoric river fish, for this book I am only going to provide recipes for a couple of other cold-blooded creatures—alligators and frogs. They're good eating and a beloved part of Louisiana food culture, and regardless of which species they actually belong to, they qualify here for seafood. The Archbishop of New Orleans recently gave the green light for Louisiana Catholics (of which there are many) to eat gator during Lent.

TIPS TO BOOST YOUR FISH AND SHELLFISH CONFIDENCE

CULTIVATE A RELATIONSHIP WITH A FISHMONGER

Think of it like this: If you have a car, you learn to treasure and trust a good mechanic. Introduce yourself to your local fishmonger and start by asking questions. Establish yourself as a savvy consumer and give them feedback. If you really loved something, tell them, and vice versa. If you can, have your fillets cut to order from a whole fish. It's impossible to know the quality of a fillet that has been precut before it reaches the market.

DON'T BE TOO WEDDED TO A PARTICULAR FISH

Adjust your recipe to whatever's the freshest thing in the case. This book will show you how to match sauces and sides with the type of fish you choose so you can think on your feet.

LEARN TO JUDGE FRESHNESS

Filleted fish should look firm, plump, and moist with no discoloration—similar to what you'd see in the case of a good sushi bar or fillets from fish you've caught yourself. If you see separation of the muscle tissue, or gapping, this is a big indication of age and mishandling.

Fresh fish should smell like seawater or a freshly opened oyster—there should be no off or "fishy" odors. Remember: If there is even a hint of a bad odor, don't buy it! I'll even take this one step further. If the market smells, leave and go somewhere else.

CONSIDER THE ORIGIN

Some countries have lax, easily circumvented, or even nonexistent laws governing catches, and some engage in farming practices that not only produce a product that damages the ecosystem but is not safe (or tasty) to eat. The US government sets catch limits to ensure the fish you're buying from the US aren't on the endangered list. US farm-raised fish have more oversight and higher standards than cheaper varieties and are therefore reliably better options.

KNOW YOUR FROZEN OPTIONS

Shrimp: This freezes a lot better than most other kinds of seafood, so if you can't get something fresh, frozen shrimp is a very good option. Look at the label to find the country of origin and whether it's farm-raised or wild-caught.

Fish: If frozen fish fillets are all you have to work with, your options for great eating are wider than you may think. Much of what's available now is flash-frozen right on the boat, and fresher-tasting than the fish that's been sitting for days on ice (which is often pre-frozen and thawed). Consider the preparation—a soup or stew that has lots of other flavors will compensate for any loss of flavor or texture, and fried is always a safe bet. Make sure it's domestic and follow the directions for thawing.

ALWAYS KEEP FISH COLD

By cold I mean iced. Fish and shellfish should be iced from the time they're caught until they are filleted one at a time on the cutting board (keep the other fillets chilled while you slice). Store them in the refrigerator, on ice until they're cooked. A lot more folks would love fish if this rule were followed.

STORE EXCESS FISH PROPERLY

Freeze seafood only if you must. A better way to preserve those fresh-out-of-the-water flavors and textures of your excess fish is to either 1) oil-poach them and use them like you would canned tuna or 2) wrap your fillets in paper towels, then in plastic wrap, and then in a bag. Put the bag on ice in your refrigerator for up to a week. Change the ice daily. Poached tuna will keep in your refrigerator for up to ten days, with a vastly superior taste than canned.

CHOOSE THE RIGHT FISH FOR THE DISH

There are two general rules in cooking finfish: Pair lean fish with richer sauces—butter and cream are good here—and pair fatty or oily fish with acidic sauces— red wine, tomatoes, fruit salsas, and smoked vegetables.

PRIORITIZE COOKING TIMES

This is probably the number one rule after "secure good fish." The margin between moist and delicious and dry and tasteless is small. You should have the rest of the meal ready to go, so the fish is the last thing you put in the pan.

I frequently stress the importance of mise en place—arranging all the items you need for your recipe, so they are in easy reach: the shallots, garlic, herbs, soft butter, measuring spoons, utensils, and so on. Follow the recipe as written so that all components of the dish are a couple of minutes away from being done before you put the fish in the pan. You want your guests to say that the fish is too hot to eat.

LEARN TO GAUGE DONENESS

Different types of fish look different when they're done. But they should all be moist and juicy. If you're sautéing a thin fillet, take it out of the pan when the flesh just turns from translucent to opaque. When you bend a piece, it should break—not flake. The flesh of a thicker fish should barely begin to separate. Beyond that point, it's probably overcooked. Remember that the fish will continue to cook after you take it out of the pan. It's better to err on the side of less done than to overcook.

SERVE FISH AT THE IDEAL TEMPERATURE

Heat your plates for hot dishes. Chill the plates in the refrigerator or freezer for cold dishes.

Unheated plates absorb the heat from the hot food and lower the temperature of your finished dishes. Here are a few ways to ensure your fish will be piping hot is when it reaches the table:

- If your oven has a warming drawer designed for this purpose, by all means use it. If not, you can stack the plates and place them in the oven on its lowest setting (below 200 degrees) for 15 minutes of so.

- If your dishwasher is empty, heat plates on a fast cycle or a heated dry setting.

- Place the dishes in a sinkful of hot water for a few minutes; towel-dry before plating.

- Zap the plates in the microwave for a couple of minutes with a cup of water on top (to keep from damaging your microwave). Just be sure the plates are microwave safe. Use oven mitts to remove them as they can get really hot.

MATCHING WINE WITH SEAFOOD: A QUICK TUTORIAL WITH GARY WOLLERMAN

Selecting a wine to pair with your meal can seem like a complex proposition, and seafood poses its own set of challenges.

The discussion about which wine should be paired with fish is often not about the fish. Coatings, sauces, side dishes, and preparation methods drive the wine-pairing decision as much as the flavor profile of the seafood. These variables make the decision a bit trickier than, say, deciding which Cabernet or Zinfandel to go with a steak. A light, spice-driven, red blend would nicely complement the heavy seasonings on a meaty blackened swordfish steak with Chili Hollandaise Sauce (page 167). But if you're more of a white wine drinker, a crisp pinot gris that contrasts those flavors and refreshes the palate may be the way to go.

Here at the restaurant, we offer about sixty wines by the glass to encourage our guests to expand their wine knowledge and learn as they go. The more you learn about wines and figure out which ones you most enjoy, the more pleasurable your overall dining experience will be.

To help you make the best wine choices when serving seafood at home, Chef Tenney (who does not imbibe) asked me and our longtime beverage manager, Terrance Green, to review the recipes that follow, and offer our suggestions. The idea was not to lay down any hard and fast rules—everyone's palate is different—but to expose you to some possibilities you may not have considered.

There are a few general guidelines to fall back on when in doubt. A rich, buttery dish calls for a full-bodied wine: fish fillets sautéed in brown butter sauce pair with an oaky, creamy Chardonnay, for example. Raw fish and lean, delicate seafood lightly dressed in a citrus- or vinegar-based sauce prefer a lighter, drier white wine—still or sparkling. Fried fish love bubbles as much as beer. Seafood dishes with spicy-sweet Asian flavors and curry seasonings call for a sweeter wine for balance, such as a Riesling or Gewürztraminer.

The vast variety of oysters invites all sorts of options for still and sparkling white wines. The hearty flavor and salinity of Gulf oysters pair well with an unoaked Chardonnay, while an Oregon pinot gris is a better match for sweeter West Coast oysters.

Smoked fish and meaty, grilled, skin-on fish would do well with a thirst-quenching rosé, while fattier, stronger-flavored fish paired with tomato-based sauces or other bold-flavored components may be better suited to a red wine than white.

Don't get hung up on a particular label or varietal. Rather, use these suggestions as a starting point for making your own wine-pairing discoveries and see where your imagination takes you from there.

WELCOME TO MY KITCHEN

STAPLE EQUIPMENT

I'm a minimalist in the kitchen, both at home and at work. I live in a small condo and don't go for fancy gadgets or more pots and pans than I really need. I wash as I go and often make an entire meal with only one pan. Here are the tools I consider essential for all my seafood-cooking needs.

10-INCH CAST-IRON SKILLET

Cast-iron pans are cheap, durable, and ovenproof, and a couple of them need to be in everyone's kitchen. This pan is vital for blackening and bronzing and is a good all-purpose sauté pan. Its smoking-hot surface does a good job of stir-frying, although it's not as good for tossing ingredients as the wok is.

SAUTÉ PANS WITH LIDS

Sauté pans with straight, relatively high sides are not good for searing and blackening, but they are the ideal tool for quickly browning a fish fillet with a simple brown butter sauce and braising fish that requires some liquid in the pan. I like stainless steel with a copper or aluminum sandwich layer that is on the bottom and comes up the sides as well. I prefer an all-metal one so I can pop it in the oven if need be. A lighter colored pan (instead of black cast iron) makes it easier to see when your butter, sugar for caramel, or roux is browning. It's good to have one with an extra-wide surface that will allow you to cook several pieces of fish in the same pan at once. A tight-fitting lid is essential for pan roasting and braising. I have some glass lids I like because I can see what's going on without removing the lid.

SAUCEPAN WITH LID

A 3-quart stainless steel saucepan with a copper or aluminum sandwich layer with a lid and an oven-proof handle is the most versatile. I use this to sear, sauté, and braise, to make small-batch soups such as oyster stew, and to reheat Creole sauces and gumbos.

EXTRA-LARGE STOCKPOT

I rely on a heavy aluminum stockpot with a capacity of 12 quarts or so to accommodate all those fish bones for making stocks, and also to have for big batches of gumbo, and for boiling shellfish for a crowd.

HEAVY-DUTY, STAINLESS STEEL MIXING BOWLS, VARIOUS SIZES

There is a world of cheap, flimsy mixing bowls on the market. Spend a very few extra dollars to get bowls that will outlast you. Stainless steel is durable and easy to clean, can withstand very high temperatures, and keeps fish and other ingredients chilled when needed. Vollrath is a good American-made brand.

IMMERSION BLENDER

This tool is incredibly useful for making quick sauces and puréeing soups in the pan they're cooked in. I recommend one with a bell cover over the blade, which concentrates the force of the blade.

METAL FISH SPATULA

I use a metal spatula with an 8- to 10-inch blade with holes or slits cut in it when cooking larger, thin fillets. You'll need one that can slide all the way under the fish so it won't break.

METAL CAKE TESTER

Those long, skinny metal pins with plastic tops are the ideal tool for getting a quick, accurate measure of fish doneness, without punching a big hole in your pristine fillet with a standard thermometer. Stick it in the thickest part of the meat for a couple of seconds, then immediately touch the tip to inside of your wrist to test. If it's warm, the fish is done. If it's cool, your fillet needs a few more minutes. If it's hot, you've probably overcooked your fish.

SHARP KNIVES AND BUTCHER'S STEEL

I own a fair amount of expensive forged knives, but I tend to use stamped stainless ones more often these days, especially for filleting fish. They are a lot lighter than forged and have composite handles and are okay in the dishwasher. Forschner is a good brand. Stainless steel is very hard and more difficult to sharpen than high carbon so plan on getting them professionally sharpened a couple of times a year and learn to use a butcher's steel to constantly hone them as you cut. An oyster knife is essential if you plan on shucking your own oysters. For deveining shrimp, I use my paring knife rather than a deveiner because I don't need another specialized tool.

THERMOMETERS

A cooking thermometer that registers 400 degrees is a good thing to have around for temping hot oil and caramel for savory sauces and candy. A standard inexpensive Biotherm model that registers up to 220 degrees works for poaching and heating butter for hollandaise. For delicate seafood, though, there are other ways to gauge doneness without mutilating the flesh—a metal cake tester for one, as previously noted.

ASIAN SERRATED PEELER

When you're in an Asian market pick up one of the little serrated peelers for a couple of bucks. It is a small, handy tool for shredding green papaya or mirlitons for salads and it is what they use on the streets of Thailand. (Mandolines will do this job, too, just not as easily.)

TWEEZERS/PLIERS

Small, spring-loaded, needle-nose pliers are the best tool for removing bones from fish. Hemostats (scissor-shaped tweezers) are best for small fish like rainbow trout.

INGREDIENTS

I love the big, bold flavors of New Orleans, the tropics, Southeast Asia, and my native Georgia. I have strong feelings about how to choose them and use them. I am partial to certain brands, especially those from New Orleans, and some, to me, are worth going the extra mile to source rather than going with a substitute. Here are some of the ones that pop up most frequently in my seafood cooking.

SALT

More important than the kind of salt you use is how you use it. Just like cooking rice with no salt in the water, you can't season the fish after it is done and expect it to taste right. Learning to season fish properly before cooking makes a tremendous difference in the outcome. A common chef's trick is to get a pinch of salt between thumb and fingers and sprinkle it about a foot above the product, rubbing fingers against thumb rapidly. Altitude—combined with this motion—makes for an even distribution.

Thicker fish need to be seasoned a bit more (since there is less surface area than thin ones) and seasoning them a little before cooking allows the salt to penetrate the flesh.

For volume measurements in the recipes, I use kosher salt (which is less than table salt by weight) and I like it for seasoning because as I get older I can see the bigger grains better. Its texture makes for good distribution. If my only

option were regular table salt, I'd just use a bit less of it.

I do use popcorn salt for some fried foods in the restaurant since it's finely ground and sticks to the surface better than regular granulated. Fancy sea salts are great on crudo (page 35), pink and black ones provide a color contrast, and rock salt is good to have on hand for oyster platter presentations. But these specialty salts aren't part of my daily cooking.

CAJUN/CREOLE SPICE BLENDS

There are dozens of mixed Cajun or Creole seasonings on the market all over the country and probably twice that amount here in New Orleans, not counting the different shrimp and crawfish boil preparations (see page 54) and ones for seasoned fish breading. I find that those labeled Cajun tend to be more straightforward, with more salt and cayenne and onion/garlic powder, and the Creole ones have dried oregano and other herb additions.

My go-to favorite is Paul Prudhomme's Magic line, of which there are many variations. Of these, my top choice is Shrimp Magic, which has complex flavors that include floral notes of sandalwood and jasmine. If you can't find it in your local store, it's well worth ordering from the Magic Seasonings website (magicseasoningblends.com).

Though not a duplicate, the recipe below is a good substitute in most dishes that call for it.

HOME CREOLE SEASONING

MAKES ¾ CUP

3 tablespoons paprika
2 tablespoons table salt
2 tablespoons garlic powder
1 tablespoon onion powder
1 tablespoon cayenne pepper
2 teaspoons black pepper
2 teaspoons white pepper
2 teaspoons dried oregano
2 teaspoons dried thyme

Combine all ingredients in a mixing bowl and store tightly covered in a cool part of your kitchen. I asked Paul Prudhomme about shelf life of his blends once and he said that if it has been stored a long time "just use a little more."

ASIAN INGREDIENTS

When Saigon fell in 1975, anyone who could left Vietnam in a hurry, and south Louisiana hosted a lot of these refugees through relief organizations. The families originally from Southeast Asia are a vibrant part of our city, and they have taken over a lot of the shrimping and longline fisheries. Their culinary contributions are felt from po'boy bread (which makes báhn mi a common sandwich) to ingredients in fine dining restaurants all over town. They have certainly influenced my cooking, both at work and at home. Pungent dried shrimp, tiny and fiery Thai red chiles, aromatic kaffir lime leaf, and fermented crab paste are flavors I've come to love and incorporate into my everyday cooking.

HOT SAUCES

There are dozens, if not hundreds, of hot sauces on the shelf here locally. Tabasco is available everywhere and the one I use most often. I also like their chipotle version and use it in my potato salad. Crystal brand is popular here as well and we offer both at Fins.

STEEN'S CANE VINEGAR

Cane syrup is a Louisiana product that's here because of our sugar industry, and cane vinegar is one of its byproducts. Both are products of the Steen Syrup Mill of Abbeville, Louisiana, which has been in operation since 1910. I find I really like its slightly sweet, smoky flavor much better than the traditional red wine vinegar for a mignonette dipping sauce for raw oysters, or malt vinegar for batter-fried fish. It's also great for vinaigrettes and barbecue sauces for meats. Outside of Louisiana, it's available on Amazon, and at Steensyrup.com.

STOCKS AND CONCENTRATES

We make our own, but store-bought chicken stock is always handy to have around. Veal stock is a whole 'nother animal. You really have to be a serious home cook to do it yourself. More Than Gourmet makes an acceptable veal demi-glace sold in concentrate form (both online and some retail). I'm pickier about my seafood stocks. They're not hard to make once you source the bones and scraps. More Than Gourmet also makes a concentrated shellfish stock that will suffice for some dishes that call for it, such as forcemeat. It is available at morethangourmet.com.

SALTED BUTTER

I love butter, and I use salted for almost all my cooking. This is largely a taste preference, but the salt also aids in the browning and is especially preferable in sautéing and making brown butter sauces (see Butter sauces, page 162). Unsalted butter refuses to brown properly. For the purposes of the recipes in this book, the amount of salt in salted butter is perfect for seasoning—yes, even in bread and dessert recipes.

LARD

If you've ever gotten hydrogenated shortening on your hands and tried to wash it off, it feels like petroleum jelly. Hot water, soap, and scrubbing, and you still have to wipe it off with a paper towel. I'm more comfortable with fats that soften at body temperature.

If I can find fresh lard, it's the best—a natural fat eaten by people for thousands of years and a perfect frying medium for fish. I also use it for biscuits, cornbread, pie dough, and many other things.

THAI CHILES

Fresh chiles provide a layer of flavor that doesn't seem to be the same as the dried ones, and I use lots of them in my cooking. But none so much as the Thai chile, or bird chile, a very hot, tiny, thin capsicum that's either bright red or green, and found in Asian markets. They also grow well in southern climates. Its flavor is comparable to cayenne or chile de arbol, and its heat level is somewhere between a jalapeño and a habanero. Heat and flavor are concentrated in the seeds and ribs.

They're often sold cheaply in big plastic bags, and a little goes a long way. Extras can be frozen. By no means touch your eyes when slicing them!

FINES HERBES AND SUBSTITUTES

This classic French herb mixture is hard to find, but if you can source it, you'll love what it does in finishing seafood dishes. A key component is chervil, a delicate

herb that tastes faintly of anise. Tarragon is similar but stronger tasting than chervil, and more readily available and makes a good substitute.

To make your own fines herbes blend, mix 2 parts chopped parsley and 1 part each of chopped chervil and chives. If you can't locate chervil, a good substitution is ¼ part each tarragon and basil.

CREOLE TOMATOES

Southern Louisiana Creole tomatoes have a very short season here—about six weeks in the late spring to early summer, and we use them in everything. They are reputed to be a higher-acid variety that benefits from our type of soil, but I think there's a lot of local pride involved in their marketing. Take advantage of whatever tomatoes are grown locally wherever you are, never refrigerate them, and you'll be happy. Most tomato-growing regions have a longer season than we do in Louisiana but nobody seems to grow really good ones year-round. Refrigeration ruins the real texture and flavor as well,

so learn to embrace seasonal produce when it's available and do what good restaurants do—make your menus with the best of what is at the market when you go. Having said that, a lot of the time canned tomatoes are what you'll use for cooking and that's just fine.

A number of the recipes in this book called for peeled, seeded, and chopped tomatoes. Here's how to do it: Core the stem end of the tomatoes and score the bottom. Dip them in boiling water for ten seconds and then in ice water. Remove the peel with a paring knife and cut the tomatoes in half through the equator. Squeeze out the seeds, flatten the halves on a cutting board, and chop.

JAZZMAN RICE

Louisiana is rice country because of our climate, and Jazzman (Jazzmen is the brand name) is a jasmine variety developed by the LSU agricultural school particularly for our growing conditions. It's a fragrant, more flavorful all-purpose rice that I often use for gumbos, shrimp creole, and any dish that would call for long grain.

RAW

RAW GULF OYSTERS WITH HOUSE COCKTAIL SAUCE

A FRENCH QUARTER CRUDO SAMPLER

SALMON TARTARE WITH HARD-BOILED EGGS, CAPERS,
AND ONION

YELLOWFIN TUNA TARTARE WITH PINE NUTS, ASIAN PEAR,
SESAME OIL, AND SEA SALT

LIONFISH CEVICHE WITH CITRUS, LIME, AND CHILE

Eating seafood raw is the best way to learn to appreciate the flavor and textural nuances each species has to offer. It goes without saying that these fish should be impeccably fresh, but beyond that, many other factors can affect an individual fish's taste: age, sex, water temperature, diet, how the fish was landed.

When GW Fins opened in 2001, I had the then-novel idea of incorporating a six-seat sushi section in our bar, on the premise that the quality of the fish in the case mirrored that of the fish we cooked on the menu. We abandoned that for several reasons—the main one being that six seats couldn't support the expense of a sushi chef. But I never gave up on the idea of stellar raw fish on the menu.

When crudo (sliced raw fish) hit the scene, it opened up a lot of new ways to serve raw fish that didn't include Japanese garnishes: different salts, oils, pickled things, herbs, edible flowers. Today we often put crudo platters of raw spearfished cobia, yellowfin tuna, and red snapper on our menus. Fat pompano is my favorite, and if you're a fan of hamachi in sushi bars, you'll love it, too. Sometimes it's fish I've speared myself.

Hawaiian poke, which has become wildly popular in recent years, is a form of crudo typically using cubed raw tuna that's tossed with soy sauce, seaweed, and various seasonings.

Tartare, which often refers to dishes made with finely chopped raw beef, can also be applied to super-fresh tuna and farm-raised salmon. I consider tartare to be a gateway to crudo—sort of like sushi rolls are an introduction to sashimi. This technique lends itself to mixing and molding all sorts of artful presentations that look more complicated than they are.

Ceviche is a classic dish throughout Latin America in which raw fish is marinated in citrus juices and spices and served chilled, usually as a first course. It's a great way to showcase an array of lean saltwater fish.

Not every fish species tastes good when eaten raw. Freshwater wild fish are prone to parasites that can make you sick and should always be cooked. Fortunately, here on the Gulf, there are many safe bets, and several options widely available just about anywhere. A little advance research before you head to the market will help. (I'll give you some places to start.)

In this chapter, I will show you a few of my favorite ways to enjoy raw fish at home that don't require the skills of a sushi master. It's all about the species, the quality of the fish, and how it's handled. Before you dive in, here are a few things to consider.

- Species that are commonly served raw are sometimes labeled sushi- or sashimi-grade. These are little more than marketing terms designed to entice sushi lovers, as there is no governmental grading system for determining fish quality. Rather, it only means that the supplier has deemed it safe to eat raw. The Food and Drug Administration offers guidelines, but it's up to individual states to adopt them as law. Another reason to seek out a fishmonger you can trust!

- The FDA advises flash-freezing most species of fish to kill or weaken parasites. Some sushi restaurants and markets are equipped with special super-cold freezers for this purpose that can reach temperatures far lower than what a home freezer can maintain. Large species of tuna are exempt from this freezing recommendation due to the extremely low risk of parasitic infection they pose, making it one of the safest choices for eating raw.

- Once you source your impeccably fresh fish, it's up to you to continue those safety measures in your kitchen. Keep your hands, tools, and your work surfaces immaculately clean. It's a good idea to wear thin rubber gloves when handling raw fish.

- To clean work surfaces, wipe them down with a mixture of bleach and water (1 tablespoon bleach per 1 gallon of water). Japanese sushi chefs dip their hands into vinegar between operations as a sanitary measure.

- Keep your fish extremely cold. I like to use nesting stainless steel bowls with ice in between to keep fish cold. Keep serving plates in the refrigerator and as soon as you arrange the fish on the plate, put it back into the refrigerator until you are ready to serve your guests.

- Use an extremely sharp knife to slice the fish. My preference is a thin-blade slicer.

- Use raw fish within a day or two of purchase and keep it wrapped in a bowl of ice in the coldest part of the refrigerator. Keep fish you've caught yourself cold throughout the trip from the boat to butchering, and they can be good at least a week held in this manner.

SEVEN GREAT FISH AND SHELLFISH FOR EATING RAW

These are the species we most often serve raw at GW Fins—five native to the Gulf and two imports. If a fish is good to eat raw, you can bet it's good cooked, too—and you'll see all these species again later in the book.

YELLOWFIN TUNA

In New Orleans, we are lucky to be only two hours north from the second largest tuna fishery in the country (after Hawaii). Our restaurant competes with sushi bars for "number one" yellowfin tuna, a rather loose term depending on the market, meaning the best of this catch that's available. (Ahi, the Hawaiian name for tuna, can refer to bigeye or yellowfin. Confusing, isn't it?) Yellowfin tuna is usually the leanest of the commercially available tunas, but in the colder months it can develop some nice fat. In general, the belly meat of any fish is going to be the richest, and the meat closest to the skin is a lighter color (fat is just insulation, after all) than the brighter red center of the loin. Everybody thinks they want the brightest red available, but the lighter colored meat has a better flavor.

Though naturally red, yellowfin tuna steaks sold in grocery store fish cases—sometimes in Cryovac-sealed portions—often have an unnatural magenta color because they've been treated with carbon monoxide (sometimes marketed as "colorless wood smoke") to "set" the color. The FDA says it's safe, but I find that tuna treated this way has a washed-out flavor and texture and avoid it.

LIONFISH

Though covered with venomous spines, this predatory species is safe to eat if properly handled—raw or cooked. The meat is mild and delicate, and highly versatile.

COBIA

Cobia is caught a lot by recreational fishermen and commercially licensed free divers here in New Orleans. It is firmer than swordfish and has a sweet flavor with a moderate fat content. It's good sautéed, grilled, blackened, or raw. Ocean Blue, a deep-water farm off Costa Rica, is a farmed variety that's perfectly acceptable.

POMPANO

If I had to pick one fish as my favorite it would be Gulf pompano (not to be confused with African pompano which is much larger and very lean). It usually shows up here in late summer and sometimes in December. The flesh is cream colored and very firm and it's loaded with sweet, delicious fat. For crudo, I like to shave thin slices and arrange them like flower petals on the plate and eat them with just a sprinkle of sea salt.

SNAPPER

American-raised red snapper is a sweet, tender fish that's great served raw, but you'll need to slice it very thinly against the grain and add a bit more garnish to augment its leanness.

FARM-RAISED SALMON

Wild salmon should only be eaten cooked. But there are some excellent farmed options that are ideal for serving raw. I prefer large Irish or Scottish Atlantics, and the tartare recipe is designed for their type of fat.

SCALLOPS

The good thing about fresh scallops, when you can get them, is they require little to no cooking. When we get the bottle cork-size Nantucket Bays, I eat them right out of the container. Larger ones just need a quick sear in the skillet or on the grill. Or, thinly slice them for crudo or ceviche.

Make sure the ones you buy are dry packed, which means they're not treated with a chemical that makes them suck up water to increase their weight. They should be glossy and firm and have no smell stronger than seawater. "Day boat" or even "diver caught" are sometimes just marketing terms that may or may not guarantee a quality product. Sometimes FAS (frozen at sea) is the way to go.

A SPEAR-TO-PLATE FEAST

Spearfishing the oil platforms off the Louisiana coast is supposedly the best big fish game shooting in the world. At Fins, we get very excited by the catch we get from spearfishermen who sometimes call us from forty miles out on the rigs asking what we want. The finest sushi restaurants in the world don't get fresher fish than what we receive from these guys.

My own introduction to the oil rigs was memorable.

I'd done about eighty dives in Florida before I finally got the opportunity to try my skill on the rigs myself. As the novice diver on the boat, I was buddied up with a more experienced diver whom I was told to meet up with around seventy-five feet under the surface.

I swam against the strong current toward the rig and grabbed onto the side. Once inside the rig, I began pulling myself down, hand over hand, through about twenty feet of thick, blinding muck. It was unsettling, to say the least. But once I got through it, the current slowed and visibility opened up. The view was magical.

The rig's cross members were covered with soft coral and all the creatures you'd see on a natural reef—from the tiny to the huge—were stacked up top to bottom: barracuda, Jacks, triggers, snappers, groupers, lookdowns, lionfish, and spiny lobsters, with cobia cruising on the outside.

Looking up at the light filtering through the sediment, and hundreds of feet down to the depths, there was almost a cathedral vibe—like an abandoned man-made structure that the fish had taken over. (If you remember the derelict alien spacecraft in Alien, it was a lot like that.) Yet this was a working oil rig.

I got so caught up in the splendor of it all I forgot about the diver I was supposed to meet and just kicked around enjoying all the wildlife. Another diver finally swam down and motioned me up. When we got to the surface I pulled off my mask and said, "That was an awesome dive!"

The boat captain was not so amused. He thought he'd seen my bubbles on the way to Florida. Turns out, my buddy got freaked out by the gumbo-like layer and hightailed it back to the boat. They thought they'd lost the chef on the first dive.

I've since learned how to load and shoot the type of guns used in the rigs. And sometimes, when the crew and I get lucky and land a pompano or an amberjack, we won't even wait until I get to the dock to reward ourselves. I pack some garnishes and oil and we cut up the nicest of our catch to eat right on the boat.

Be aware that cutting a chunk out of a fish you just speared is going to be different than a sushi bar selection of that same fish a couple of days later. Not bad, just different.

Before rigor mortis (when the fish gets hard as a board) comes and goes, the meat has a crunchy, corrugated texture. Some people actually claim that fillets from a four- or five-day-old fish are preferable, but unless you catch them yourself, you'll probably never have the opportunity of off-the-spear taste. However, the condition of the fish when caught, the length of time taken to land it, and the amount of time between catching and cutting and eating can also affect that ultra-fresh taste and texture.

RAW GULF OYSTERS WITH HOUSE COCKTAIL SAUCE

SERVES 1 OR 2 AS AN APPETIZER

I was a raw oyster fan long before I came to New Orleans. I remember my dad feeding them to me in front of the cooks at a restaurant he managed in North Carolina when I was three or so, just to freak them out. I still really love them, and today my usual dosage is up to about three dozen.

Cocktail sauce heavy on horseradish, Worcestershire, and hot sauce is the favorite accompaniment around here. But I usually like oysters as is, without even a squeeze of lemon, or sometimes with a little mignonette. If I feel like a fancy feast of sea flavor, I have been known to top them with a little uni and caviar. No matter how you like the eat them, they are a perfect appetizer—always light and refreshing.

Oyster shucking is a little daunting if you've never done it before. I highly recommend watching some YouTube videos first before shucking them yourself.

Special equipment: Oyster knife, oyster-shucking gloves (or a small bar towel you don't mind getting dirty), a large, deep platter for serving

Rock salt

1 dozen live oysters in their shells (or however many you can eat), held on crushed ice until ready to serve

Optional garnishes and accompaniments: lemon wedges, horseradish, House Cocktail Sauce (page 158), Cane Vinegar Mignonette (page 158), saltines

Set out a large, deep serving platter. Add a layer of rock salt. This will hold the shells upright.

To shuck an oyster, hold it with the rounded part of the shell away from you. Place the tip of the oyster knife at the base of the hinge and twist, using downward pressure. When the shell pops, hold the oyster level and work the knife, levering back and forth to remove the top shell. Flick any debris from the edges away using the liquid from the oyster, and cut the muscle attaching the meat to the shell. Place each oyster within its half shell on the rock salt platter, reserving the liquid in the shell. Serve with desired accompaniments.

SUGGESTED WINE PAIRING: Serve with Avissi Prosecco (Veneto, Italy), a crisp, easy-going sparkling wine with acid and minerality that complement the oysters' briny-sweet character. Cold beer is also always a safe bet.

A FRENCH QUARTER CRUDO SAMPLER

SERVES 4 TO 6 AS AN APPETIZER

Crudo is simply fish that is sliced and served raw with little, if any, adornment.

Tuna, cobia, lionfish, and fat pompano are some of the local fish we serve at the restaurant because they have a soft, buttery texture that's ideal for eating this way. Farm-raised salmon, snapper, and scallops are also good choices. Avoid tail pieces for crudo—they contain the most connective tissue that is hard to chew. Instead, use the more tender part from the belly or loin.

Use a very sharp, thin-blade slicer for cutting crudo. This is especially important with smaller fish like pompano and snapper.

For serving, garnish with something simple to accentuate and not mask the flavors and textures of the fish. This is where your creativity comes in. Think salty, crunchy, fatty, or acidic. You can start with sea salt and olive oil, taste, and maybe add a sliver of preserved lemon peel or thinly sliced chile, some dill flowers, or savory whipped cream. Or present the slices arranged on a chilled platter with a variety of garnishes and let your guests pick. Just remember to start tasting with a minimal amount of ingredients—you're trying to enjoy the natural flavors of the fish, not cover them up. As in cooked fishes, fattier ones will marry better with acids and heat, and leaner ones with savory whipped creams and flavorful oils.

Special equipment: thin rubber gloves; a small, very sharp knife

CRUDO

3 to 4 ounces Gulf pompano fillet

3 to 4 ounces lionfish fillet (or dry-pack sea scallops)

3 to 4 ounces cobia fillet

3 to 4 ounces American red snapper fillet

3 to 4 ounces yellowfin tuna (preferably belly or loin meat)

GARNISHES

Flaked sea salt

Really good extra-virgin olive or avocado oil

Thinly sliced preserved lemon peel

Slivered fresh mint

Thinly sliced Fresno or Thai chile

Dill or cilantro flowers

Finely diced Kalamata olives

Whipped cream (lightly flavored with chile oil, saffron, lavender, or wasabi)

Caviars or fish roe

Using a very sharp knife and wearing rubber gloves, slice each fish thinly against the grain if it's perceptible—often it's hard to determine. The fish listed here are already tender, so it really doesn't matter. I tend to shave pompano more thinly than the others—about $1/8$ inch thick—because I like the texture better that way. Slice and taste a few pieces to see what works for you.

Keep the other fish cold while you work. Arrange on a chilled platter, sprinkle lightly with sea salt, and dribble a little oil over the top. Decorate with garnishes as desired, or serve them in small bowls and let guests garnish their own.

SUGGESTED WINE PAIRING: *Serve with Sokol Blosser pinot gris (Willamette Valley, Oregon), a light white wine to complement the delicate flavors and textures of the raw fish.*

NO-WASTE TARTARE

Tartare is a great way to utilize scraps and trim from tuna and farm-raised salmon. Bits of tender belly or loin are ideal and need only be chopped. But for total utilization, you can also use the tougher meat clinging to the bones of tuna, or from the tail of the salmon—the part of the fish that moves the most—which are full of connective tissue. You may be able to get these pieces from your butcher at a bargain rate. The trick is to scrape the meat off these smaller, sinewy pieces with a spoon or small, serrated knife, discard the tissue, and mix these fine bits of meat in with the chopped belly or loin. I love the contrast in textures. As an aside, exposure to air causes the tuna meat to "bloom," so the more surface area you create the more this happens. This is a good thing, as blooming allows the meat to develop a vibrant red color and makes for a great presentation. If scraps and trim are not available, just follow the raw purchasing rules and tell the butcher you're planning to eat it raw.

SALMON TARTARE WITH HARD-BOILED EGGS, CAPERS, AND ONION

4 SERVINGS AS AN APPETIZER OR 2 SERVINGS AS A MAIN COURSE

I learned how to make this rich-tasting and striking-looking tartare from John Carver, who now owns the wildly successful Red Ash in Austin, Texas. We worked together in the late 1980s, when he was the executive chef at the Fish Market at Lenox and I was the sous chef. Back then, towering appetizers like this one—layered with fish tartare, egg yolk, and egg white, and "iced" with a layer of caviar—were indicative of expense-account dining. The combination holds up just as well today, and it's still one of the best I know of to showcase impeccably fresh and responsibly farmed (aquacultured) salmon. It's also quick and easy to make. I like the striated belly meat for this—it's the fattiest and most flavorful.

Special equipment: thin rubber gloves; a small, very sharp knife; 4 ring molds about 2 inches in diameter and 1 ½ inches deep, or 2 larger molds, about 3 ½ inches in diameter (see NOTE)

8 ounces farmed Scottish or Irish salmon (not wild salmon), preferably the striated belly meat

2 tablespoons finely diced Vidalia onion

2 large hard-boiled eggs (see Tip)

1 teaspoon minced fresh chives

1 tablespoon drained, chopped small capers

2 tablespoons extra-virgin olive oil

2 tablespoons heavy cream

Pinch of sea salt

1 teaspoon finely chopped chervil (or parsley)

1 ounce domestic sturgeon caviar, optional

Edible flowers and/or microgreens for garnish

Before proceeding, follow the raw fish handling guidelines (page 29). Set a small bowl in a larger bowl of ice to chill. Place another small bowl and 2 or 4 serving plates in the refrigerator to chill.

Wearing rubber gloves, set the salmon on a dark surface, such as a black napkin (I find that I can see what I am doing better). Cut the salmon into 2- or 3-inch chunks. If using the belly meat or fillet, cut the pieces into very fine dice. If using the tougher tail meat, use the tip of a spoon or a small, sharp knife to scrape the flesh from the white sinew then discard the tough tissue. Place the fish in the bowl over ice.

Place the onion in a clean cloth napkin and bring up the corners to form a bundle in your hand. Rinse the bundled onion under cold water then squeeze dry to cut the sharpness of the onion.

Peel the eggs and set them on a paper towel or napkin (this will absorb moisture and make them easier to handle). Cut the eggs in half, separate the egg white and yolk, and chop each very finely, keeping them separate. Add the onion, chives, capers, and olive oil to the salmon in the chilled bowl; keep on ice. This can be covered and refrigerated for several hours until you're ready to serve.

Whisk the cream in the small chilled bowl from the refrigerator until soft—not stiff—peaks form. Add the salt and chopped herbs and carefully combine.

Set each mold on a piece of parchment paper and divide the salmon mixture equally between them. Add a thin layer of diced egg white, then yolk, and if you're flush enough, add a layer of caviar. (Alternately, you can sprinkle the egg and caviar over the top or mix it in.) Dollop a spoonful of whipped cream in the center of each of the chilled plates and spread it out with the bottom of a spoon to about a 4-inch diameter circle. Slide the mold onto the plate in the center of the whipped cream and unmold the tartare. Repeat with the rest of the molds. Garnish with edible flowers or microgreens, if desired.

SUGGESTED WINE PAIRING: Mistinguett Brut Rose (Spain). The soft bubbles in this dry cava brighten the raw salmon. Or breakout the Dom Pérignon or your favorite champagne.

Note: You can get cooking ring molds at most cookware stores. Or you can do what I do and make them yourself out of 2-inch PVC pipe cut into 1 ¹/₂-inch sections. (A clean, empty tuna fish can with the bottom cut out will also do the trick.)

TIP: PERFECT HARD-BOILED EGGS

Place the egg in a small pot and cover with cold water. Bring to a boil and let boil for 5 to 15 minutes, depending on the altitude of where you live. Remove from the pot into a bowl of ice water and, when cool enough to handle, peel and return the egg to the ice water—this prevents the yolk from greening.

YELLOWFIN TUNA TARTARE WITH PINE NUTS, ASIAN PEAR, SESAME OIL, AND SEA SALT

4 SERVINGS AS AN APPETIZER OR 2 SERVINGS AS A MAIN COURSE

This more contemporary tartare is one of the most popular starters at Fins. Like the salmon version, it's easy to make, with contrasting colors and textures for an eye-catching presentation. I like to mold it, but it can also be scooped out directly onto the plate, or made into quenelle (egg-like) shapes with two spoons.

Special equipment: 4 ring molds about 2 inches in diameter and 1 ½ inches deep, or 2 larger molds, about 3 ½ inches in diameter; a small, very sharp knife

½ pound super-fresh yellowfin tuna steaks, very cold

½ cup ¼-inch-diced, peeled Asian pear

¼ cup chopped toasted pine nuts

¼ teaspoon toasted sesame oil

½ teaspoon kosher salt

Freshly ground black pepper

1 avocado, cut in small dice just before using (optional)

WASABI DRESSING

1 tablespoon wasabi powder

2 tablespoons seasoned rice wine vinegar

8 tablespoons canola oil

Optional garnishes: sweet soy sauce, avocado oil, coriander blossoms

Set a small bowl in a larger bowl of ice to chill. Place 4 serving plates in the refrigerator to chill.

Wearing rubber gloves, set the tuna on a dark surface, such as a black napkin (I find that I can see what I am doing better). Cut the tuna into 2- or 3-inch manageable chunks. If using the belly meat or fillet, cut the pieces into very fine dice. If using the tougher tail meat, use the tip of a spoon or a small, sharp knife to scrape the flesh from the white sinew then discard the tough tissue. (A mixture of the two gives you an interesting texture contrast.)

Transfer to a small bowl and mix with the pear, pine nuts, sesame oil, salt, and pepper. If you have four small molds (see note on page 37), set each one on a piece of parchment paper and divide the tuna mixture equally between them. You can do this a few hours ahead of time and chill in the refrigerator, but serve it the same day. If you're using diced avocado, add this at the last minute to prevent browning.

For the dressing, in a small bowl, whisk together the wasabi powder and the vinegar until smooth. Slowly dribble in the oil and whisk until smooth.

When ready to serve, slide the mold, if using, onto a serving plate and unmold the tartare. Repeat with the rest of the molds. Or, form the mixture into quenelles and divide among the plates. If desired, garnish the plates with a drizzle of sweet soy sauce, avocado oil, wasabi dressing, and coriander blossoms. Or you can add a dollop of savory cream whipped with a little wasabi mustard powder.

SUGGESTED WINE PAIRING: *Serve with Craggy Range Sauvignon Blanc (Martinborough, New Zealand), a light, dry, minerally white wine with citrus and apple notes. A sweet or dry white wine would pair nicely with this dish, as would a sparkling rosé.*

RAW

LIONFISH CEVICHE WITH CITRUS, LIME, AND CHILE

4 SERVINGS AS AN APPETIZER

A quick soak in citrus juice and spices is an easy way to add flavor to most mild, lean, saltwater fish. It's especially good with lionfish. It is also great with either bay scallops or thinly sliced sea scallops. To avoid a pickled taste, combine lime juice with less acidic orange juice, and let it marinate for only a few minutes. We often garnish ceviche with our local satsumas, a member of the mandarin family favored here for its exceptionally sweet flavor and delicate texture, when they're in season. But any citrus will be delicious.

½ cup freshly squeezed orange juice

½ cup freshly squeezed lime juice

1 teaspoon sugar

½ teaspoon salt

1 teaspoon finely minced shallot

½ teaspoon finely minced Fresno chile, seeds and all (if substituting Thai chile, reduce the amount to ¼ teaspoon)

½ cup peeled, seeded, and diced cucumber, preferably European or Persian (I prefer the flavor, and the meat-to-seed ratio is better)

½ pound skinless lionfish fillets, cut in ½-inch-wide strips and spanked (not pounded) with the heel of a French knife

About ½ cup citrus supremes for garnishing: satsumas, blood oranges, Meyer lemons

Mix the citrus juices with the sugar and salt in a small bowl. Add the shallot and chile. (Don't prepare the marinade more than a few hours ahead of marinating the fish.)

Add the cucumber and the fish and toss to coat with the juices. Place in the refrigerator for 15 minutes to an hour, making sure to stir several times while it marinates. Serve in chilled martini glasses or on small plates and garnish with the citrus supremes.

SUGGESTED WINE PAIRING: *Serve with WillaKenzie Pinot Gris (Willamette Valley, Oregon), a white wine high in acidity with bright fruit flavors to match the citrus and spice. Champagne, beer, and most stainless steel-made wines will work well with this dish. Stay away from oak.*

HOW TO SUPREME CITRUS

A supreme is a segment of citrus without any pith or membrane attached, which makes for a more refined garnish presentation. Supreming is the method of removing the pith and the membranes of citrus fruits, leaving only the segments.

Using a very sharp knife, slice off the top and bottom of the fruit then slice off the skin and white pith from top to bottom along the curve of the fruit.

Set the fruit on its side and slice along one of its membranes, toward the center. Then slice along the adjacent membrane to release the segment. Place the supreme in a bowl and repeat with the next membrane, until all segments have been removed. Save any juice for another use.

POACHED AND BOILED

OIL-POACHED TUNA

POACHED KING SALMON WITH CARROTS AND LEEKS IN VIN BLANC

TUNA-MUFFULETTA-NIÇOISE SALAD WITH CRISPY POACHED AND FRIED EGG

LOUISIANA-STYLE BOILED SHRIMP IN THE SHELL

STONE CRAB CLAWS WITH CREOLE MUSTARD CREAM

SOUTHERN SHRIMP ROLL

VERACRUZ SEAFOOD COCKTAIL

Poaching and boiling involves cooking seafood in a liquid bath—one slowly and gently, the other quickly and furiously. If done correctly, both are wonderful ways to respect the natural textures and flavors of very fresh fish or shellfish. These are the techniques I turn to most often when I have an excess of fresh tuna or shrimp, which happens frequently here in Louisiana, and want to be able to serve it multiple ways over several days, warm or chilled.

POACHING TIPS

- Poaching is a delicate method of infusing fresh fish with subtle flavor by simmering it in water, stock, oil, or butter. The trick is to balance that poaching medium with the right amount of acid from white wine, beer, citrus juice, or vinegar and the flavor extraction from aromatics such as onions, celery, herbs, and spices.

- Poaching works best with firm fish at least ½ inch thick, such as tuna, salmon, or lobster. Peeled shellfish such as shrimp (especially the delicate, prized Royal Reds) or lobster that's been parboiled long enough to release its shell, are delicious poached in melted butter.

- Choose a pan wide enough to hold fish steaks in a single layer for even cooking. Add just enough liquid to cover by about an inch.

- Equally important as your cooking medium is not letting the temperature of the liquid rise above 160 degrees F during the cooking. There are several ways to do this. The easiest and most reliable is to bring the liquid to a boil, turn off the heat, then immediately add the fish. The liquid will quickly cool down to its proper temperature, while still being hot enough to cook the fish perfectly. Use a thermometer to regulate the temperature of the liquid. If it cools down too much, simply turn up the heat until it reaches the desired temperature and then turn it off.

- Test the fish for doneness by gently pinching the thickest part. If the flesh separates, it's done. Err on the side of underdone.

- Carefully remove the fish with a slotted spatula to keep it from falling apart.

- Don't toss out the poaching liquid! Drizzle a few spoonfuls over the cooked fish for extra moisture and flavor or use some of it to make a quick butter sauce.

BOILING TIPS

I've heard there is a culinary tradition in the upper Midwest where lake trout and other finfish are actually boiled. We Southerners shudder to think of it. I do love our Yankee tourists when they bite into a fresh Gulf fish. In this chapter, boiling will be reserved for creatures in their shells.

- Use a pot large enough to fill three-quarters full with water while completely covering the shellfish and allowing for some circulation.

- Like poaching fish, it's a good idea to add some acid and aromatics to the water. Lemon juice, beer, wine, or vinegar are all fine additions for acidulating the water. Aromatics and seasonings can include powdered and boil-in-the-bag commercial blends, garlic cloves, bay leaves, and parsley stems. But most of all, add plenty of salt—more than you think you'll need! (For more on seasonings and sources, see page 24.)

- Take care not to overcook. Follow the timetables given in this chapter. Whole crabs and crawfish are best drained immediately and served hot, right out of the pot. Peel-and-eat shrimp are good hot or chilled.

OIL-POACHED TUNA

MAKES 2 1/2 CUPS

Louisiana has the second largest tuna fleet next to Hawaii, so there is a plentiful supply and I'm always looking for different ways to cook it. If I have more than I can use right away, I might poach it in oil with seasonings, which means I can refrigerate it for up to ten days and use it in salads. I typically do this with yellowfin, but it's also a great technique for blackfin or any other variety of tuna. You can also poach tuna in highly seasoned broth, but poaching in oil allows you to store it longer and carries the flavors of the aromatics better. Open your mind to a cold mayo salad with almost any big fish cooked this way. Once you try this, you may never open another can of tuna again.

Special equipment: thermometer

2 cups olive oil or canola oil

1 Fresno or jalapeño chile, split open lengthwise, with seeds

1 large sprig thyme

2 bay leaves

10 peppercorns

1 lemon, thinly sliced, peel, seeds and all

1 pound fresh fatty tuna, cut into 1-inch chunks (Wahoo and thick redfish are good substitutes for tuna)

In a medium saucepan, combine the oil, chile, thyme, bay leaves, peppercorns, and lemon. Heat over medium-low heat to 160 degrees F.

Add the tuna and poach for 10 to 15 minutes, or until cooked medium—slightly pink inside. With a slotted spoon, transfer the tuna to a container, let cool slightly, and refrigerate. Let the oil cool to room temperature, about 1 hour.

Pack the tuna into a smaller container and cover with the reserved cooled oil until it is immersed. Cover and refrigerate up to ten days. Discard any remaining oil.

BUTTER-POACHED SHRIMP OR LOBSTER

Butter poaching, like oil-poaching, is a great way to add flavor and richness to seafood. Lobster Butter Sauce (page 163) is a wonderful poaching medium and cooking shrimp or lobster in it enriches it even more for later use.

Raw shrimp can be peeled, but the claws and smaller parts of raw lobsters are resistant to shelling. I recommend blanching lobster for 3 or 4 minutes in boiling water which will make shelling easier.

In a medium saucepan, heat the Lobster Butter Sauce over medium-low to about 160 degrees F and poach 5 minutes for shrimp and about 10 minutes for blanched lobster depending on the size. Test for doneness by cutting a piece in half and tasting for firmness. If they're a little undercooked, return them to the hot butter sauce for a couple more minutes. Be sure to chop and add the flavorful tomalley (the light green innards) and any roe from the lobsters cooked in a little of the sauce for a great complement.

Note: Maine lobster or Royal Red shrimp poached in Lobster Butter Sauce is delicious served warm, with some of the lobster butter, on the same Sally Lunn rolls (page 175) used for the Southern Shrimp Roll (page 55).

POACHED KING SALMON WITH CARROTS AND LEEKS IN VIN BLANC

SERVES 2 AS A MAIN DISH

The natural richness of a fatty fish like wild-caught Pacific king salmon stands out when gently poached until meltingly tender in a delicately flavored liquid. Paired with colorful spring vegetables and herbs and drizzled with buttery wine sauce, this makes an easy entrée for two that is quite elegant, and needs only a salad and crusty bread (for sopping up the rich juices) for a complete meal. If skin and a few bones bother you, farmed Atlantic salmon fillets can be substituted—just get a thick piece. Be sure to have all the vegetables prepped and set out before you begin because once you start cooking, things start to go pretty fast. (And if you don't want to bother with the butter sauce, just add a few tablespoons of the flavorful poaching liquid to each serving bowl.) Boiled baby Yukon potatoes makes a great side dish.

Special equipment: thermometer

POACHING LIQUID

1 cup sliced white mushrooms (or stems)

2 bay leaves

12 peppercorns, crushed

Stems from 1 bunch parsley (about 20; reserve leaves for another use)

4 teaspoons kosher salt

1 cup white wine

About 6 cups Fish Stock (page 128) or water (enough to cover the fish)

SALMON AND VEGETABLES

½ cup finely julienned carrots

¼ cup finely julienned leeks

½ cup trimmed and thinly sliced white or chanterelle mushrooms

2 lemons, juiced

2 tarragon sprigs

2 (5- to 7-ounce) King salmon fillets or steaks (Halibut, sablefish, or hog snapper can be used in place of salmon)

1 teaspoon chopped chervil or ¼ teaspoon finely chopped fresh tarragon

POACHING LIQUID Combine mushrooms, bay leaves, peppercorns, parsley stems, salt, and white wine in a large saucepan wide enough to hold the fish steaks in a single layer. Cover with stock or water. Set the saucepan over medium heat and let simmer for 20 minutes, allowing the aromatics to infuse the poaching liquid. Strain off the poaching liquid into a bowl and discard the aromatics. Return the strained liquid to the pan.

SALMON AND VEGETABLES Put the carrots, leeks, and mushrooms in a soup bowl, pour in enough poaching liquid to cover the vegetables, and cover with plastic wrap. Microwave on high for 3 minutes, until vegetables are tender.

Strain any juices from the vegetable mixture back into the pot with the poaching liquid. Set vegetables aside.

Bring the poaching liquid to a boil and stir in the lemon juice and tarragon sprigs. Set aside ¼ cup of the liquid for the Vin Blanc Butter Sauce.

Leave the pan on the burner and turn off the heat. Add the fish steaks to the poaching liquid. (Add a little more water or stock if necessary to completely submerge.) Check the temperature of the broth every few minutes—you want to maintain between 150 and 160 degrees F (turn the heat to low if needed).

The fish should be cooked medium rare to medium (about 140 degrees F in the thickest part on a probe thermometer) in 10 to 15 minutes. Err slightly on the underdone side; carryover heat will do the rest.

When the fish steaks are done, add the cooked vegetables to the pot. With a slotted fish spatula, carefully place each steak in the center of a heated pasta bowl and arrange the vegetables around the outside. Drizzle with the Vin Blanc Butter Sauce, if using, or just pour a couple of ounces of broth into the bowl. Garnish with the chervil or tarragon.

VIN BLANC BUTTER SAUCE

2 tablespoons white wine

1 teaspoon finely diced shallot

¼ cup poaching liquid

3 tablespoons salted cold butter, cut in chunks

VIN BLANC BUTTER SAUCE While the salmon is poaching, pour the wine in a small saucepan, add the shallot, and bring to a boil over medium heat and allow the wine to reduce until the pan is almost dry. Add the poaching liquid and bring to a boil. Take the pan off the heat and add the cold butter, one piece at a time, and whisk vigorously until emulsified. Pour the sauce into a heated cup to keep warm. Or you can pour the hot liquid into a large ceramic coffee mug, add the butter all at once, and blend with an immersion blender.

SUGGESTED WINE PAIRING: Serve with Moillard Saint Véran Meursault (Côte-d'Or, France). Because French Chardonnays are light on oak, this wine will allow the flavor of the mushrooms and leeks to come forward.

TUNA-MUFFULETTA-NIÇOISE SALAD WITH CRISPY POACHED AND FRIED EGG

SERVES 4 AS A MAIN DISH

Here's a New Orleans riff on the Mediterranean classic, tuna niçoise, using fresh oil-poached tuna and a salad based on the olive relish we use for our muffuletta sandwiches. Instead of using hard-cooked eggs, I like to poach the eggs so their centers are still runny. I dredge them in breadcrumbs and fry them until crisp. At the restaurant, we often use sea beans—a salt marsh plant that tastes like a salty green bean—in place of the traditional green beans, which we then dip in the batter we use for our fish tacos and deep-fry until crispy. Even though this recipe involves multiple components, each one is fairly simple and all can be done ahead of time—even the eggs, which can be poached and refrigerated, then rolled in the breadcrumb mixture and quickly fried a few minutes before serving.

Special equipment: thermometer

POTATOES AND BEANS

½ pound haricot verts or thin, fresh green beans, trimmed

¾ pound small Yukon Gold potatoes

CRISPY POACHED AND FRIED EGGS

4 large eggs

About 2 cups vegetable oil for frying

1 cup all-purpose flour

1 egg, beaten with 1 tablespoon water to make an egg wash

1 cup panko breadcrumbs

SALAD

4 to 6 ounces spring greens

½ cup Sherry Vinaigrette (page 169)

1 cup Italian Olive Salad (page 189, or purchase premade)

1 recipe Oil-Poached Tuna (page 45), sliced

Place 4 dinner plates in the refrigerator to chill.

POTATOES AND BEANS Bring a pot of salted water to a boil. Have an ice bath ready. Add the beans and cook 3 to 5 minutes or until tender-crisp and still bright green; drain. Cool in an ice bath, drain again, and refrigerate until ready to use.

Meanwhile, place the potatoes in a medium pot and cover with salted water. Bring to a low boil over medium heat and cook until tender, 12 to 15 minutes.

Drain, let cool slightly, slice into ¼-inch-thick slices, and set aside.

CRISPY POACHED AND FRIED EGGS To poach the eggs, bring a medium pot of salted water to a simmer and have a bowl of ice water ready. Crack the eggs, one at a time, into a small measuring cup and carefully slide them into the water. Poach for 3 to 4 minutes, or until the whites are barely set. Using a slotted spoon, transfer each egg into the ice water, and let sit until ready to use. Drain the eggs on paper towels and trim off any loose pieces of egg. These can be made ahead, covered, and refrigerated until ready to use.

To fry the eggs, pour about 2 inches of oil into a heavy saucepan and heat to 350 degrees F. Place the flour, egg wash, and panko into each of three shallow bowls. Dredge each egg, one at a time, in the flour. Dip each egg into the egg wash until the flour is sticky, and immediately roll them in the panko bread-crumbs until covered. Add the eggs to the hot oil and quickly brown them, turning carefully to brown the other side. Transfer the fried eggs to paper towels to drain.

SALAD In a medium bowl, quickly toss the greens in the vinaigrette and divide them between the chilled plates. Overlap sliced potatoes around the greens and scatter them with some of the olive salad. Arrange the green beans around the plate. Place the tuna on top of the lettuce and add a little more of the olive mixture. Place an egg on each plate, drizzling with a little more dressing if desired.

SUGGESTED WINE PAIRING: SERVE WITH Bridesmaid Sauvignon/ Sémillon Blanc Blend (Napa, California), a clean-tasting, medium-bodied wine that lets these wide-ranging flavors shine on their own.

LOUISIANA-STYLE BOILED SHRIMP IN THE SHELL

SERVES 10 AS A MAIN DISH, 1/2 POUND PER PERSON

The many different methods of boiling shellfish, the ingredients used, and their garnishes and accompaniments are a continual source of contention in Louisiana. I will probably add to the arguments, but here is a basic method that I think works the best.

Shrimp in the shell cook pretty quickly. Once they're done, dump a gallon of ice into the pot to stop the cooking. Rinse them in some of the cooled cooking liquid while peeling and deveining to retain flavor.

The seasoning blend I use is based on the local favorite, Zatarain's. They also make a dry mix I really like. (For more on seasonings and sourcing, see page 24.) My dad used to pour the seasoning blend directly into the cooking water with the peel-and-eat shrimp, and he was a strong believer in eating this shrimp warm from the pot. You can use his method or tie this mixture in a muslin or cheesecloth bag.

The peeled, cooked shrimp can be used for a simple shrimp cocktail or shrimp rémoulade.

Special equipment: a small piece of cheesecloth or muslin and twine (optional)

SEASONING BLEND

4 tablespoons mustard seeds

2 tablespoons coriander seeds

1 tablespoon whole allspice

2 tablespoons dill seeds

1 teaspoon whole cloves

1 tablespoon crushed red pepper flakes

6 bay leaves

SEASONING BLEND If desired, place the mustard seeds, coriander seeds, whole allspice, dill seeds, cloves, red pepper flakes, and bay leaves on a piece of cheesecloth, pull the ends together and tie with twine to make a bag.

SHRIMP Place cheesecloth bag of seasonings in a stockpot with water, salt, lemons or vinegar. Alternately, add the spices directly to the water. Bring to a boil. Add the shrimp and stir to combine.

By the time the water returns to a boil, the shrimp should be done. Remove the pot from the heat. If serving hot, drain the shrimp immediately, reserving some of the liquid, if desired. Let folks peel their own shrimp as they eat, with desired accompaniments and some of the seasoned liquid in a bowl for dipping.

SHRIMP

1 gallon water

1 cup kosher salt, plus more, to taste

2 lemons, cut in half, or 1 tablespoon of white or cider vinegar

5 pounds (16 to 20 per pound) shell-on, wild-caught American shrimp, preferably from Louisiana, thawed if frozen

1 gallon ice

House Cocktail Sauce (page 158), optional

White Rémoulade Sauce (page 159), optional

Hot sauce, optional

Lemon wedges

Saltines

To prepare chilled shrimp, add ice to the pot to stop the cooking and cool the liquid; do not drain. Peel all the shrimp first. To devein them, cut a shallow (⅛ inch or less) slit from the center of the top of the shrimp, down to the tail. Lay the shrimp flat on the counter and use the tip of the knife to open the cut to remove the vein.

Rinse out any remaining black particles in the shrimp in the cooled cooking liquid. Taste and, if you'd like more spice or salt, soak the peeled shrimp in the liquid as you continue deveining the rest of the shrimp. Store in a covered container set in a bowl of ice in the refrigerator until ready to serve.

SUGGESTED WINE PAIRING: *Serve with Monchhof Estate Riesling (Mosel, Germany), a sweet, white wine high in acidity, with peach, citrus, and floral notes that harmonize well with light seafood and balance the assertive spice.*

Note: Other Seasoning Options

In other areas of the country, the seasonings added to the water can be subtle—salt, parsley stems, and bay leaf, for example. Pickling spice is okay, too, and Old Bay—whose primary flavor is celery seed—has its fans. But in Louisiana, we make our seasonings aggressively hot with cayenne. With dozens of boil seasonings here to choose from, I often use the local favorite, Zatarain's dried Crawfish, Shrimp, & Crab Boil, which contains all the seasonings you need in a box: salt, hot red pepper, dried lemon, and other seasonings (see page 24). I use the powders and bagged whole spices as opposed to the liquid boil, which tastes nasty to me.

HOW TO HAVE A CRAWFISH BOIL FOR A CROWD

Crawfish boils in New Orleans are a big part of the local culture. They are very casual. The backyard method usually involves two sawhorses and a door or big piece of plywood placed on top covered with a thick layer of newspaper. The cooker, which is a propane ring and a large tall pot with a basket, is common garage equipment. The forty-pound sack(s) of live crawfish are purged by immersing in cold water, at which time any trash from the swamp is removed along with any dead crawfish. The seasoning (most often, Zatarain's) is placed in the water, and when it's at a rolling boil you add the basket and finally the crawfish.

When the water returns to a boil, they are done. Turn off the heat and let them sit in the seasoned liquid for a few minutes, and then remove the basket and dump the steaming crawfish on the covered table. I subscribe to the western Louisiana method of sprinkling the same dried shrimp/crab/crawfish boil liberally over the crawfish at this point. I realize this is absolute heresy to many New Orleanians who swear by more complicated methods, but to me it works.

It's also common to add corn on the cob, new potatoes, mushrooms, garlic cloves, and andouille sausage to this mix. Other shellfish may make it into the same pot, as well. If you go this route, I advise cooking them separately in the seasoned boiling liquid as they all cook at different rates. Then dump them together at the end.

CRAWFISH-EATING 101

Standing around the newspaper and crawfish–covered table, it's easy to spot the crawfish-peeling novice. A Louisianan will probably be eating five or six bugs while you are struggling with your first one. Fortunately, there are hundreds to practice on. Never rely on others to do the work—you not only miss the chance to learn but you'll inhibit their eating. Every man for himself! Every woman for herself!

Hold the crawfish in your nondominant hand and twist off the head with the other. Pinch the tail longways, which loosens the meat, and peel off the top segment of the shell. Grasp the top part of the meat (after you get a little better you'll do this with your mouth) and ease out the meat. Pop it in your mouth. Between every five or so tails, suck the delicious fat out of the heads. Some folks make orderly rows of the discarded heads that record their prowess, but I get busy eating a few pounds before digging in to the potatoes, corn, sausage, and the like. Like cutting chiles, don't touch your (or anyone else's) mucous membranes until you've thoroughly washed your hands.

HAVE IT YOUR WAY

Here are some cooking times and yields for putting together whatever feast you like.

LARGE/JUMBO SHRIMP: ½ pound per person (¾ pound with heads); about 2 to 3 minutes (when water returns to a boil)

LIVE CRAWFISH: 3 to 4 pounds in the shell per person; about 8 minutes

LIVE BLUE CRABS: 2 pounds in the shell per person; about 8 to 10 minutes. Start boiling crabs in barely warm water—if you drop them into boiling water, the claws come off and you have to fish them out of the pot.

LIVE LOBSTER: ½ to 1 per person; 8 to 10 minutes for a one-pounder; add 2 minutes for each additional pound

SMOKED OR FULLY COOKED SAUSAGE (andouille, kielbasa, hot Italian): ⅛ to ¼ pound per person; 3 to 4 minutes

NEW POTATOES (or halved larger ones): 20 to 25 minutes

CORN ON THE COB: cut in thirds: ½ to 1 cob per person; 4 minutes

Suggested pairing: Serve with your favorite ice-cold beer.

HOW TO PREPARE MAINE AND SPINY (OR ROCK) LOBSTERS

To cook, fill a good-size pot with a lid halfway full of water. Cover and bring to a boil. Place the lobsters in the boiling water, cover and cook for 8 to 10 minutes. Serve whole, letting each person crack their own. Or, if you're planning to use the meat in a cold dish, remove the lobsters and place in enough ice water to cover. Allow to chill and then remove shells.

To crack and shell lobster, follow these steps.

Use a kitchen towel to protect your hands from the sharp parts and tear off the tail, arms, and claws. This is the part with the meat.

Put the tail down on the board and, using the heels of your hands, crush it. You can then break it open from the bottom. You can also cut the softer bottom of the tail with scissors or shears.

Slice the tail longways down the middle and remove the vein. Place the cut side down and slice, keeping the shape somewhat intact.

Break off the claws and, holding it by the fat part, break off the thumb. Place the claw on the board and carefully whack the rounded bottom part with the heel of a French knife so it cuts through the shell and not so much into the meat. Twist the knife and the shell should separate. Hold it by the pointed end and shake out the claw.

Break the arms in two and placing the sharp edge up, cover with a towel, and crush with the heel of your hand. Poke the meat out with your finger or a small fork. Place all the meat on a plate, cover, and refrigerate.

STONE CRAB CLAWS WITH CREOLE MUSTARD CREAM

SERVES 12 AS AN APPETIZER

Stone crabs are a seasonal delicacy prized for the sweet, tender claw meat from their famous giant claws. They're harvested primarily in Florida from October to May by removing only the largest claw, then returning them to the water where their claws regenerate. (There is a small stone crab fishery south of New Orleans that produces a few.) They're boiled on the boats before shipping and are usually served cold, with a sauce for dipping. Just crack and eat. (Be aware that there's a hard center membrane in the meat, so bite carefully.) If you're buying them fresh, note that they have a very short shelf life, so make sure there's no ammonia smell.

This sweet, tangy mustard sauce recipe is based on one I used to do at the Fish Market in Atlanta. We called it "Better Than Joe's" in reference to a similar one served at Joe's Stone Crab, the famous century-old restaurant in Miami that made these giant claws famous. This recipe makes a lot, but it keeps in the refrigerator for weeks and is also good slathered on ham or chicken sandwiches, or as a dipping sauce for smoked sausages.

CREOLE MUSTARD CREAM

3 ¼ cups mayonnaise

6 tablespoons honey

¼ cup plus 2 tablespoons Creole mustard, or other grainy mustard

1 ½ teaspoons dry mustard

4 ½ teaspoons A–1 steak sauce

4 ½ teaspoons fresh lemon juice

½ teaspoon Tabasco Sauce

3 tablespoons half-and-half

About 3 dozen stone crab claws (about 3 per person, or as many as you can eat)

CREOLE MUSTARD CREAM Place the ingredients into a large bowl and blend with a whisk or with an immersion blender. Chill until ready to serve. This sauce is also great on chilled lobster, crab, or shrimp.

To crack the claws, place the claws rounded side up on a cutting board and, using a hammer, hit the center of the claw with a sharp tap. (Do this in a plastic bag to catch sharp shells and keep the juice from splattering.) It takes a little practice to get the right amount of force—you want to avoid smashing the meat but have to break the shell. Carefully remove the pieces of shell—the edges are very sharp. The knuckles have pointy parts and on the point is where you want to tap them. They'll probably separate from the claw but that's okay. When all the shell is removed, plate the meat, wrap with plastic wrap, and refrigerate. When ready to serve, place on a platter or individual plates with bowls of the mustard sauce and open some champagne.

Suggested pairing: Serve with Veuve Clicquot Ponsardin Brut (Reims, France). This bubbly is made from Pinot Noir, Pinot Meunier, and Chardonnay grapes. Combined they are bright and structured, with soft bubbles—a wonderful match for the delicate crab and creamy mustard dipping sauce.

HOW TO PICK CRABMEAT

Blue crabs have two distinct types of meat: the white lump meat in the body and the darker claw meat. Fingers are the whole peeled claw that has the pincers attached and cartilage in the middle so they're finger food—hold by the hard claw part and eat the meat off.

Once blue crabs are cooked, break them in half with your hands or a heavy knife. Twist and pull the crab legs away from the body. Use a nutcracker if necessary for larger crabs, and to crack the claws. Use a mallet or a flat meat tenderizer to lightly crack open the claws without shattering them. Pull them apart and use a small fork or chopsticks to remove the claw meat. Use a thin metal pick to pick out the rest of the crab. Repeat with the legs, and then pick out the body meat.

SOUTHERN SHRIMP ROLL

4 LARGE ROLLS

I seek out local food wherever I travel, and what I remember from the eastern coast of Canada are the fried clams, berry pies, and, of course, the lobster rolls. Lobster roll purists have strong opinions about whether to use side-slit or top-slit buns and they might freak out about some of the dressing ingredients in this recipe, but I'm going for big Southern flavor here. I've opted to use our local shrimp instead of lobster and boost the spice with Creole seasoning. Fresh Sally Lunn rolls take it over the top. If you're avoiding bread, this salad is also fantastic stuffed into a ripe tomato.

½ cup mayonnaise

¼ cup stringed and finely diced celery

1 tablespoon finely diced roasted and peeled red pepper (page 191)

1 lemon, juiced (about 2 tablespoons)

1 teaspoon Chef Paul Prudhomme's Magic Seasoning Blends Shrimp Magic or Home Creole Seasoning (page 24)

¼ teaspoon kosher salt

1 tablespoon chopped fresh parsley

1 pound Louisiana-Style Boiled Shrimp in the Shell (page 50), peeled, deveined, and chopped into ½-inch chunks

4 large Sally Lunn Rolls (page 175) or other soft roll

1 tablespoon butter (plus more, as needed)

Mix together the mayonnaise, celery, roasted red pepper, lemon juice, Shrimp Magic, salt, and parsley in a large bowl. Fold in the shrimp and return to the refrigerator until ready to serve.

Slice the buns almost all the way through. Melt the butter in a large skillet over medium heat. Place as many of the buns as will fit, cut side down, on the hot surface for a minute or so, until lightly browned. Fill the buns with a heap of shrimp salad. Repeat with remaining buns.

SUGGESTED WINE PAIRING: *Serve with Kris Pinot Grigio (Delle Venezie, Italy), a simple grape for a simple dish. Refreshingly flavorful and aromatic, this uncomplicated white wine also goes well with grilled salmon, seafood pastas, and salads.*

VERACRUZ SEAFOOD COCKTAIL

SERVES 4 TO 6 AS AN APPETIZER

I once opened a Ruth's Chris Steak House in Cancún. It was there that I had my first cóctel de mariscos (seafood cocktail— kind of a cross between a chilled soup and ceviche) with shrimp, octopus, conch, and crabmeat. It was served in a big beer goblet and was really refreshing in the heat. I make it with octopus sometimes, which is a feat to cook without turning it to rubber. I find that frozen squid is available much more widely and it's easier to cook successfully. It's best to eat this within a few hours of making it as ketchup mixed with citrus juice tends to take on the texture of applesauce the longer it sits. It's not bad, just thick.

SEAFOOD

12 ounces frozen cleaned squid, tubes and tentacles (or use octopus)

2 quarts water

1 tablespoon kosher salt

1 teaspoon cracked black pepper

2 bay leaves

6 parsley stems (reserve the leaves for another use)

½ cup large-dice sweet onion

12 ounces (16–20 or 21–25) wild-caught American shrimp, peeled and deveined

1 quart of ice

½ pound jumbo lump crab or crab fingers (page 54), optional

½ pint fresh oysters, optional

TOMATO BASE

1 cup ketchup

¼ cup tomato juice

6 tablespoons freshly squeezed lime juice

2 tablespoons freshly squeezed orange juice

1 teaspoon Tabasco Sauce

¼ cup large-dice roasted red pepper

2 tablespoons chopped cilantro, plus a few sprigs for garnish

1 avocado, peeled and sliced (for serving)

SEAFOOD Thaw the squid under cold running water for 5 to 10 minutes and separate the tentacles. Feel the center of each to check for small pieces of beak and remove them. Run water inside the tubes and remove any stray debris with a finger. Slice the cleaned tubes in ¼-inch pieces. Place them in a bowl and mix them together with the tentacles.

In a large pot, bring the water to a boil over high heat. Add the salt, pepper, bay leaves, and parsley stems and stir. Lower the heat and simmer for 5 minutes. Add the onion and continue to simmer until slightly softened, about 3 minutes longer. With a slotted spoon, remove the onion, spread out on a plate, and put in the refrigerator.

Raise the heat and return the liquid to a boil. Add the shrimp and cook for 2 or 3 minutes, until the shrimp are just beginning to turn pink. You don't want them all the way done—the lime juice in the sauce will finish "cooking" them.

With a slotted spoon, transfer the shrimp to a large bowl. Return the liquid to a boil, add the squid, and cook for another 3 minutes. Transfer the squid to the bowl with the shrimp, add the ice, and pour the cooking liquid over them. There should be enough ice to completely cool the mixture. Let the shellfish sit in the water while you make the tomato base. (You can prepare the seafood the day before and chill in the refrigerator.)

TOMATO BASE In a medium bowl, mix together the ketchup, tomato juice, citrus juices, Tabasco, roast pepper, and the cooled onion. Mix in the cilantro and refrigerate for 1 hour, or until very cold.

To serve, drain the squid and shrimp and add it to the sauce, along with the crab and/or oysters, if using. Serve in chilled footed glass goblets or glass bowls. Garnish with avocado slices and cilantro sprigs.

SUGGESTED WINE PAIRING: *Serve with Boizel Brut Rose (Epernay, France), a dry, sparkling rosé that makes a refreshing starter paired with ice-cold seafood cocktail. This one has a pale-salmon tint, medium-fine bubbles, and strawberry aromas.*

SAUTÉED, SEARED, BLACKENED, AND BRONZED

RAINBOW TROUT WITH SWISS CHARD, OYSTERS, AND COUNTRY HAM

SPECKLED SEA TROUT MEUNIÈRE

PARMESAN-CRUSTED FLOUNDER WITH BROWN BUTTER, ASPARAGUS, CAPERS, AND CRABMEAT

HORSERADISH-CRUSTED CATFISH FILLETS

SHEEPSHEAD À LA FRANÇAISE WITH SUMMER CORN AND TOMATO

SHRIMP SAUTÉED IN BBQ BUTTER

SEARED YELLOWFIN TUNA WITH BABY BOK CHOY, STICKY RICE, AND GINGER-SOY BUTTER SAUCE

SEARED SEA SCALLOPS WITH MANGO-MELON SALSA AND PASSION FRUIT BUTTER SAUCE

BLACKENED SWORDFISH WITH CHILI HOLLANDAISE SAUCE

BRONZED COBIA WITH HOT AND SOUR MUSTARD GREENS IN POTLIKKER BROTH

Sautéing is the easiest and fastest method of cooking thin fillets of lean fish, and the one we use most often at the restaurant for its speed and versatility. The short cooking times do not leave much room for error, however. Throughout this book, I stress the importance of having all the side dishes ready and your tools and ingredients organized and prepped before you start cooking the fish. For these dishes, that's not just a suggestion—it's a requirement for success. Those rules hold true for the other pan-to-plate techniques covered in this chapter, which work well with shellfish and thicker cuts of fish.

Searing means browned slightly on the outside and raw in the middle, so it's only used with the freshest and highest quality fish. This can be done in a very hot pan or on the grill. Yellowfin tuna, wahoo, and diver-caught sea scallops are excellent prepared this way.

Blackening, the method developed and popularized by Chef Paul Prudhomme some forty years ago, is better for fattier fish that hold up to the intense heat and heavy spices. It's not a difficult technique, but really needs to be done outside unless you have a high-capacity exhaust system vented to the outdoors.

Bronzing is a not-so-black version of blackening that is less likely to set off the smoke detector.

There are several tricks to achieving that lightly crispy exterior and moist interior you're after, while keeping the fillet intact. Every stovetop and pan is different, so it's important to understand what you have to work with and adjust heat and cook times accordingly.

TIPS

- For more even cooking, use a heavy sauté pan—not Teflon—and heat it before adding the oil. Then wait a few seconds to add the butter. The oil raises the smoke point of the butter so it won't burn too fast. The oil/butter combination allows you to gauge the ideal moment to add the fish. You know you're ready when the butter melts immediately and starts to foam and brown slightly, and you start to smell the wonderful aroma. If the oil smokes, or the butter browns immediately and sputters madly, the pan's too hot and needs to be removed from the heat until it calms down a little.

- Before you begin, make sure that your pan is wide enough to accommodate the fillets comfortably. Avoid overcrowding since adding cold fish cools off the pan. The thinner the fillet, the wider the pan you'll need. If you see that they aren't going to all fit, use two pans (use the same amount of fat for each pan, whether you're cooking two servings or four).

- If you don't want to have to monitor two pans at once, brown one side of each fish in a sauté pan, then place the fish, uncooked side down, on a baking sheet coated with vegetable oil spray. Just before you're ready to serve, finish in a preheated 375-degree oven for 3 or 4 minutes. (More on this oven-finished method in the Braised, Roasted, and En Papillote chapter.)

- Lightly dust the fillets with flour rather than dredge them as for frying. You want just enough flour to aid in the caramelization and seal in the juices without masking the flavors of the fish. Depending on the fish and the preparation, you might dip it into seasoned flour and shake off the excess, or just sprinkle the surface with a teaspoon or two.

- To test for doneness, pinch the fattiest part of the fillet. When it begins to separate, it's done. If it's still elastic, it's not done. If it flakes easily, it's probably overcooked. It's best to err on the underdone side as it will continue to cook after you take it out of the pan.

FOUR GREAT BASIC BUTTER SAUCES FOR FISH

Lean fish loves butter. And there's no better place for this marriage to take place than in a skillet or sauté pan. Cooking fish in butter adds more flavor and color to the fish than oil alone would. A butter sauce adds just the right finishing touch as soon as you flip your crispy fillet onto a warm plate. See the Sauces and Dressings chapter, page 156, for recipes and more information.

I rely on four types of butter sauces for most of my fish dishes, all of which are represented in this chapter.

BROWN BUTTER SAUCE This is simply butter that's allowed to melt in a hot pan until the milk solids start to brown and take on a rich, nutty taste. The trick is keeping it from burning. A light-colored pan can help you gauge this.

BEURRE MONTÉ Chefs often call this "magic butter." It's a fast method of blending cold butter with a little hot water or hot stock to form a silky, emulsified sauce that's incredibly versatile and used throughout this book. This technique, and its variations, are covered on page 162.

COMPOUND BUTTER This is cold butter mixed with other flavorings, formed into a log, and chilled or frozen until ready to use. A few slices can be added directly to the top of a fillet, or whisked into pan juices for a sauce.

HOLLANDAISE SAUCE Here, melted butter is enriched and emulsified with egg yolk, resulting in the most luxurious sauce imaginable.

RAINBOW TROUT WITH SWISS CHARD, OYSTERS, AND COUNTRY HAM

SERVES 4 AS A MAIN DISH

Farm-raised rainbow trout fillets are mild, easily and quickly sautéed, and lend themselves to a variety of garnishes. This is one of my favorite ways to fix them. Bits of salty, smoky country ham pull the flavors of the fish, the oysters, and the chard together. I ship in country hams from Virginia for the restaurant, but finely julienned prosciutto (not sliced too thinly) or tasso ham work almost as well in this application. Spinach is a fine and more delicate alternative to the chard if you prefer. This recipe is for four servings, so if your pan isn't large enough to accommodate all the fillets, see the first two tips on page 60. They cook so quickly they should stay warm over the warm bed of greens.

CHARD

2 ounces country ham

1 large bunch Swiss chard (12 to 16 ounces) or spinach

2 tablespoons salted butter, plus more if needed

½ pound stemmed and sliced shiitake mushrooms

1 cup fresh, shucked oysters

FISH

4 (5-ounce) skin-on, boneless rainbow trout fillets (sheepshead, lionfish, and snapper are good alternatives)

Kosher salt and freshly ground black pepper

2 tablespoons all-purpose flour

2 to 4 tablespoons olive or canola oil

2 to 4 tablespoons salted butter

CHARD If using sliced country ham, sauté in a skillet on medium-high heat for 3 minutes per side, then finely julienne it. Set aside. Wash the chard; cut the leaves from the ribs and slice the leaves into bite-size pieces.

Melt the butter in a large sauté pan over medium-high heat. Add the mushrooms and cook for 3 minutes, until tender (add a little more butter, if needed.) Add the chard and cover the pan so it steams a little to soften the greens for a couple of minutes, or until tender. Stir in the julienned ham and the oysters and cook until the edges of the oysters start to curl, about a minute. Remove from the heat and place this mixture in a bowl. Cover and keep warm.

FISH Rinse and wipe out the pan and return it to the burner on medium heat. (Use two skillets if necessary, or sauté fish in batches.) Season the top side of the fish with salt and pepper; dust with flour. Add 2 tablespoons oil to each skillet then 2 tablespoons butter. If the butter is browning too quickly, remove the pan from the burner and wait a few seconds before adding the fish. (If the butter burns, dump it out, wipe out the pan, and start over.)

Place the seasoned fillets, skin-side up, in the hot pan and cook undisturbed, 2 to 3 minutes.

With a spatula, lift a fillet to check for color. When they are golden brown, tilt the pan toward you so the oil drains to the bottom and turn the fillets away from you so you don't splash oil onto yourself. Gently flip with spatula and cook, skin side down, for 2 or 3 minutes longer.

While the fish is cooking, check the flavor of the chard mixture. Country ham is very salty, but if you're using prosciutto it may need a little seasoning.

Divide the chard-oyster mixture equally between 4 large warmed pasta bowls and place the trout fillets, skin side down, on top. Drizzle with the browned butter.

SUGGESTED WINE PAIRING: *Serve with Copper River Pinot Noir (Willamette Valley, Oregon), a nice, light red with bright fruit and earthy flavors that pairs well with the oysters, Swiss chard, mushrooms, and country ham.*

SPECKLED SEA TROUT MEUNIÈRE

SERVES 2 AS A MAIN DISH

The first fish recipe you need to master is a little like learning to properly fry an egg or a pancake, and about as easy. A meunière sauce is nothing more than browned butter with a squeeze of lemon and some fresh parsley. You can amaze your friends with this one method. In French cuisine, sole is the fish that made this dish famous. Here in New Orleans, Galatoire's popularized their own version a hundred years ago with Trout Amandine, using speckled trout, a fish native to the Gulf, and adding slivered almonds to the garnish. Restaurants all over this city, and well beyond, have their own takes on this dish, and once you get the hang of it you can go in a thousand directions using whatever fish looks best at your market.

2 (5- to 6-ounce) speckled trout fillets or other fillets from a smallish fish (Alternatives are catfish, drum, or sole)

Kosher salt and freshly ground black pepper

½ cup all-purpose flour

1 tablespoon olive or canola oil

3 tablespoons salted butter, plus more if needed, divided

½ lemon, juiced

1 tablespoon chopped fresh parsley

OPTIONS TO ADD TO THE BROWNED BUTTER/LEMON JUICE MIXTURE

¼ to ½ cup sliced almonds for classic Trout Amandine

½ cup blood orange segments, 4 ounces cooked lump crabmeat, 1 tablespoon minced parsley, and 1 tablespoon orange juice

4 ounces crawfish, ½ cup corn kernels, ¼ cup diced roasted red pepper

¼ to ½ cup chopped pecans

Lightly season the fish fillets with salt and pepper and dust with the flour. Set a large sauté pan on medium heat. When hot, add the oil then 1 tablespoon butter. If the butter is browning too quickly, remove the pan from the burner and wait a few seconds before adding the fish. (If it burns, dump it out, wipe out the pan, and start over.)

Place the seasoned fillets skin side up (the flat side, if skinned) in the hot pan and cook undisturbed, for 3 to 4 minutes. With a spatula, lift a fillet to check for color. When they are golden brown, tilt the pan toward you so the oil drains to the bottom and turn the fillets away from you so you don't splash oil onto yourself. Gently flip with spatula and cook, skin side down, for 2 or 3 minutes longer.

Remove the fillets to a heated plate. Reduce heat to medium and add the rest of the butter. Using a fork or whisk, scrape the crusted bits off the bottom of the pan while the butter is browning. (If the melted butter has blackened bits, dump it out, quickly wipe out the pan, and add fresh butter.)

When the butter is medium brown (just past the color of light brown sugar), add the lemon juice and parsley, and other additions if desired.

Immediately pour over the fish fillets and serve.

SUGGESTED WINE PAIRING: *Serve with DeLoach Chardonnay (Russian River, California). The oak and butter in this wine is a perfect match for the browned butter and toasted almonds.*

PARMESAN-CRUSTED FLOUNDER WITH BROWN BUTTER, ASPARAGUS, CAPERS, AND CRABMEAT

SERVES 2 AS A MAIN DISH

Dredging fish fillets in finely grated cheese instead of flour is an easy way to add extra flavor and crunch without a bunch of extra ingredients. For this recipe, a seasoned cast iron skillet is essential for forming a crispy, golden crust that does not stick. (Teflon doesn't work, trust me.) Finish with a simple meunière sauce, or dress it up as I suggest here. This is not a hard dish, but you do need to have everything ready as it comes together really fast.

3 tablespoons vegetable oil, divided

1 tablespoon capers, drained

6 large spears asparagus, with bottom third of each spear peeled

2 (5- to 6-ounce) flounder or other thin fish fillets (Alternatives are sheepshead, snapper, or trout)

Vegetable oil spray

½ cup very finely grated Parmesan cheese

2 tablespoons salted butter

1 lemon, juiced

1 teaspoon minced parsley

4 ounces jumbo lump crabmeat, picked through

Line a small plate with a paper towel. Heat 1 tablespoon of the oil in a small skillet on medium-high heat. Add capers and fry for just a few seconds, until the buds open and they become crispy. Quickly remove with a slotted spoon and drain on paper towel.

Meanwhile, bring a large pot of salted water to a boil over high heat. Have a large container of ice water ready. Add the asparagus to the boiling water and let boil for 3 minutes until tender-crisp but not limp. Remove the asparagus with tongs (keep water hot for reheating) and transfer to the ice bath to stop cooking. Drain on paper towels.

Place a cast iron skillet large enough to accommodate both fillets on medium heat. Coat the fillets liberally with the vegetable oil spray. Spread the grated cheese on a plate and dredge the skinless (or rounded) side of the fillets in it, coating well.

Add the remaining 2 tablespoons of oil to the hot pan then place the fish, cheese side down, in the hot oil. Do not disturb for about 4 minutes.

Put about a tablespoon of the cheese directly into the skillet as a test at the same time you add the fish. When you can slide a spatula under that fried cheese medallion, you can carefully loosen the fillets and turn them. A golden brown, fried cheese crust that completely coats the fish is what you're looking for here. (Lower the heat if it's browning too quickly.) Cook about 2 minutes on the uncoated side.

While the fillets cook, return the asparagus to the pot of hot water for another minute or so to reheat. Move the fillets to a warm plate. Wipe the pan out with a paper towel; immediately return it to the heat and add the butter. When the butter is medium brown (take care not to burn), add the lemon juice, parsley, and crabmeat. Turn off heat.

Using tongs, divide the hot, drained asparagus between 2 heated plates. Place the fish on top of the asparagus spears, spoon the brown butter and crabmeat mixture over the fish, and sprinkle with the fried capers.

SUGGESTED WINE PAIRING: Serve with Freemark Abbey Chardonnay (Napa Valley, California), a very clean, balanced, refreshing wine, with pear and apple aromas. An oak-aged chardonnay is always a safe bet with mild white fish and crabmeat.

HORSERADISH-CRUSTED CATFISH FILLETS

SERVES 4 AS A MAIN DISH

A generous smear of Dijon mustard and horseradish, and a coating of Japanese breadcrumbs add just the right balance of tang, heat, and crunch to transform a common, mild-flavored fish fillet into an uncommonly delicious entrée. It's not hard to make, but the temperature of your pan is critical. Too hot and the crust will over-brown before the first side of the fish is done, and if not hot enough, the coating will become soggy from the oil and butter. If you're cooking more fillets than your pan will accommodate, see first two tips on page 60. I can think of no better side dish to serve with this than Creamy Mashed Potatoes with Chicken Skin Crackling "Gravy" (page 177).

1 cup panko breadcrumbs

1 tablespoon chopped parsley

¼ cup prepared horseradish

¼ cup Dijon mustard

4 (5- to 7-ounce) catfish fillets (Alternatives are hogfish, snapper, speckled trout, and sheepshead)

Kosher salt and freshly ground black pepper

2 to 4 tablespoons olive or canola oil

2 to 4 tablespoons salted butter

Mix the panko and parsley in a small dish. Mix the horseradish and Dijon well in another small dish. Lay out the catfish on a dinner plate and season liberally on both sides with salt and pepper, placing them skin side down.

Smear a heaping tablespoon of the mustard-horseradish mixture in a thick, even layer on each fillet. Pour the panko crumbs evenly over the fish and press to firmly adhere.

Set a large, heavy skillet on a burner over medium heat. (Use two skillets if necessary.) When hot, add 2 tablespoons of the oil then 2 tablespoons of the butter. When the butter hits the oil, it should melt immediately and start to foam a bit. If the oil smokes—or if the butter goes crazy, browning and sputtering madly—remove the pan from the heat until it calms down a little.

Place the fish, crust side down, in the skillet and cook on medium heat until the crust is golden brown; turn and continue cooking for several minutes longer, until browned and cooked through. Total cook time should be about 7 minutes.

SUGGESTED WINE PAIRING: Serve with Château Goudichaud Blanc (Bordeaux, France). The tart flavors in this wine play well with the horseradish and mustard. A French sauvignon blanc would also be a good choice.

SHEEPSHEAD À LA FRANÇAISE WITH
SUMMER CORN AND TOMATO

SERVES 4 AS A MAIN DISH

Sheepshead are among the most popular species in New Orleans based on fish market sales, even if they're often listed on menus as bay snapper or speckled trout. They're mild and sweet with a firm texture that makes them an ideal candidate for sautéing. We made the decision when we opened Fins to call them sheepshead, which was unusual at the time, but a lot of restaurants have gotten on board since.

In this preparation, the egg wash is on the outside of the flour-dusted fish, sealing in the flavor with the lightest batter you can imagine. These fillets pair really well with two quick, contrasting sauces that taste like summer and dress up the plate in a hurry. Tomato Fondue is tomato based, with a pungent dose of garlic and basil; Corn and Red Pepper Butter Sauce is a creamy butter sauce enriched with fresh corn kernels and roasted red pepper.

2 large eggs

1 tablespoon cold water

1 tablespoon chopped fresh parsley

1 cup all-purpose flour

4 (4- to 6-ounce) sheepshead fillets (Alternatives are catfish, rainbow trout, skate wings, or any thin, white fillet)

Kosher salt and freshly ground black pepper

1 or 2 tablespoons olive or canola oil

1 or 2 tablespoons salted butter

Tomato Fondue (page 161), warm

2 ounces sheep's feta, or soft goat cheese, crumbled

Corn and Red Pepper Butter Sauce (page 163), warm

Small basil leaves for garnish

Set a large sauté pan over medium heat. See the first two tips on page 60 if all fillets won't fit at the same time. Crack eggs into a large mixing bowl and whisk well. Whisk in water and parsley and beat until light and somewhat foamy. Set aside. Place flour in a shallow dish beside the egg mixture.

Season fillets with salt and pepper and dust with flour on both sides, shaking off excess. Place fillets in the egg mixture.

Add 1 tablespoon of the oil then 1 tablespoon of the butter to the sauté pan or pans if using two. When the butter foams, drain the excess egg from the fillets and add fillets to the pan, one at a time. Shake the pan like you're making an omelet and cook for 2 or 3 minutes until fillets begins to turn golden brown, then flip with a spatula and cook until lightly browned on the other side. This is a thin fillet, so it cooks at about the same rate as the egg gets golden brown.

Divide the Tomato Fondue among four heated wide pasta bowls and dot with feta. When the fish is lightly browned on both sides, place on top of the Tomato Fondue and spoon the warm Corn and Red Pepper Butter Sauce around the fish. Garnish with basil leaves.

SUGGESTED WINE PAIRINGS: Serve with Orogeny Pinot Noir (Russian River, California). The Tomato Fondue and fresh herbs will bring more flavors out of this medium-bodied wine that's not too complex, but not at all simple. If you prefer a white wine, a Chardonnay from this region would be an excellent alternative.

SHRIMP SAUTÉED IN BBQ BUTTER

SERVES 4 AS A MAIN DISH

Calling this dish BBQ only makes sense in New Orleans—there's nothing barbecued about it, but that's its name here. There are endless variations. At Fins, we serve this over grits enriched with goat cheese, along with bread for dipping. It's also great over rice. This is an easy recipe you can whip up on a moment's notice if you already have the prepared butter in your freezer. The flavors are big, and the aroma will have everyone heading to the kitchen.

BBQ BUTTER

4 tablespoons plus 4 sticks (1 pound) salted butter, softened, divided

6 tablespoons minced shallots

6 tablespoons minced garlic

2 tablespoons freshly squeezed lemon juice

1 tablespoon finely chopped fresh rosemary

1 tablespoon paprika

1 teaspoon finely chopped fresh thyme

1 teaspoon Worcestershire sauce

1 ½ teaspoon kosher salt

1 ½ teaspoons freshly ground black pepper

Pinch of cayenne pepper

SHRIMP

2 pounds (16–20 count or larger) wild-caught American shrimp, peeled and deveined

2 teaspoons Chef Paul Prudhomme's Magic Seasoning Blends Shrimp Magic or Home Creole Seasoning (page 24)

2 tablespoons olive or canola oil

2 tablespoons salted butter

½ cup amber beer, plus more, as needed (we use Abita)

½ recipe BBQ Butter

Goat Cheese Grits (page 174), warm

2 tablespoons chopped parsley

Plenty of hot, crusty bread

BBQ BUTTER Melt 4 tablespoons butter in a small sauté pan on medium-low. Add the shallots and garlic; sauté until soft but not browned. A lid helps this process so they steam a little while cooking. Spread this mixture out on a plate and refrigerate.

Place the remaining butter in the bowl of an electric mixer and whip until light and fluffy. (You can do this with a wooden spoon if you soften the butter to room temperature first.)

Reduce the mixer speed to low and add lemon juice, rosemary, paprika, thyme, Worcestershire sauce, salt, black pepper, and cayenne, along with the cooled shallot mixture. Whip on high for another minute. Divide mixture in half, cutting half of it into chunks; set aside.

Save the other half of mixture for later use by rolling it into a 2-inch-diameter log in waxed paper or plastic wrap. Refrigerate or label, date, and freeze up to 6 months.

SHRIMP Season the shrimp lightly with the Shrimp Magic seasoning. Set a large, heavy skillet or sauté pan on medium-high heat. When hot, add the oil, then the butter. When the butter foams, add the seasoned shrimp and sauté quickly for 2 minutes. Turn and continue cooking for 1 minute.

Add the beer and reduce by half. Turn down the heat to medium-low. Make sure there is enough reduced liquid to keep the temperature at a simmer. If it's all cooked off, the heat will rise quickly and the compound butter will break when you stir it in.

Whisk all the chunks of BBQ butter into the simmering beer and stir until the mixture has a creamy consistency.

Put a big scoop of grits in the center of large warmed bowls, and divide the shrimp and sauce equally on top. Garnish with parsley, serve with bread, and drink the rest of the beer for a job well done.

Suggested Pairings: Serve with En Route Les Pommiers Pinot Noir 2015 (Russian River, California). The red fruits of plum and cherry, notes of sage, and elegant tannins complement the sweet shrimp, garlic, and spices. Or, you can't go wrong with the Abita Amber used for deglazing the pan. This smooth, malty, Munich-style lager is a popular local accompaniment for many dishes, such as this one.

SEARED YELLOWFIN TUNA WITH BABY BOK CHOY, STICKY RICE, AND GINGER-SOY BUTTER SAUCE

SERVES 4 AS A MAIN DISH

One of my favorite things to do with the buttery-tender heart of the yellowfin tuna loin, besides eating it raw, is to cut it into block-shaped steaks, season it, and sear it for just a few seconds on all sides, leaving the middle raw, like an extremely rare steak. In this presentation I fan the rosy-centered tuna slices over quickly stir-fried Asian vegetables, and then tie those flavors together with a salty-sweet, ginger-spiked butter sauce. Since the tuna isn't hot in the middle, everything else for the dish needs to be. Use the freshest, highest-quality tuna you can get for this dish.

4 (5-ounce) blocks yellowfin tuna (An alternative is wahoo)

Chef Paul Prudhomme's Magic Seasoning Blends Shrimp Magic, Home Creole Seasoning (page 24), or kosher salt and freshly ground black pepper

8 heads baby bok choy (or about 6 cups rough-chopped bok choy from about ½ head regular size)

2 tablespoons toasted sesame oil, divided

12 large or 20 small trimmed and sliced chanterelle or shiitake caps

1 Thai chile, stemmed and minced, with seeds (or 1 teaspoon minced jalapeño or Fresno chile)

Kosher salt

Sticky Rice (page 184), warm

Ginger-Soy Butter Sauce (page 164), warm

Set the tuna on a plate and season liberally with the Shrimp Magic, Creole seasoning, or salt and pepper. Let stand for about an hour to achieve room temperature.

Quarter the heads of baby bok choy, leaving the stem intact to hold them together. Clean by immersing them in cold water and shaking vigorously. Dry the bok choy in a salad spinner if you have one; if not, shake off as much water as you can and drain on paper towels. They should be as dry as possible when they hit the hot oil.

Heat a 10-inch heavy skillet (or wok if you have one) on high until very hot. Add about 2 teaspoons sesame oil to the pan (it will be smoking) and quickly sear the blocks of tuna for 10 seconds on each side. Transfer to a cutting board and let them rest for a few minutes. Using a very sharp knife, slice each block into 5 or 6 pieces and reassemble them into their original shape.

Return the pan to medium-high heat. When hot, add the rest of the oil, then add the bok choy. Stir-fry, tossing often, for 3 minutes, or until tender-crisp. Add the shiitakes and the chile, season with a little salt (the soy butter is salty so don't overdo it), and continue to stir a few more minutes, until the mushrooms are tender and most of the liquid has evaporated.

Heat the oven to broil. Place the sliced tuna on a baking sheet and broil for about 30 seconds, just long enough to warm slightly without losing its red color. Divide the Sticky Rice and the bok choy mixture among four heated plates, overlap tuna on top and spoon the Ginger-Soy Butter Sauce liberally over the tuna.

SUGGESTED WINE PAIRINGS: *Serve with Mt. Beautiful Dry Riesling (New Zealand), an off-dry white wine with great fruit flavors and a touch of sweetness that pairs well with the ginger-soy butter. Stag's Leap Viognier from Napa Valley would also make a fine complement.*

SEARED SEA SCALLOPS WITH MANGO-MELON SALSA AND PASSION FRUIT BUTTER SAUCE

SERVES 4 AS A MAIN DISH

If you're lucky enough to get your hands on real Nantucket Bays or other impeccably fresh scallops, try them in a simple dish like this one. Here they are paired with a light, bright salsa and a tropical-flavored butter sauce. I make this only when I can get small melons (honeydew, Crenshaw, casaba, Santa Claus) in late summer at their season's peak. Use at least two types of melons, but the more the merrier. This is a combination hot and cold dish, so warm your serving plates but don't get them as hot as you would for other dishes.

Special equipment: 8 metal or wooden skewers

MANGO-MELON SALSA

½ cantaloupe, peeled

½ honeydew, peeled

1 large mango, peeled

2 large limes, juiced

2 tablespoons honey

1 teaspoon chopped cilantro

1 teaspoon chopped mint

½ teaspoon kosher salt

¼ teaspoon Sambal or Sriracha or ¼ diced Thai chile, seeds and all

SCALLOPS

1 pound dry-pack sea scallops, (or Nantucket Bay scallops)

Kosher salt

Vegetable oil spray

1 teaspoon olive or canola oil

Passion Fruit Butter Sauce (page 164) keep warm

Cilantro leaves for garnish

MANGO-MELON SALSA Cut cantaloupe, honeydew, and mango in pencil-width julienne pieces about 2 inches long. Place lime juice, honey, cilantro, mint, salt, and chile sauce or chopped chile in a medium bowl. (If you're using fresh chiles, it will take longer for the heat to permeate the dressing.) Stir to dissolve the honey.

Add the julienned fruit, toss and hold at room temperature until ready to serve. Or cover and refrigerate up to four hours. If made the day before, keep the dressing separate and delay adding the herbs until you mix in the fruit.

SCALLOPS Check over scallops and cut or gently pull off the side muscle (that little rectangular piece of tissue) if attached. Divide scallops evenly into 4 portions. Use 2 skewers per portion to thread scallops (so they don't spin on a single skewer) and season lightly with salt. Coat liberally on both sides with vegetable oil spray.

Heat a large heavy-bottom sauté pan or skillet on high.

Divide the salsa into the middle of four warmed plates. Some juice is good and combines well with the butter sauce.

Put the oil in the hot skillet and swirl to coat the bottom. Place the 4 skewers into the pan and sear for 2 minutes until they form a nice brown crust. Turn and repeat on the other side. Immediately place on top of the salsa, remove the skewers, and drizzle with 2 tablespoons of the Passion Fruit Butter Sauce. Garnish with cilantro leaves.

SUGGESTED WINE PAIRING: *Serve this with Moises Pinot Gris (Willamette Valley, Oregon), a white wine with tropical notes to match the flavors of this dish.*

BLACKENED SWORDFISH WITH CHILI HOLLANDAISE SAUCE

SERVES 4 AS A MAIN DISH

Blackened fish was a 1980s craze started by Paul Prudhomme that is not as popular as it once was. Before you dismiss this technique, give it a try. Start with a dense fish with some fat and a decent thickness. A well-seasoned cast iron skillet is essential. There are some seasoning blends on the market labeled for blackening, but I find that the Shrimp Magic seasoning blend I use for everything works perfectly—the blackening is all in the technique.

This dish can produce a great deal of smoke and shouldn't be done inside unless you have a heavy-duty exhaust system. Preheating an outside grill on high with the cover closed and the empty skillets inside the grill works well. When done correctly, this dish is delicious as is, but is even better topped with a mouth-tingling hollandaise sauce and served over a bed of spinach.

6 tablespoons salted butter

4 (5- to 7-ounce) skinless, thick-cut swordfish steaks (Alternatives are grouper, mahi mahi, and tuna)

4 tablespoons Chef Paul Prudhomme's Magic Seasoning Blend Shrimp Magic or Home Creole Seasoning (page 24)

Chili Hollandaise Sauce (page 167), warm

Heat 2 large, seasoned, cast iron skillets to smoking. Melt the butter in a shallow soup bowl in the microwave for about 1 minute. Set the fish steaks on a plate. Sprinkle 1 tablespoon of the seasoning on 1 side of each steak. Dip the seasoned side in the butter, and then place the fish, seasoned side down, in the prepared pans. Cook for about 4 minutes, until fish begins to blacken, and pour the leftover butter from the bowl on top of the steaks. Turn and continue cooking for an additional 3 or 4 minutes, depending on the thickness of the fish, just until flesh begins to separate when pinched. Remember that the fish will continue cook once removed from the smoking-hot pan, so err on the underdone side. If the fish is quite thick and starts to burn before it's done, reduce the heat or remove from the burner and let the fish cook through with the residual heat. Serve the blackened fish steak with Chili Hollandaise Sauce.

SUGGESTED WINE PAIRING: Serve with Carter Oak Old Vine Zinfandel (Napa, California), always a good bet with its heavy spicy flavors. A full-bodied white, such as Kim Crawford Unoaked Chardonnay 2015 (Marlborough, New Zealand), is also good.

BRONZED COBIA WITH HOT AND SOUR MUSTARD GREENS IN POTLIKKER BROTH

SERVES 4 AS A MAIN DISH

I am a traditionalist when it comes to Southern greens. I like to cook turnip or mustard greens (I'm not a fan of the tougher collards) with pork, onion, and a little chile spice, and season them with a splash of vinegar at the table. Besides the predictable fried chicken or catfish, I might pair them with a meaty cobia steak seasoned with Creole spices and then bronzed in a skillet to caramelize the surface, without blackening it and setting off your smoke alarm. While the greens cook, whip up a quick batch of old-time Hot Water Cornbread. The crunchy fried nuggets are just the thing for sopping up potlikker, the savory liquid in the pot, which also makes a wonderful juice for the fish just by mixing in some rice vinegar and reducing it a bit.

GREENS

1 or 2 large bunches of mustard or turnip greens (at least 8 cups cleaned leaves with stems removed; see Tip)

1 tablespoon plus 2 teaspoons kosher salt, divided

8 thick slices of good bacon, finely chopped

½ cup diced yellow onion

1 jalapeño, Fresno, or small Thai chile, finely chopped, seeds and all

1 bay leaf

1 tablespoon sugar

½ teaspoon freshly ground black pepper

6 cups water

Hot Water Cornbread (page 174)

GREENS Tear the leaves off their stems. Immerse the torn greens into a sink full of cold water and clean them thoroughly. If there is any sand residue in the sink, repeat the process again. Drain in a colander.

Fill your largest pot half-full of water, add a tablespoon of salt, set over high heat and bring to a boil. Pack the cleaned greens into the pot just for a minute and drain off the water. This is to shrink the volume so you use less liquid to cook them in.

Cook the bacon in a large saucepan on medium heat, stirring frequently. When it starts to brown, add the onion and chile. Lower the heat and cook until the onion is somewhat soft but not browned, about 5 minutes.

Stir in the wilted greens and add the bay leaf, sugar, 2 teaspoons salt, and black pepper, along with 6 cups of water. Cook until the greens are tender and the liquid is reduced to about 4 cups. Depending on the size of the greens, this should take at least 30 minutes. Keep warm.

Drain off 2 cups of the potlikker and taste it. You want a rich bacon flavor with the tang of the greens, and a decent level of heat from the chile and black pepper. You may need to add a teaspoon or two of diced chiles, depending on the heat desired. Be sparing with the salt—the vinegar seems to accentuate the salt content.

While the greens are cooking, make the Hot Water Cornbread.

TIP:

If you bought turnip greens with the turnips still attached, peel them, cut them into large dice, and cook them right along with the greens—they'll taste great. You can also cook them separately by browning them in butter in a skillet over medium heat and finishing them in a 350-degree F oven for 10–15 minutes, or until tender.

FISH AND POTLIKKER BROTH

4 tablespoons salted butter

4 (5-ounce) cobia steaks cut at least ¾ inch thick (Alternatives are any large, moderately fat fish such as Louisiana barracuda, Spanish mackerel, or salmon)

1 tablespoon Chef Paul Prudhomme's Magic Seasoning Blends Shrimp Magic or Home Creole Seasoning (page 24)

2 cups reserved potlikker from cooked greens

¼ cup rice vinegar

FISH AND POTLIKKER BROTH Heat a skillet over high heat. Melt the butter in a shallow soup bowl in the microwave for about 1 minute. Set the fish steaks on a plate. Sprinkle Creole seasoning on one side of each steak. Dip the seasoned side in the butter then place the fish, seasoned side down, in the hot skillet and cook for 4 minutes. Turn, cover the pan with a lid, reduce the heat to low, and cook on low heat for an additional 4 to 5 minutes, depending on the thickness of the fish.

In a saucepan, bring the potlikker to a boil and add the vinegar.

Using tongs, put about a half a cup of drained greens in the center of 4 warmed pasta bowls. Divide the broth, top with the cobia steaks, and add 6 rounded coffee spoon-size pieces of cornbread per bowl.

SUGGESTED WINE PAIRING: Serve with Margerum M5 Rhone Blend, (Santa Barbara, California), a minerally, medium-bodied red with black cherry and pepper flavors that stands up well to full-flavored fish and pungent greens.

GRILLED AND SMOKED

SMOKED RAINBOW TROUT WITH HORSERADISH CREAM

GRILLED REDFISH ON THE "HALF-SHELL" WITH SMOKED TRI-COLOR PEPPER AND GRILLED ONION SALSA

WHOLE GRILLED BRANZINO WITH BABY SQUASH AND PEPPERS

GRILLED GROUPER WITH PINEAPPLE-BASIL GLAZE AND SPICY SWEET POTATO-CORN HASH

WOOD-GRILLED SCALLOPS WITH MUSHROOM RISOTTO, SAUTÉED MUSHROOMS, AND MUSHROOM BUTTER SAUCE

SHORT-SMOKED SALMON FILLETS WITH CHARRED ONION AND CHIPOTLE BUTTER SAUCE

SMOKED SIZZLING OYSTERS

I live on the second story of an old French Quarter building and I often cook on the balcony on the smallest Weber grill they make. Skewered scallops, shell-on shrimp, or any quickly grilled fish only necessitate a couple of handfuls of charcoal, and the tight-fitting lid lets me add bits of wood for smoke. It's a convenient way to cook dinner for myself, and maybe a few friends, in practically no time, without messing up the kitchen. Thicker, fattier fish tend to grill better than thin, lean fillets. They have a lot of flavor on their own, especially when infused with wood smoke. For these dishes, I lean toward light, fresh-flavored salsas, salads, and slaws or a few pats of flavored butter for elevation rather than rich, complicated sauces and garnishes. For each of these recipes, I suggest sides that not only complement the flavors of the fish, but can be made ahead so you can get everything plated while the fish is good and hot when you're ready to serve it.

GRILLING TIPS

- Clean your grill rack and spray it with vegetable oil spray. Propane grates are fixed so you can spray them while hot. A good way to control the heat with propane is to turn off half the burners. If the fish gets too hot directly over the flame you can just move it over a bit.

- Use the same amount of charcoal each time. You can't set a precise temperature like an oven, so by using the same amount, you'll get used to the heat it generates and you'll be better able to judge how long it takes your fish to cook. You want just enough fire to cook your fish, which isn't much, but you do want it hot enough for caramelization. I find that about 20 briquettes does the trick for up to 4 (6-ounce) fillets or 2 small whole fish; if you're grilling for a crowd, or cooking larger fish, you'll need to adjust accordingly.

- When the coals are covered with white ash, spread them out on one side to make an even bed corresponding to the area of the grill you'll be grilling on. Spray the grill again and add a pinch of wood twigs or chips if you want a little extra smoke flavor.

- Fillets cook faster than whole fish and skin-on sides. You can control a fire that's a little too hot by adjusting the grill dampers.

- Thinner fish will cook faster, so higher heat is needed to get the same degree of browning.

- Spray the grill and both sides of the fish liberally with vegetable oil and let a crust form before moving the fillet. If you're after crosshatched grill marks, give the fish a quarter turn as soon as a crust is formed enough so it doesn't stick.

- Cooking with a lid converts your grill into a very hot oven. The heat is circulating all around the fish as well as from the coals underneath it, so be careful to avoid overcooking.

- Judging doneness takes some practice. Timing varies with the type and size of fish, the heat of your grill, and your personal preference. The cake tester method on page 23 works well here, or go for 125 to 130 degrees on an instant-read thermometer. Or just give it a pinch—if the fish separates slightly, it's done.

SMOKED RAINBOW TROUT WITH HORSERADISH CREAM

SERVES 4 AS A MAIN COURSE OR 6 TO 8 AS AN APPETIZER

Freshwater rainbow trout is a reliably easy fish to source and is a great fish to hot-smoke. The preparation of the fire and low temperature required are trickier at first than preparing the fish. Since you'll be cooking this with the skin on and removing it before serving, don't worry about getting it too smoky. It's very mild and pairs well with the horseradish.

A barrel smoker with a water pan under the top grill is the easiest equipment to use for this recipe. You need some distance from the heat source, so a small grill doesn't work nearly as well. Ideally the cook temperature is about 200 to 250 degrees F. If all you have is a propane grill, you can still cook on it by turning one burner on low and placing the fish as far away from the heat as you can. A tin can makes a fine chip holder for that type of grill—just set it over the flame.

Special equipment: barrel smoker with a water pan, or a propane grill with a cover; charcoal, wood chips, cast iron skillet or perforated tin can, wood chips, microplane

2 whole, skin-on rainbow trout, bone and head removed (Alternatives are mullet, speckled trout, and the collar and cheeks from a tuna or other 8 pound or larger fish)

Kosher salt and freshly ground pepper

1 lemon, halved

2 tablespoons good olive oil

1 (2-inch) piece of fresh horseradish

Vegetable oil spray

Horseradish Cream (page 168)

4 generous handfuls of mixed microgreens

Sherry Vinaigrette (page 169)

Light a charcoal or propane grill as directed (see GRILLING TIPS, page 80).

Open the fish and season the flesh with salt and pepper. Squeeze the lemon over the surface and spread a tablespoon of olive oil on each fish. Using a microplane, grate about a teaspoon of horseradish on each fish, distributing it as evenly as you can. Close up the fish and spray both sides of the skin with vegetable oil spray.

Add chips to the fire, cover the grill, and when the smoke is built up, place the fish as far from the heat source as you can. If you have a probe thermometer that you can insert into a top flue, you'll want to reach 250 degrees F. Cook time will vary widely due to temperature variations. What you're looking for in doneness is firm to the touch, which could be as little as 10 or as long as 20 minutes. If you have an electric smoker that has a thermostat it will be on the longer side. If you do have a probe thermometer the internal temperature should be 160 degrees F.

Remove the fish from the grill and refrigerate.

When the trout is chilled, trim off the tail and about a half-inch of the belly. It's easier to skin whole and you should be able to peel off the skin with your fingers. Start at the big end and gently pull down and it will probably come off in one piece. Use a table knife or spatula to carefully separate the sides from each other. Put them in the refrigerator covered with plastic wrap. They will be good for three to four days at this point.

Remove the chilled trout fillets from the refrigerator and cut them lengthwise with a very sharp slicer. Pull these strips apart with your fingers about an inch each. They will naturally separate into chevron shapes. This presentation is entirely for visual effect, so if you'd rather, just cut them into 1-inch chunks. Return them to the plate and back into the refrigerator. Chill four plates for serving.

Divide the fish onto the center of the four plates in a little mound and divide the cream in spoonfuls over the fish.

Cover with a handful of microgreens. Drizzle with vinaigrette and serve.

WINE SUGGESTION: Serve with Blindfold White Wine (Oakville, California). This Chardonnay-based blend layered with a variety of other full-bodied whites has stone fruit flavors that work well with the cold smoked trout.

GRILLED REDFISH ON THE "HALF-SHELL" WITH SMOKED TRI-COLOR PEPPER AND GRILLED ONION SALSA

1 SIDE OF REDFISH PER PERSON

Louisiana anglers swear by this tried and true method of cooking redfish. Because of their heavy scales and thick skin, the fish, which typically weigh 6 to 8 pounds each, are filleted into two pieces and then cooked skin side down without scaling on a closed grill. The usual portion per person is half a fish. The thick, unscaled skin acts as a container for the fish, and you eat it right out of the "shell." This is a great way to keep the flesh from falling apart or drying out while cooking, but since the meat doesn't come in contact with the grill, there isn't any caramelization and that's where a huge amount of flavor comes from. To get that flavor, we changed the process slightly and started grilling them flesh side down.

This recipe serves 1 person, but it's easy to scale it up to serve as many people as you like. It makes for a great casual backyard meal served with assertive accompaniments like Smoked Tri-Color Pepper and Grilled Onion Salsa.

Special equipment: charcoal or propane grill, charcoal, a few wood chips (optional)

1 side of redfish per person, scales on (Alternatives are red snapper, sheepshead, black drum, or other thick-skinned fish)

1 teaspoon Chef Paul Prudhomme's Magic Seasoning Blends Shrimp Magic or Home Creole Seasoning (see page 24) per side

Vegetable oil spray

Tri-Color Pepper and Grilled Onion Salsa (page 190)

Light a charcoal or propane grill as directed (see GRILLING TIPS, page 80), using about 30 briquettes.

The skin and scales shield the flesh from the heat so it takes a bit more heat to cook it through.

Season the flesh side of the fish with Shrimp Magic, spray liberally with vegetable oil, and place on the grill, skin side up. Cook for about 4 minutes, just enough to get a little caramelization. Turn the fish skin side down and cover the grill. Cook until the thickest part of the fillet can be separated with a fork, 6 to 8 minutes.

Serve on the biggest plate you have with a bed of Tri-Color Pepper and Grilled Onion Salsa, and eat it right off the skin!

SUGGESTED WINE PAIRING: Serve with Girard Petite Sirah (Napa Valley, California), a red wine with bright acidity and notes of bacon and espresso, which highlights the smoky, robust flavors of the hearty fish and the salsa.

SPOTLIGHT ON REDFISH

Redfish is a mild-flavored, medium-textured fish that's abundant in Louisiana, and there are dozens of ways to cook them. They were hardly known outside the region until the 1980s when Chef Paul Prudhomme put blackened redfish on his menu at K-Paul's Louisiana Kitchen. Customers went wild for them, and demand skyrocketed nationwide. Schools of redfish were targeted by spotter planes and rounded up by the thousands in huge nets by commercial fishermen happy to sell them to this new market. There was no limit because, up until that point, there was no demand. Concerned about the health of the resource, Chef Paul switched to blackening yellowfin tuna. Today redfish are protected game fish that can no longer be harvested commercially anywhere in the state. The wild redfish we serve in the restaurant is almost always from Mississippi, but sometimes from as far off as the Carolina coast. But recreational game limits here are still generous, and redfish often turns up at backyard cookouts or in a pot of Court Bouillon (page 134).

WHOLE GRILLED BRANZINO
WITH BABY SQUASH AND PEPPERS
1 FISH PER PERSON

Branzino, a tender, silver-skinned Mediterranean fish also known as European sea bass, is being farmed in the US, and has become increasingly available in markets. They're great for grilling. There are many ways to handle cooking whole fish on the grill. What they should all produce is a crispy intact skin and a juicy interior. This recipe is one of the simplest, using few ingredients and really showcasing the flavor of the fish. You don't need a lot of heat to grill a smallish fish—20 charcoal briquettes should do the trick. A covered grill will channel the heat all over the surface of the fish so it doesn't have to be directly over the coals.

There are two different ways of scoring a fish to cook it whole. One is done with a very sharp knife or a new, single-edged razor blade by making shallow slices about a quarter of an inch deep in a crosshatch pattern on both sides. The other (which definitely works better if you're deep-frying) is to make deep slices diagonally through the skin all the way to the bone, 4 or 5 slices per side. The slicing method exposes more surface area both to the heat and the seasoning so it cooks faster. It's also easier to stand the whole fish up on the grill in a swimming position so it cooks without needing to be turned. The shallow scoring is better if you're laying the fish down directly on the grill. Spray oil is your best friend to prevent sticking, both on the grill and the fish.

Tender vegetables can be placed on the grill alongside the fish for an easy side. A drizzle of flavored oil makes a fine, fresh enhancement that doesn't mask the beauty of this simple dish.

Special equipment: charcoal or propane grill, charcoal, a few wood chips (optional)

1 whole branzino (1 ½–2-pound) per person, cleaned and scored (Alternatives are red snapper, speckled trout, pompano, or freshwater bass)

Kosher salt and freshly ground black pepper

Fines herbes (page 25), or any combination of chopped herbs, such as parsley, basil, chives, tarragon, chives, or chervil

Vegetable oil spray

Halved baby squash (1 or 2 per person)

Red or yellow bell peppers, cut in wedges (½ per person)

2 tablespoons good olive oil

½ lemon or lime

Citrus Chile Oil (page 167)

Cilantro Purée (page 166)

Light a charcoal or propane grill as directed (see GRILLING TIPS, page 80), using about 20 briquettes. Season the fish liberally with salt and pepper on the skin and exposed flesh, and rub some of the fines herbes into the cuts.

Spray the grill grates, fish, and vegetables heavily with vegetable oil spray.

Place the fish upright on the grill if sliced, and on the side if scored, surround with the vegetables, and cover the grill. If it's upright you won't need to move it at all during the 10 minutes or so of cooking. Resist the impulse to turn the fish too early—what you're striving for is golden brown, crispy skin that is attached to the fish and not stuck to the grill. After 4 minutes or so, ease a spatula under one edge and gently lift it to check if it's ready to turn. If so, carefully turn it over, along with the vegetables, and continue cooking for an additional 4 minutes. To test for doneness, use the cake tester method or internal thermometer as directed on page 94. If fish isn't quite to the muscle separation point when removed from the grill, resting covered on the counter for 2 minutes should complete the cooking. To serve, plate on a big dinner plate or platter and drizzle with olive oil and a squeeze of lemon. Lightly cover with freshly chopped herbs. Garnish with Citrus Chile Oil and Cilantro Purée.

SUGGESTED WINE PAIRING: *Serve with La Sirena Dry Moscato Azul (Napa, California), a clean, dry (not sweet) Muscat with floral and fruit flavors and a little spritz. This unusual wine goes beautifully with most any light seafood dish, from sushi to grilled fish.*

GRILLED GROUPER WITH PINEAPPLE-BASIL GLAZE AND SPICY SWEET POTATO-CORN HASH

SERVES 4 AS A MAIN DISH

Grouper, like snapper, comes in literally dozens of commercially available varieties. Reds, yellow edge, and scamp are fine fish, but are a little delicate and are best sautéed. Black, gag, Warsaw, or snowy are great for the grill. Black grouper is hands down my favorite for this dish. It has a sweet flavor and a meaty texture with enough fat to stay juicy. It's usually at least ten pounds, so the size of the "flake" is large as well. (Generally, the larger the fish, the larger and more defined the individual pieces within the fillet. At this size, "flake" really isn't the right word.)

We often glaze grouper and other grilled fish with a flavored compound butter that can be made ahead and refrigerated or frozen. The sweet potato hash pairs well with the tropical flavors of the butter.

Special equipment: charcoal or propane grill, charcoal, a few wood chips (optional)

PINEAPPLE-BASIL COMPOUND BUTTER

1 (6-ounce) can pineapple juice

10 basil leaves

8 tablespoons (1 stick) salted butter, room temperature

1 tablespoon finely diced fresh pineapple (optional)

SPICY SWEET POTATO-CORN HASH

1 large sweet potato, peeled and cut into ½-inch dice

2 tablespoons salted butter

1 tablespoon diced shallot

2 tablespoons diced poblano pepper

1 tablespoon diced red pepper

1 teaspoon Chef Paul Prudhomme's Magic Seasoning Blends Shrimp Magic or Home Creole Seasoning (page 24)

2 ears sweet corn, cut off the cob

½ teaspoon salt

1 cup vegetable oil for frying

PINEAPPLE-BASIL COMPOUND BUTTER Put the pineapple juice in a small sauté pan and simmer on medium heat until reduced to 2 tablespoons. Watch it carefully when it gets thick, and stir it off the sides with a rubber spatula. Spread it onto a dinner plate to cool quickly in the refrigerator. Roll the basil leaves up into a cylinder and slice them as thinly as you can.

Whisk the cooled pineapple reduction into the soft butter vigorously until incorporated. Stir in the basil and mix until equally distributed. Add the diced pineapple if using.

Place a 10-inch section of plastic wrap on the counter and spread the butter in the center. Roll the butter into a log shape about the size of a stick of butter and refrigerate.

SPICY SWEET POTATO-CORN HASH Place the sweet potatoes in a bowl, cover with cold water, and let soak while you prepare the rest of the ingredients.

Melt the butter in a large sauté pan or skillet on medium heat. Add the shallot and cover to "sweat" for a couple of minutes, removing the lid once or twice to stir. Add the poblano, red pepper, and seasoning and continue cooking for 4 minutes, or until tender. Add the corn and salt, cover, and reduce the heat to low.

Drain the sweet potatoes and heat the oil in a small, heavy-bottom saucepan to about 300 degrees F. (The sugar content of potatoes varies and some will brown at that temperature, but that's ok.) Carefully add the diced potatoes to the hot oil and cook until fork-tender, about 5 minutes. Remove them with a slotted spoon and drain on paper towels. (You can do this step of the recipe ahead of time and refrigerate.)

Raise the heat of the covered vegetables and stir in the cooked potatoes. Keep warm.

GROUPER

4 (4- to 5-ounce) grouper steaks
(Alternatives are gag, Warsaw, or
snowy grouper; tripletail, amberjack,
and mahi mahi)

Kosher salt and freshly ground pepper

Chef Paul Prudhomme's Magic
Seasoning Blends Shrimp Magic or
Home Creole Seasoning (page 24)

Vegetable oil spray

GROUPER Light a charcoal or propane grill as directed (see GRILLING TIPS, page 80), using about 20 briquettes.

Season the fish with salt, pepper, and Shrimp Magic, and coat liberally with vegetable oil spray. Grill for 2 or 3 minutes on each side, rotating the steaks slightly for a crosshatch pattern if desired. After getting some surface caramelization on both sides, move fish to a cooler part of the grill and cover for 2 or 3 minutes more, or until done. "Done" may feel a little different in a bigger fish—somewhat firmer than a thinner more tender fish— since the size of the muscle structure is different. If the fish separates slightly when you give it a pinch, it's done.

Divide the hash among plates and set a grouper fillet atop each. Top with a pat of Pineapple-Basil Compound Butter.

SUGGESTED WINE PAIRING: Serve with Supernatural Sauvignon Blanc/Sémillon (Hawke's Bay, New Zealand), a dry white wine that balances the sweetness and the spice. When blended with Sémillon grapes, sauvignon blanc matches up well with more complex seafood dishes.

WOOD-GRILLED SCALLOPS WITH MUSHROOM RISOTTO, SAUTÉED MUSHROOMS, AND MUSHROOM BUTTER SAUCE

SERVES 4 AS A MAIN DISH

The earthy flavors of wild mushrooms have a natural affinity for almost any seafood on the grill, especially with a little wood thrown into the fire. Grilled scallops require so little work that I don't mind investing some extra time on the front end making one of my favorite mushroom-based side dishes to go with them: risotto cooked in homemade mushroom stock, garnished with as many different kinds of sautéed mushrooms as I can lay my hands on, and finished with a creamy mushroom-infused butter sauce.

All the heavy lifting can be done well in advance, making for a fast feast the day you're planning to serve it. But you do need to be organized. Follow Fins' shortcut method of partially cooking risotto the day before, using stock that's already labeled and refrigerated (see page 178).

Special equipment: charcoal or propane grill, charcoal, a few wood chips, 8 small bamboo skewers

1 pound dry-pack sea scallops

Kosher salt

Vegetable oil spray

Water, as needed

Wild Mushroom Risotto (page 180), warm

Mushroom Butter Sauce (page 165), warm

Chopped fines herbes (page 25) or fresh parsley for garnish

Light a charcoal or propane grill as directed (see GRILLING TIPS, page 80), using about 20 briquettes, adding wood chips to coals when they're covered in ash.

Check over scallops and cut or gently pull off the side muscle (that little rectangular piece of tissue) if attached and line up scallops for skewering in equal rows. Use two skewers per portion (so they don't spin on a single skewer) and season lightly with salt. Spray liberally on both side with vegetable oil spray.

Grill the skewers, covered, for about 2 minutes on each side.

Meanwhile, stir a little water into the warm risotto if it has become too dry. Put a big spoonful of risotto in the center of a large warmed soup bowl or plate. Top liberally with the sautéed mushrooms and slide the scallop portions off the skewers onto the risotto. Top with a couple of tablespoons of the Mushroom Butter Sauce and garnish with freshly chopped fines herbes or parsley.

SUGGESTED WINE PAIRING: *Serve Gary Farrell Pinot Noir (Russian River, California), a woodsy and complex pinot noir, which is a natural match for the intense fungi flavors.*

SHORT-SMOKED SALMON FILLETS WITH CHARRED ONION AND CHIPOTLE BUTTER SAUCE

SERVES 4 AS A MAIN DISH

"Short-smoked" is menu verbiage for the cold-smoking process, which just means a lot of smoke and not much fire. The smoking process flavors the fish and tones down the fatty flavor of farmed salmon or any fat fish. I also use it on freshwater bass that may have a grassy flavor from a farm pond. The spicy, smoky flavor of chipotle and charred onion in the creamy butter sauce complements these flavors really well, as would Sweet Corn and Red Pepper Butter Sauce (page 163), pictured here.

If all you have is a propane grill, you can use a pie tin to light the charcoal in. Some sort of perforated metal pan, sieve, or even an old piece of window screen comes in handy to move the fish in and out of the smoker in one operation.

This is great with Crawfish and Corn Spoonbread (page 151).

Special equipment: *covered grill or smoker, charcoal, wood chips, perforated metal pan or screen*

4 (5- to 6-ounce) salmon fillets (preferably Irish or Scottish Atlantic farm-raised) (An alternative is freshwater bass)

¼ cup teriyaki sauce

Vegetable oil spray

Charred Onion and Chipotle Butter Sauce (page 166), warm

Put the fillets in a shallow pan and pour on the teriyaki sauce, turning the portions several times to coat them all over. Remove them after 3 minutes (any longer and the fish could absorb too much sugar, causing it to darken on the grill). Place on a screen or large sieve.

Make a very small charcoal fire by lighting 6 or 8 briquettes in a perforated tin can or a cast iron skillet. When the coals are covered in white ash, put a handful of chips directly on the coals and close the top of the grill, leaving a small crack in the vent so the fire isn't totally extinguished from lack of oxygen. The grill will immediately start filling with smoke, and you want a large amount built up.

Quickly lift the top of the grill and place the tray, sieve, or screen holding the fish as far from the coals as you can and put the lid back on. Smoke for 4 minutes and move the tray back to the refrigerator. Remove the grill grate.

At this point you can add enough charcoal to grill the fish. Twenty briquettes are plenty to cook four pieces of fish in a covered grill.

When the coals are covered with white ash, spray the grill grate with vegetable oil spray and place it back on the fire. Spray the fish liberally on both sides as well and cook, covered, about 4 minutes on each side. Salmon is best cooked medium or medium-rare. Serve with Charred Onion and Chipotle Butter Sauce.

SUGGESTED WINE PAIRING: *Serve with* Mer Soleil Chardonnay *(Santa Lucia Highlands, California). The ripe fruit flavors and tropical scents of this buttery wine balance the rich, spicy flavors of this dish.*

SMOKED SIZZLING OYSTERS

SERVES 8 TO 12 AS AN APPETIZER

I wanted to recreate the sizzle and the flavor of New Orleans char-grilled oysters, but I didn't have the space or equipment to do it. So I came up with this method, where the raw oysters are briefly cold-smoked to give them a smoky flavor and instantly cooked on 800-degree shells. You can do this at home, too, as long as you have a propane grill with a cover and the shells are completely cleaned and dried. (You also need to plan for this several days in advance to allow oyster shells ample time to dry.) Be sure to have everything else ready for the dish ahead of time: warm French bread, quartered lemons, extra butter for dipping, open champagne, etc.

Special equipment: propane grill with a cover, charcoal, hickory wood chips, cast iron skillet or perforated tin can, oyster knife

4 dozen fresh oysters

2 tablespoons Chef Paul Prudhomme's Magic Seasoning Blends Shrimp Magic or Home Creole Seasoning (page 24)

4 cups rock salt

1 pound (4 sticks) butter, melted

1 or 2 tablespoons chopped fresh parsley

2 lemons, quartered

Warm French bread for serving

Shuck the oysters (see page 33), transfer to a container, and refrigerate.

Clean the shells thoroughly with a metal scrub pad to remove any adhered particles. Rinse and then place on a baking sheet in a 350-degree F oven for at least 6 hours or overnight. (This gets rid of all the moisture so they won't explode at a higher temperature).

When ready to cook, make a very small charcoal fire by lighting 5 or 6 pieces of charcoal in a perforated tin can or a cast iron skillet. When the coals are covered in white ash, place a handful of hickory chips on the coals and close the lid of the grill to cut off as much air as you can and build up a good head of smoke.

Place the oysters in a metal colander or sieve and season liberally with the Shrimp Magic. When the smoke is rolling, quickly open the lid, place the colander as far from the coals as you can get it, and shut the lid. (Work fast—this operation should take only about a second so you won't lose smoke). Smoke for 3 or 4 minutes, transfer the oysters to a container, and refrigerate. (This can be done the day before.)

Spread the dried shells out in the grill and close the lid.

About an hour before serving, turn the grill on high with the cover down to heat the shells.

Place 1 cup of rock salt on each of 4 large serving platters for sharing and set them close to the grill. Heat the melted butter to very warm.

Just before you're ready to serve, drop the smoked and seasoned oysters into the melted butter.

With tongs, carefully place 12 sizzling shells on each plate.

With the tongs, drop the warm, buttery oysters on the hot shells, spoon a little melted butter on each one and top with chopped parsley. Serve with lemon wedges and French bread for dipping.

SUGGESTED WINE PAIRING: *Serve with Remy Pannier Muscadet (Loire, France). This clean, dry, white wine with smoky, saline aromas and flavors of honeysuckle and lemon brings out the best in oysters without overpowering them.*

BRAISED, ROASTED, AND EN PAPILLOTE

BRAISED SPANISH MACKEREL WITH GLAZED TURNIPS, CABBAGE, THAI CHILES, AND RED WINE SAUCE

MUSSELS AND ITALIAN SAUSAGES BRAISED IN WHITE WINE

WHOLE RAINBOW TROUT STUFFED WITH EGGPLANT RAGOUT

MACADAMIA AND PEPPERCORN-CRUSTED SWORDFISH

POMPANO EN PAPILLOTE WITH OYSTERS, ROCKEFELLER SPINACH, AND MELTED TOMATO

RED SNAPPER EN PAPILLOTE WITH BRAISED FENNEL, TOMATO, OLIVES, AND FETA

ome tastes are learned, like stinky cheese, single malt Scotch, and Maduro cigars.

Many members of the fish world also fall into this category. I like to think of these as "grown-up food." Unlike the bland, nondistinctive fillets we cut our teeth on at our first fish fry, the fish species featured in this chapter are fuller-flavored, with meatier textures that stand up to hearty pairings such as bacon and cabbage, or anchovies and eggplant. They may prefer a bold Cabernet to a sauvignon blanc, and an earthy sauce made with veal stock and mushrooms rather than a beurre blanc.

These recipes are slightly more involved than a quick sauté or turn on the grill, and are the next step in cooking more complicated dishes with a few more ingredients building on the same technique. Because each finishes in the oven, or in a covered vessel at a lower heat, there's less hand-eye coordination as in some of the lightning-fast dishes in previous chapters. Those last minutes spent in the oven can give you time to assemble the rest of the meal's components. Some of these recipes are whole meals in and of themselves, with everything hot and in one place for serving.

Some are insulated in sturdy nut crusts, parchment paper or foil, or their own fatty skins to shield them from drying out, and also giving you the option to partially cook them ahead and finish in the oven. These dishes are also a great way to go if you're serving more guests than one skillet can accommodate.

HOW TO GAUGE DONENESS

It's harder to tell the moment a fish is cooked to perfection when it's not right in front of you. One way to test the doneness of a fish roasting in the oven (especially if it's wrapped in parchment) is to use the chef's trick of inserting a metal cake tester into the center, touching it to your lower lip for a second or two, and seeing if it is very warm, but not hot. You can use an instant-read thermometer, but I don't advise it as it can tear the flesh. If you do, shoot for about 130 degrees F (a little less for medium-cooked salmon). Remember that the temperature will continue to rise out of the oven, so if you allow it to come to the standard recommended 145 degrees F your fish will likely be overcooked.

If thick steaks aren't quite to the muscle separation point, resting covered on the counter for two minutes should complete the cooking. Err on the side of slightly underdone, and you may find you like your fish medium-well instead of well-done.

Here is a rundown of the terminology of the techniques that apply. For roasting a whole fish, see page 101.

BRAISED This is a cooking method using both dry and wet heat. Fish steaks or fillets are first browned on both sides in a pan on the stovetop, and then covered in a little stock or sauce and other ingredients. The pan is then covered and simmered either in the oven, or on low heat on the stovetop until done. Since almost any fish is going to cook in 10 minutes or so using this method, make sure you choose vegetables or garnishes that cook at the same rate as the fish. Mussels and clams can be braised in a deep pot and covered with a lid to finish on top of the stove. The Cajun Court Bouillon (page 134), where pieces of fish are sautéed first then finished in a brothy Creole sauce, would also qualify as a braise.

PAN-ROASTED This is a restaurant menu term which really just means starting the fish in a sauté pan on top the stove, cooking one side of the fish and then turning (and usually adding additional ingredients) and finishing in a hot oven. Fillets that are crusted with nuts or seeds are usually finished this way as well.

PAPILLOTE This is a preparation for mild- to medium-flavored fish done classically in a heart-shaped folded parchment paper, allowing the fish to steam in its packet with vegetables, herbs, and sauces. The vegetable may be blanched or raw, depending on the recipe. I like to sauté one side of the fillets first in a sauté pan or mark them on the grill before wrapping them to add an extra layer of caramelized flavor. You can also do this in foil, campfire-style, for a less dramatic presentation. This method allows you to get a head start on the cooking by refrigerating the packets and popping them in a hot oven to finish at the last minute. It's also a great method to use if you're having a dinner party and want all the fish to come out hot at the same time.

BRAISED SPANISH MACKEREL WITH GLAZED TURNIPS, CABBAGE, THAI CHILES, AND RED WINE SAUCE

SERVES 4 AS A MAIN DISH

Spanish mackerel, a fish that's abundant in the Gulf of Mexico, is regarded by many as a trash fish and not worth fooling with. Like its better known cousin, the king mackerel, it has a high fat content, which makes it more perishable but also lends itself well to full-flavored garnishes and sauces, as long as it's very fresh. King mackerel is more esteemed than Spanish probably because of its somewhat lower fat content and hence its longer shelf life. But unless you're in an international market, king is likely not going to be available. Other fatty fish, like salmon, will work just as well in this big-flavor dish. I love the hot chiles with the earthy taste of the cabbage and turnips browned in the bacon fat, along with the astringency of the reduced red wine sauce.

RED WINE SAUCE

1 cup red wine

1 bay leaf

1 large sprig of fresh thyme

5 crushed peppercorns

½ cup chopped mushroom stems or pieces (or 1 tablespoon dried morel or porcini)

4 tablespoons salted butter, chilled

VEGETABLES

8 slices thick bacon, diced

½ to 1 head Napa cabbage (the smaller the better)

4 small turnips, peeled and cut into 1-inch dice (about 1 cup)

2 Thai chiles, split down the middle, stem attached

½ pound stemmed shiitake mushrooms

FISH

4 (5- to 6-ounce) Spanish mackerel steaks (Alternatives are cobia, mullet, bluefish, salmon, or any full-flavored fatty fish)

Kosher salt and freshly ground black pepper

1 to 2 tablespoons olive or canola oil

RED WINE SAUCE Pour the red wine into a small saucepan with the bay leaf, thyme, peppercorns, and mushrooms. Bring to a boil, and reduce to ¼ cup. Remove from heat and allow to cool slightly for a couple of minutes. Whisk in the butter to make a creamy emulsion and press through a fine strainer. Reserve warm but not hot.

VEGETABLES Cook the bacon in a large cast iron skillet on medium heat until crisp. Remove from skillet with a slotted spoon and drain on paper towels; set aside. Meanwhile, slice off the top of the cabbage (reserve for another use), leaving 4 or 5 inches from the bottom. Slice lengthwise into 1-inch wedges with the core intact to hold each wedge together. Raise the heat in the skillet and brown the cut cabbage wedges and turnips in hot fat, turning with tongs to caramelize as much surface area as you can. Add the chiles and mushrooms; cook and stir a few more minutes, until tender. Spoon this mixture into a large bowl, and rinse and clean the skillet under running water with a brush or scrub pad.

FISH Heat the oven to 375 degrees F. Season the fish with salt and pepper. Return skillet to the burner on medium heat, and when it's hot, add 1 tablespoon of the oil, swirl to coat, and brown the fish steaks for 2 minutes on each side. Put the cabbage and turnips back into the pan, cover with a lid or several thicknesses of foil, and bake for about 5 minutes. (If all the fish won't fit in one skillet, brown the fish in two batches and transfer them to a baking dish large enough to accommodate the fish and vegetables.)

Divide the cabbage, turnips, juices, and crispy bacon among four heated pasta bowls. Place the mackerel on top and add 2 tablespoons Red Wine Sauce.

SUGGESTED WINE PAIRING: *Serve with Duckhorn Merlot (Napa Valley, California). Fatty fish, smoky bacon, and earthy vegetables call for a big red wine such as this one with silky tannins and flavors of strawberry, plum, and cherry.*

MUSSELS AND ITALIAN SAUSAGES BRAISED IN WHITE WINE

SERVES 2 AS A MAIN DISH

Mussels are a super quick, delicious seafood that don't require much in the way of ingredients to be world class. Those usually available are farmed on PEI (Prince Edward Island). Bangs Island mussels are preferred, if available, as they are usually meatier and bigger. Shellfish are sold with tags denoting origin and harvest date, and sometimes a shipping date. They are transported in refrigerated trucks from the East Coast. I consider myself lucky if the harvest date is within a week. They're usually sold in grocery stores in 2-pound mesh bags so they are easy to pick up and smell. They should smell really good, like fresh seawater. If they are going to be a main course with a salad, figure at least one pound per person.

8 ounces Italian sausage links or andouille

¼ pound linguine

1 (2-pound) bag mussels (An alternative is small clams, but they require longer purging)

1 tablespoon diced shallot

1 teaspoon minced garlic

¼ cup white wine

1 tablespoon freshly chopped fines herbes (page 25) or parsley

2 tablespoons salted butter

Pinch of freshly ground black pepper

Preheat oven to 375 degrees F.

Pierce sausage thoroughly with a skewer or toothpick and lay it out on a baking sheet. Roast about 15 minutes and remove from the oven. Allow to cool before cutting into 1-inch chunks. It will be slightly underdone but will finish in the dish. If you are opting for andouille, which is a fully cooked sausage, you still need to brown it a bit in the same manner, just not as long.

Bring a large pot of salted water to a boil. Add linguine; cook according to package directions and drain in a colander.

Meanwhile, clean the mussels by first discarding any cracked or broken ones. They are supposed to be alive so if you pinch shut any open ones they should "clam up" (now you know where that expression came from). Put them in a mixing bowl, cover with cold water, and soak for 15 minutes to purge of sand and grit. (This is less of an issue with farmed mussels as they are raised in suspended beds.) Lift them out of the water and reexamine them again for cracks or gapers that refuse to close. You'll probably notice protruding, dark hair-like beards in some of them, which you can pull out. Drain well.

This process goes quickly, so if you're planning on having some hot bread or a salad to go with the dish, get those ready before you start roasting.

Heat a large pot on high. Add all the mussels and cover. After 3 minutes, remove the lid. A lot of the shells will be open. Add the shallot, garlic, and wine; recover, and continue cooking for an additional 4 or 5 minutes. Remove from heat. Stir in half the herbs and all the butter. Add cooked pasta, sausage, and pepper.

Lift mussels out of the broth and arrange them pointy side down inside two heated pasta bowls. Discard ones that are still closed. Carefully divide the remaining liquid, pouring it slowly to decant it, leaving any residual grit in the pot. Plate the pasta in the middle of the bowl and top with sausage and the remaining herbs.

SUGGESTED WINE PAIRING: Serve with Simonnet-Febure (Chablis, France). The minerality and fruit aromas of this oakless French Chardonnay are a great fit for this dish.

WHOLE RAINBOW TROUT STUFFED WITH EGGPLANT RAGOUT

SERVES 4 AS A MAIN DISH

Farm-raised rainbow trout are a uniform size and cook quickly. They are usually sold as two completely boneless, skin-on fillets joined at the backbone with the head on for presentation, but if you prefer not to have your fish looking back at you, remove the head. They make an easy and impressive entrée when stuffed and baked, and hold up to big flavors, like the one suggested here. The fish cooks by the time the stuffing is hot. Don't be afraid of anchovies—they belong in the same class of flavor as fish sauce, in that you may not like them by themselves, but they marry well with the roast garlic and eggplant in this bread stuffing.

EGGPLANT RAGOUT

Vegetable oil spray

1 (1-pound) eggplant

2 tablespoons olive oil

1 bay leaf

8 cloves garlic, peeled

5 anchovy fillets, preferably Spanish, finely diced (rinsed if very salty)

1 tablespoon beef and veal demi-glace (Demi-Glace Gold brand), optional

1 cup stock (fish, chicken, or mushroom)

2 tablespoons chopped basil

¼ teaspoon finely chopped thyme leaves

1 roasted and peeled red bell pepper (page 191), diced

3 tablespoons salted butter

1 ½ cups cubed and dried French baguette (20 to 30 minutes in a 200-degree F oven)

TROUT

4 whole rainbow trout, deboned, head on or off (Alternatives are branzino and speckled trout)

Kosher salt and freshly ground black pepper

2 tablespoons melted butter

EGGPLANT RAGOUT Preheat oven to 350 degrees F. Coat a rimmed baking sheet with vegetable oil spray. Cut the eggplant lengthwise down the center and place, cut side down, on the baking sheet. Bake 30 to 40 minutes, or until eggplant is fork-tender. Set aside to cool.

Heat olive oil in a small saucepan on medium-low heat, add bay leaf and whole garlic cloves and cook until cloves are browned and soft. Finely dice the anchovy fillets and add them to the garlic. Add demi-glace, if using, and transfer mixture to a mixing bowl. Mash garlic with a fork.

Heat stock to boiling and remove from heat. Transfer baked eggplant to a cutting board and scoop out pulp with a spoon; discard skin. Chop or mash eggplant finely and add it to the ingredients in the bowl. Blend vigorously; add basil and thyme, roast pepper, butter, and the hot stock.

Fold in the bread and stir until it soaks up the juices and the mixture stiffens. (If you are making this ahead, cover and refrigerate at this point. Warm in a saucepan or the microwave when ready to use.)

TROUT Preheat oven to 400 degrees. Coat a rimmed baking sheet with vegetable oil spray. Lay the trout on a clean work surface or cutting board and open them up. Season with salt and pepper and divide the stuffing equally between the fish, spreading it to within an inch of the edges. Fold sides together and spray skin sides with vegetable oil spray.

Put stuffed trout on a baking sheet with space around each and place in oven for 10 minutes. Transfer from pan to warmed plates with a long metal spatula. Brush with butter and serve.

SUGGESTED WINE PAIRING: *Serve with Château du Seuil Bordeaux 2014 (Graves, France), a French Bordeaux that pairs well with the bold flavors of the eggplant ragout.*

HOW TO ROAST A WHOLE FISH OR LARGER FISH PARTS

Roasting whole fish at a high temperature turns the skin crispy and keeps the fish moist and juicy inside. Anything cooked this way needs to be impeccably fresh. Any slight odor, even in the gills, is magnified when cooked whole, but it's a great method for right-out-of-the-water fish. This can be done entirely in a 500-degree oven or covered grill, or started on top the stove and finished in the oven. Often small fish are scaled and deeply scored so that seasoning can penetrate the meat before cooking. Follow the procedure for the Whole Grilled Branzino (page 84), setting the scored and seasoned fish upright (or flat) on a pan coated with vegetable oil spray. Add vegetables such as sliced small squash, onions, or peppers to the pan if you like. And garnish with Citrus Chili Oil (page 167), Cilantro Purée (page 166), homemade pesto, or a good olive oil. Whole snapper or lionfish are excellent cooked this way as well. If you don't have access to whole fish that fresh, you can apply this technique to a beheaded and deboned rainbow trout and fill its cavity with herbs and lemon slices, or a stuffing such as the one suggested in this chapter. This is also a good way to cook a grouper or swordfish collar (use a slightly lower temperature—400 to 425 degrees F).

MACADAMIA AND PEPPERCORN-CRUSTED SWORDFISH

SERVES 4 AS A MAIN DISH

I did a version of this dish when I was a chef at Chops, a high-end steakhouse in Atlanta. The meaty texture of the sword-fish paired with the crunch of the nuts and the peppercorns fit right into that steakhouse menu.

It's important to use raw macadamias. If you use toasted nuts, which are already a little browned, the crust can get too dark. Raw nuts are usually more available in health food stores and I always taste for rancidity before buying. They should be fatty and sweet with no aftertaste of old oil. If you can't find raw macadamia nuts, raw cashews work just fine. This dish is a natural with mashed potatoes, and even better with a drizzle of Quick Veal Jus (page 168) or Red Wine Sauce (page 97). For a great garnish, dredge thinly sliced onions in seasoned flour and fry in 325 degree F oil until golden brown, as shown in the photograph.

CRUST

1 tablespoon peppercorns

½ cup raw macadamias or cashews

1 tablespoon rice flour (all-purpose can be substituted)

FISH

4 (5-ounce) swordfish steaks (Alternatives are cobia, king mackerel, barracuda, mako shark, black grouper, or almost any firm, medium-fat fish)

Kosher salt

Vegetable oil spray

2 tablespoons olive or canola oil

1 tablespoon salted butter

CRUST Put the peppercorns on a cutting board and crush with the bottom of a heavy, flat pan. Press down firmly and rock the pan back and forth.

Put the nuts in a food processor with the rice flour and pulse on high until they are match head size, about a minute or less. The flour keeps them from turning into nut butter, but be careful not to over-process. (If the nuts clump up in a ball, mix in a little more rice flour to separate the mixture.) Combine with the peppercorns and place this mixture evenly on a dinner plate. Preheat oven to 375 degrees F.

FISH Season swordfish liberally on both sides with salt and spray well with vegetable oil spray. Dredge one side firmly into the nut mixture. Place steaks crust side up on a plate. Spread any remaining nut mixture equally on the steaks.

Heat a heavy-bottom sauté pan with an ovenproof handle on medium heat. Add the oil and then the butter. When the butter starts to foam, carefully place the fish in the pan, crust side down, and cook for 3 to 4 minutes, until lightly browned. (Do not over-brown the crust as it will pick up additional color when you put it in the oven.) Use a small spatula to gently turn each steak. If some of the crust falls off at this point, you can reapply it with a spoon.

Place the pan in the oven to finish cooking for an additional 5 minutes. After 3 minutes or so, if they look like they're browning too much, cover the pan with foil. (See Note.)

SUGGESTED WINE PAIRING: Serve with Penfolds bin 138 Shiraz Grenache (Barossa Valley, Australia), a blend that nicely complements the peppercorn and veal jus in this dish.

Note: Did the nuts burn? Don't panic. Quickly make another batch of the nut and peppercorn mix. Heat a small sauté pan, add 2 tablespoons of butter and add the nut mixture, stirring it constantly until golden brown, about 2 minutes. Remove the pan from heat. Scrape off any overcooked nuts from the cooked fish, top with the new mixture, and no one will be the wiser.

POMPANO EN PAPILLOTE WITH OYSTERS, ROCKEFELLER SPINACH, AND MELTED TOMATO

4 SERVINGS

Pompano en papillote was made famous here in New Orleans at Antoine's to celebrate a Brazilian balloonist. Fillets of pompano were wrapped in parchment with a seafood sauce and tightly sealed, then baked in the oven where they puffed up slightly as they filled with steam, like balloons. Guests got to open their own packages, and it was fun to have that aroma hit everyone at the table. The herbs, wine, and vegetables flavor the fish as it steams in its own juices, and it makes a great presentation. Wrapping it in foil does the same thing, but it's not nearly as pretty.

At Fins, we do many versions of this—usually with pompano but any mild to medium-flavored fillet will work. This presentation is loaded with flavors that capture the essence of the French Quarter. Although it contains multiple components, it goes together very quickly because we parcook the fish to caramelize the exterior a bit—either on the grill or in the sauté pan—and cook the creamed spinach in advance. Once the fish are wrapped in their packets, you can refrigerate them for several hours and pop them in the oven a few minutes before you're ready to serve. This would be an impressive choice for a dinner party where it's much more convenient than sautéing fillets one by one.

ROCKEFELLER SPINACH

2 (18-inch) pieces of parchment paper

2 tablespoons salted butter, divided

12 ounces cleaned spinach leaves

1 tablespoon diced shallot

3 Spanish anchovies, rinsed and finely diced

2 tablespoons Pernod or Herbsaint, divided

½ cup heavy cream

Kosher salt and freshly ground black pepper

For the papillote, fold parchment paper pieces in half, and starting at the top of the fold draw a half-heart shape big enough to use all the paper. You shouldn't have much to trim off if you make the line as big as the paper allows. Using scissors, cut along the line. You want a clean cut.

ROCKEFELLER SPINACH In a large skillet over medium heat, melt 1 tablespoon butter. Add the spinach and sauté until tender. Remove from the heat; tilt the pan and press the spinach to squeeze and drain all the excess moisture out; set aside.

Wipe out the skillet. Melt remaining butter over medium-low heat; add shallot and sauté until soft but not browned. Add anchovies and continue to cook for a couple of minutes. Add half the Pernod and reduce to almost dry. Add the cream, raise the heat to medium high and reduce by half. Add the remaining Pernod. Season with a pinch of salt and pepper. Cool.

Squeeze and drain cooked spinach one more time to remove liquid. Finely chop the spinach and add to the cream mixture. Set aside.

FISH

½ cup all-purpose flour

4 (6- to 8-ounce) skin-on pompano or other lean fish fillets (Alternatives are snapper, grouper, tripletail, or redfish)

Kosher salt and freshly ground black pepper

4 tablespoons salted butter

4 tablespoons vegetable oil

Vegetable oil spray

1 large tomato, peeled, cored, seeded, and cut into 1-inch dice

16 fresh oysters

4 large sprigs tarragon

Oyster Butter Sauce (page 163), optional

FISH Preheat oven to 375 degrees F. Place the flour in a flat dish. Season the fish liberally with salt and pepper. Dip fish fillets in the flour to coat on both sides. Heat a large sauté pan to high and add 1 tablespoon each of butter and vegetable oil. Add a floured fillet and sauté about 2 minutes on each side until light golden. Transfer to a clean dish. Repeat with remaining fish, adding more butter and oil as needed. Set aside.

To assemble the papillote, lay the parchment hearts flat on the counter. Divide and place the spinach mixture on the center of one half of each heart, leaving a 1 ½-inch border. Arrange ¼ of tomato, 4 oysters, and 1 tarragon sprig around the spinach and place a fish fillet on top of the spinach on each heart.

Fold the paper over the fish. Starting with the round edge at the top of the heart and working your way around to the point, fold and crease the edges together so each fold overlaps the one before and the packet is sealed. If needed, watch a YouTube video to see how it is done.

Spray a baking sheet with vegetable oil spray and set the packets on top. Lightly mist spray over them as well. (Up to this point, this can be done ahead of time and refrigerated.)

Place the baking sheet with the packets in the preheated oven and cook for 6 to 8 minutes if they were at room temperature and for 10 to 12 minutes if they were refrigerated.

Slide the packets onto plates and serve immediately. You may provide each guest with scissors or a sharp knife to let them cut the paper themselves—the aroma is part of the experience—or if you prefer, you can quickly transfer the contents onto a warm plate, making sure to serve all the juices. Serve with Oyster Butter Sauce on the side, if desired.

SUGGESTED WINE PAIRING: *Serve with Lagar de Indra Albariño (Rias Biaxas, Spain), a white wine that can stand up to the Rockefeller sauce.*

RED SNAPPER EN PAPILLOTE WITH BRAISED FENNEL, TOMATO, OLIVES, AND FETA

2 SERVINGS

This parchment-wrapped fish preparation goes together quickly with little precooking of ingredients. Any snapper, lean small grouper, or tripletail will work well with these flavors.

This entrée is light with subtle Mediterranean flavors punctuated with briny bursts of olive. The tomato and feta melt together a bit and mix with the juices of the fish and fennel. Milder green olives such as Castelvetrano or Picholine may be substituted for the Kalamatas, though you'll probably have to pit them. Once you get the hang of this cooking method, you can add or subtract ingredients at will.

2 (18-inch) pieces of parchment paper

2 (5-ounce) skin-on red snapper fillets, scored (see note) (Alternatives are tripletail, mahi mahi, or scamp grouper)

Kosher salt and freshly ground black pepper

2 tablespoons all-purpose flour

2 tablespoons canola oil

2 tablespoons salted butter

1 small head fennel, bulb only, sliced crosswise ⅛-inch thick

1 large ripe tomato, peeled, seeded, and diced in 1-inch chunks

8 pitted Kalamata olives, cut in half lengthwise

6 ounces sheep's milk feta cheese

Vegetable oil spray

For the papillote, fold parchment paper pieces in half, and starting at the top of the fold draw a half-heart shape big enough to use all the paper. You shouldn't have much to trim off if you make the line as big as the paper allows. Using scissors, cut along the line. You want a clean cut.

Preheat the oven to 375 degrees F.

Heat a large sauté pan or skillet on medium. Season the fish lightly with salt and pepper and dust lightly with flour on both sides. Add the oil to the hot pan, swirl, and then add the butter. When the butter foams, shake any excess flour off and place the fish skin side down in the pan. Cook 3 or 4 minutes, or until the skin is golden brown and crispy. Turn fish and add fennel to the pan.

Cook the flesh side of the fish for 2 minutes and remove to a plate. Remove the fennel with a slotted spoon and place on a separate plate.

To assemble the papillote, Put the paper on the counter with the rounded side facing to your right. For each serving, place a fillet 1 inch away from the folded side in the center and scatter the rest of the ingredients over the fillet. Fold the paper and line up the edges on the rounded side. Starting at the fat end of the heart, make a 2-inch fold and crease it. Continue folding and creasing around the edge so that each fold overlaps slightly to seal the packet. If needed, watch a YouTube video to see how it is done.

Spray a baking sheet with vegetable oil spray and set the packets on top. Lightly mist spray over them as well. (Up to this point, this can be done ahead of time and refrigerated.)

Place the baking sheet with the packets in the preheated oven and cook for 6 to 8 minutes if they were at room temperature and for 10 to 12 minutes if they were refrigerated.

Slide the packets onto plates and serve immediately. You may provide each guest with scissors or a sharp knife to let them cut the paper themselves—the aroma is part of the experience—or if you prefer, you can quickly transfer the contents onto a warm plate, making sure to serve all the juices.

SUGGESTED WINE PAIRING: *Serve with E. Guigal Châteauneuf-du-Pape (Rhone, France). Any wine from this region is capable of extracting all the different complex flavors in this dish.*

HOW TO SCORE A SKIN-ON FISH FILLET

We remove the skin for most of our fish fillets at Fins, but some are delicious to eat when crisped in a skillet or on a grill. I especially like the pretty red skin of snapper. Before you sauté or grill a fish fillet with the skin on, pat it very dry and make shallow cuts ½ inch apart, just through the skin with a very thin, sharp knife, first lengthwise then crosswise, to form a crosshatch pattern. This keeps the skin from curling and allows the seasoning to penetrate the flesh, while creating extra-crispy bits of edible skin.

FRIED

NEW ORLEANS BEER-BATTER FISH AND BRABANT POTATOES

CORNMEAL-CRUSTED CATFISH WITH BUTTERMILK
HUSH PUPPIES

CRAWFISH FRITTERS WITH RED PEPPER JELLY

FRIED FISH TACOS WITH CHIPOTLE SLAW

TEMPURA-FRIED LOUISIANA WHITE SHRIMP WITH
CHILI AIOLI

FLASH-FRIED WHOLE LIONFISH WITH
VIETNAMESE FLAVORS

SOFT-SHELL CRAB BLT

FRIED OYSTER SLAW DOG

CHICKEN-FRIED ALLIGATOR WITH MASHED POTATOES AND
CHICKEN SKIN CRACKLING "GRAVY"

The first time I ever held a fishing pole was at my grandfather's farm in the West Virginia mountains. I had a spinning reel and got so excited when I caught a fish I ran it up the hill to drag it out of the water instead of reeling it in. We caught mostly bream and catfish that we ate pan-fried in lard with cornbread and coleslaw on the side. I find this meal just as mouth-watering now as I did then.

My fish-frying repertoire has expanded quite a bit over the years.

Like rice and pasta, fried food is either just right or not worth a damn. The correct oil or fat, temperature, breading, and size of the pieces being fried have to align to achieve the desired color, texture, and flavor.

This is not to say frying is difficult. Once you have the equipment and technique down, it's a quick and very efficient method of transferring heat.

The supposed health risks associated with eating fried food, perhaps to excess, are in my mind countered by its deliciousness. It seems there are a growing number of folks who seem to believe that if they eat the right food they will be skinny and pretty and live to be 120.

I say, eat real food and enjoy it!

BREADING

DRY BREADING Standard breading procedure is something I remember from culinary school. This usually involves a dip in flour, then a wet wash, and then in crumbs or meal, or back into the flour. I season the food to be fried before the first step and also add seasoning to the final mixture. The wash can be any liquid— milk or buttermilk, eggs, or some combination thereof. Leaving the floured product in the wash for a minute makes the flour sticky and this causes the final layer to adhere uniformly. The rule "dry hand, wet hand" keeps your fingers from forming an ever-increasing layer of breading. A handful of flour or crumbs keeps the finished pieces dry and separate.

WET BREADING A wet batter, either a thick one with beer, or a thin tempura, is different in that the pieces are first dusted in flour and then dipped in the batter. Pieces are placed in the oil differently, too, especially if you're not using much. It requires holding them in your fingers and waving them through the hot fat for a few seconds to partially harden the breading so when you release them they won't all stick together. Since smaller amounts at a time are introduced to the hot oil, you can use less oil, and shallow-fry if you prefer. Spooning the oil over the not-quite-submerged surface still gets the job done.

FRYING TIPS

- Choose thinner fillets for frying. Consider the size and shape of food to be deep fried—it has to cook internally in the same time as its outside coating browns. A fairly thin fillet is best—too thick and the outside will brown while the center remains raw.

- Use the proper oil. I recommend a processed neutral oil that can be heated past the frying temperature called for in the recipe to allow for the temperature drop when you put your cold food in the hot oil. Peanut, corn, safflower, canola, and soybean all work well for 350- to 375-degree F frying. If I can find fresh lard, it's the best—a natural fat eaten by people for thousands of years and a perfect frying medium for fish. Coconut oil has a similarly high smoke point that produces extra-crispy results. Olive oil has a low smoke point and does not work well for high-temperature frying. Bacon grease has a relatively low smoke point and is really only suitable for thin fish. But it does add a wonderful flavor. One way to get that bacon flavor is to add twenty-five percent bacon grease to an oil with a high smoke point.

- Use the proper size cooking vessel. A deep cast iron skillet works fine for small quantities, but a Dutch oven or a heavy saucepan with a fryer basket is better suited for larger quantities. I've not had much luck with the small electric counter-top fryers because the heat recovery time is too slow for more than the smallest amounts.

- You'll also need a thermometer that registers at least 400 degrees F. Keep checking the temperature of the oil and adjust as needed throughout the process. Overloading your hot fat with cold ingredients will drastically lower the heat and result in a soggy product. Recovery time also depends on the size and amount of oil and your heat source.

- If you're using an electric stove, sometimes the best way to quickly regulate the heat is to move the pan off the burner until it cools a bit.

- Reuse the oil. When you're finished and cleaning up, the oil needs to be cooled and strained. If this is a method you're likely to use again soon, the oil can be covered and stored in the refrigerator for reuse for months.

- Be careful. Hot oil has a potential of igniting, especially if you're frying outside on a propane grill (or in Louisiana, a turkey fryer). Never try to put out an oil fire with water. A fire extinguisher is a must.

- Serve fried foods immediately. As is the case with most of the dishes in this book—only more so—fried food has to be served immediately, so it is important to organize around that fact. Like making pancakes for a crowd, this may necessitate the guests being seated while you're still manning the stove.

NEW ORLEANS BEER-BATTER FISH AND BRABANT POTATOES

SERVES 4 AS A MAIN DISH

Here is Fins' answer to British fish and chips. We pair Creole-seasoned batter-fried fish strips with the twice-fried, garlicky potatoes locals know as Brabants. Malt vinegar is a traditional accompaniment, but I think a shallot-infused mignonette sauce made with Louisiana's homegrown Steen's cane vinegar (see page 25) is even better.

Brabant Potatoes (page 176)

BEER BATTER

1 cup all-purpose flour

1 cup cornstarch

1 tablespoon Chef Paul Prudhomme's Magic Seasoning Blend Shrimp Magic or Home Creole Seasoning (page 24)

2 teaspoons kosher salt

1/8 teaspoon baking powder

1/8 teaspoon baking soda

1 (12-ounce) bottle cold Abita Amber beer, or other light beer

3 or 4 tablespoons ice water, or as needed

FISH

About 1 quart vegetable oil for deep-fat frying

1 cup all-purpose flour

1 pound black drum fillets, cut in finger-size strips (Alternatives are brook trout, bream, crappie, sunfish, and catfish)

Kosher salt, and freshly ground black pepper

Chef Paul Prudhomme's Magic Seasoning Blend Shrimp Magic or Home Creole Seasoning (page 24), to taste

Cane Vinegar Mignonette (page 158)

Keep the potatoes warm in a 200-degree oven while you fry the fish.

BEER BATTER Fill a large container with ice. Set aside. Mix together the flour, cornstarch, Shrimp Magic, salt, baking powder, and baking soda in a metal bowl. Add the beer, stir to incorporate, then thin with ice water to the consistency of heavy cream. Reserve on ice; stir before using. (This can be made up to a day in advance and refrigerated.)

FISH Pour oil into a Dutch oven or deep-fat fryer and heat to 350 degrees F. Line a tray with paper towels and set near the fryer. Pour the flour onto a plate.

Season the fish with salt, pepper, and Shrimp Magic. Dust with flour, dip it into the Beer Batter, and shake off any excess. Carefully lower the pieces into the hot oil and fry 2 to 3 minutes or until golden brown on all sides and cooked through. You can fry several pieces of fish at one time, but don't crowd the pan. With a slotted spoon transfer the fried fish to the paper towel–lined tray to drain.

Serve with Brabant Potatoes with Cane Vinegar Mignonette for dipping.

SUGGESTED WINE PAIRING: *Serve with Charles Smith Kung Fu Girl Riesling (Columbia Valley, Washington), a subtly sweet white wine that works with fried fish and the garlicky potatoes.*

CORNMEAL-CRUSTED CATFISH WITH BUTTERMILK HUSH PUPPIES

SERVES 4 AS A MAIN DISH

This simple recipe for pan-fried fish is not much different from how I remember it as a kid. Catfish are delicious fried in a relatively a small amount of fat in a heavy skillet, or deep-fried. Either way, it's worth getting a smaller pot of oil going at the same time to deep-fry some hush puppies to go with them.

I find a breading mixture of corn flour or masa harina (finely ground cornmeal used to make tortillas) and cornmeal for crunch is good for all manner of fried seafood, from oysters to catfish. It's perfectly permissible to use one of the seasoned fish fry mixtures that are popular here in Louisiana (I like Zatarain's) with the addition of about 20 percent cornmeal. I was raised on straight cornmeal, but I find that coating a bit too gritty. For extra flavor, source fresh stone-ground cornmeal from a local farmers market if you can, or order online.

Hush puppies are basically deep-fried cornbread in the form of finger food, and they are a perfect accompaniment to fried fish. They are richer and crispier than baked cornbread. Unlike the more rustic Hot Water Cornbread (page 174), wheat flour provides some structure, but I feel that hush puppies should taste predominantly of corn, so I use finely ground corn flour or tortilla flour instead—which is convenient since I'm also using those for the fish coating. Additions are endless—crawfish tails, oysters, corn, roast peppers are all good—but I like the plain ones best. Small ones cook a little faster and provide more crunch.

BUTTERMILK HUSH PUPPIES

1 cup cornmeal (preferably freshly ground)

½ cup all-purpose flour

½ cup corn flour or masa harina

1 teaspoon Chef Paul Prudhomme's Magic Seasoning Blends Shrimp Magic or Home Creole Seasoning (page 24)

1 teaspoon baking powder

1 teaspoon sugar

1 teaspoon kosher salt

⅛ teaspoon baking soda

1 large egg

1 cup buttermilk

½ cup finely diced yellow onion

¼ cup finely diced green onion

1 tablespoon melted lard or bacon grease

3 to 4 cups vegetable oil for deep-fat frying

Preheat the oven to 200 degrees. Line a baking sheet with paper towels and set near the stove.

BUTTERMILK HUSH PUPPIES Mix together the cornmeal, flour, corn flour, Creole seasoning, baking powder, sugar, salt, and baking soda in a medium bowl.

In another bowl, beat the egg with the buttermilk, fold in the onions, and then quickly stir into the dry ingredients until just incorporated. Add the grease and stir a couple more times. Don't overmix.

Pour oil into a medium-size heavy saucepan until oil is about 3 inches deep; heat to 375 degrees F.

To fry the Hush Puppies, scoop some batter out with one coffee spoon and scrape with another and then drop into the hot oil. Fry 6 or 8 at a time. If they don't turn themselves, flip them over in about 3 minutes and continue to cook for another couple of minutes. Remove to the paper towel–lined baking sheet and keep warm in the oven while you finish frying the fish and remaining hush puppies. Eat while piping hot.

continued

CATFISH

2 cups corn flour or masa harina

½ cup cornmeal

2 tablespoons Chef Paul Prudhomme's Magic Seasoning Blends Shrimp Magic or Home Creole Seasoning

1 cup milk

4 (5- to 7-ounce) catfish fillets (Alternatives are brook trout, bream, crappie, and sunfish)

Kosher salt and freshly ground black pepper

1 cup all-purpose flour

½ cup lard, bacon grease, or high-temperature oil

Accompaniments: Lemon wedges, Mom's Coleslaw (page 184), My Favorite Tartar Sauce (page 159), House Cocktail Sauce (page 158), and Zydeque Potato Salad (page 191)

CATFISH Mix together corn flour, cornmeal, and seasoning in a large bowl. Pour the milk in a wide, flat bowl. Season the fillets with salt and pepper, and then dredge in flour. Dip each floured fillet into the milk for a couple of minutes to soften the flour and make it sticky. Dredge in the cornmeal mixture to coat thoroughly on both sides. Leave in the bowl until ready to fry.

To fry the fish, heat a large cast iron skillet over medium-high heat and add the lard. When sizzling, lift a few pieces of fish out of the breading, shaking off the excess, and add to the skillet (don't crowd the pan). Cook until a golden brown crust forms, about 4 minutes. Turn and continue cooking for 2 to 3 minutes on the other side. Remove to the paper towel–lined baking sheet and keep warm in the oven.

Serve with lemon wedges, Mom's Coleslaw, My Favorite Tartar Sauce, House Cocktail Sauce, and Zydeque Potato Salad.

SUGGESTED WINE PAIRING: *Serve with Sonoma-Cutrer Rosé of Pinot Noir 2017 (Russian River, Sonoma County, California), an easy-drinking rosé, when an ice-cold beer just won't do the trick.*

CRAWFISH FRITTERS WITH RED PEPPER JELLY

MAKES 3 DOZEN

These crunchy nuggets are delicious for snacking, or as a garnish for fried or grilled fish. These are best eaten piping hot.

3 to 4 cups vegetable oil for deep-fat frying

¾ cup all-purpose flour

1 tablespoon baking powder

1 tablespoon Paul Prudhomme's Magic Seasoning Blends Shrimp Magic or Home Creole Seasoning (page 24)

1 egg, lightly beaten

1 tablespoon finely diced jalapeño (with seeds) or poblano pepper (seeds removed)

½ cup milk

½ pound cooked, chopped domestic crawfish tails (An alternative is blue crabmeat)

2 tablespoons red pepper jelly

Pour oil into a medium-size heavy saucepan until oil is about 3 inches deep; heat to 350 degrees F. Line a tray with paper towels. Whisk together flour, baking powder, and seasoning in a mixing bowl. Stir in the egg and diced pepper, until incorporated, and thin with milk. Add crawfish tails and gently incorporate into the batter.

Shortly before you're ready to serve, scoop the batter 1 teaspoon at a time and fry in hot oil until golden brown, about 3 minutes.

Meanwhile, gently melt the pepper jelly in a small saucepan or in a coffee mug in the microwave.

When fritters are done, remove with a slotted spoon and drain on paper towels. Place in a heated bowl and toss with warm pepper jelly. Serve immediately.

SUGGESTED WINE PAIRING: *Serve with J Vineyards Cuvée Sparkling Wine (Russian River, California). With flavors of Asian pear and lemon, this champagne marries exceptionally well with fried foods and the spicy-sweet sauce.*

FRIED FISH TACOS WITH CHIPOTLE SLAW

MAKES 8 TACOS

This is my favorite way to stretch a meager catch of fish to feed a bunch of people. For several years, we've served these tacos to about 10,000 people of the half million or so who come the French Quarter Festival along the river using the speckled trout, sheepshead, or drum that are so common in this area. Lately I have also been making this recipe with lionfish for different events. It works well with just about anything white and flaky, including freshwater bass. The key is keeping the batter really cold, and having a nicely seasoned slaw to pair with it, and filling the tortilla with about as much slaw as fish.

CHIPOTLE SLAW

1 cup mayonnaise

1 chipotle pepper in adobo, finely chopped

1 tablespoon adobo sauce

2 tablespoons fresh lime juice

1 teaspoon Chef Paul Prudhomme's Magic Seasoning Blend Shrimp Magic or Home Creole Seasoning (page 24)

1 pinch kosher salt

Freshly ground black pepper

2 cups shredded green cabbage

½ cup finely sliced red bell pepper

½ cup chopped green onions

¼ cup finely chopped cilantro leaves

CHIPOTLE SLAW In a mixing bowl, whisk together the mayonnaise, chipotle pepper, adobo, lime juice, seasoning, salt, and pepper until mixed thoroughly. Combine the cabbage, bell pepper, green onions, and cilantro in a large bowl. Pour the mayonnaise mixture over the slaw ingredients and gently combine with a wooden spoon. Cover and refrigerate until ready to use. (This can be made a day ahead, but keep the dressing and slaw ingredients separate until the last minute.)

FISH

About 1 quart vegetable oil for deep-fat frying

1 cup all-purpose flour

1 pound speckled trout, cut in finger-size strips (Alternatives are lionfish, snapper, bass, grouper, catfish, and drum)

Kosher salt

Freshly ground black pepper

Chef Paul Prudhomme's Magic Seasoning Blend Shrimp Magic or Home Creole Seasoning (page 24), to taste

1 recipe Beer Batter (page 111)

TO ASSEMBLE

8 (5-inch) corn tortillas

Optional garnishes: diced avocados, diced tomatoes, chopped green onions, diced cilantro

FISH Pour oil into a Dutch oven or deep-fat fryer and heat to 350 degrees F. Line a tray with paper towels and set near the fryer. Pour flour onto a plate.

Season the fish with salt, pepper, and Shrimp Magic. Dust with flour, dip in the batter, and shake of any excess. Carefully lower the pieces into the hot oil and fry 2 to 3 minutes or until golden brown on all sides and cooked through. You can fry several pieces of fish at one time, but don't crowd the pan. With a slotted spoon, transfer the fish to the paper towel–lined try to drain.

TO ASSEMBLE Heat a medium skillet or griddle to high; add a tortilla and heat on both sides until a few brown spots appear, about 30 to 60 seconds.

Place a spoonful of slaw on each corn tortilla then place one or two pieces of fish over the slaw. Fold and serve with garnish of choice.

SUGGESTED WINE PAIRING: *Serve with Burly Sauvignon Blanc (Napa Valley, California), a crisp, fruit-forward sauvignon blanc that is a good bet for seafood, salads, and complex flavors.*

PANFISH FOR ONE

I like to go backpacking alone at times, and have been known to stay away a week. It's great to unplug and let life slow down. You don't get that effect when you're in a hurry, and adjusting to fishing, cooking, and gathering firewood is the best therapy.

Panfish refer to edible game fish and are, by definition, any variety small enough to fit in a pan. They are usually cleaned, scaled, and pan-fried, often with the small bones intact. Sometimes the smallest ones are crispy fried and the fins and small bones eaten whole. (Generally anything ¾ pound and bigger I fillet.) Some people freak out at the idea of getting a fish bone in their mouth, but once you learn skeletal structure, this is less of a problem.

Even though I'm pretty well supplied with basics when I backpack, I don't bread panfish the same way as when I'm in the kitchen. I usually pack some seasoned corn flour mixed with a little cornmeal in a 1-gallon plastic bag and just drop the scaled and gutted fish right in. The juices from the fish cause enough breading to adhere, and I love to fry them in reserved bacon fat or some lard brought for that purpose. Add some reconstituted dried mushrooms and sliced shallots to the pan for more flavor.

TEMPURA-FRIED LOUISIANA WHITE SHRIMP
WITH CHILI AIOLI

SERVES 4 AS A MAIN DISH, 8 AS AN APPETIZER

I love the look of fried shrimp with the heads attached (including the long feelers). I've been schooled by my Vietnamese friends that the meat on the inside is the most flavorful, and I agree. To preserve the delicacy and visibly distinctive features of the shrimp, I dip them in tempura batter, which is much thinner than beer batter. I use flavorless soda water instead of beer. But the flavor difference is so minor you may use them interchangeably. If you can't find head-on shrimp, leave the tails on—it gives you something to hold onto as you wave them through the batter. I also like to serve shrimp cooked this way with Vietnamese Green Apple Salad, page 188), as pictured here.

CHILI AIOLI

1 cup mayonnaise

1 teaspoon Asian chili paste

½ teaspoon kosher salt

1 lime, juiced

SHRIMP

2 pounds fresh head-on Louisiana white shrimp (Alternatives are any head-on or headless shrimp and frog legs)

Chef Paul Prudhomme's Magic Seasoning Blend Shrimp Magic or other Creole seasoning, to taste

Cornstarch for dusting

TEMPURA BATTER

1 cup cornstarch

½ cup all-purpose flour

½ cup rice flour

1 tablespoon Chef Paul Prudhomme's Magic Seasoning Blend Shrimp Magic or Home Creole Seasoning blend (page 24)

1 teaspoon kosher salt

½ teaspoon freshly ground black pepper

1 teaspoon baking soda

¼ teaspoon baking powder

12 ounces cold club soda

3 or 4 tablespoons ice water, or as needed

About 6 cups vegetable oil for deep-fat frying

CHILI AIOLI Mix together all ingredients in a small bowl until well-blended; cover and chill until ready to serve.

SHRIMP Clean the shrimp, leaving the heads intact (or leave the tails on if using headless.) Devein and season with Shrimp Magic. Refrigerate until ready to use.

TEMPURA BATTER Fill a large container with ice. Set aside. Mix together the cornstarch, flour, rice flour, Shrimp Magic, salt, pepper, baking soda, and baking powder in a metal bowl. Add the club soda and stir to incorporate. This should be a slightly thinner batter than beer batter—thin with iced water as needed. Reserve on ice; stir before using. (This can be made up to a day in advance and refrigerated.)

Pour oil into Dutch oven, deep-fat fryer, or large, heavy-bottom saucepan and heat to 325 degrees F. Line a tray with paper towels and set near the fryer.

Remove the shrimp from the refrigerator. Dust the shrimp with cornstarch and shake off the excess. Stir the batter (the cornstarch has a tendency to settle to the bottom) and carefully place the shrimp in the batter.

Pick up the shrimp by the heads, two at a time, and allow to drain well. Holding the heads, gently wave them into the hot oil, releasing them after a few seconds. This allows the batter to harden slightly and prevents the shrimp from sticking together. Quickly repeat this process until all the shrimp in one batch are frying (don't crowd the fryer). Cook for about 3 minutes, until golden brown, and remove to drain on paper towels.

Serve with the Chili Aioli.

SUGGESTED WINE PAIRING: *Serve with Adelsheim Pinot Gris (Willamette Valley, Oregon), a clean, crisp white that lends itself well to seafood, spice, and rich sauces.*

Variation: Fresh frog legs are a treat. The smaller ones (no bigger around than your little finger) are delicious dipped in tempura batter, fried like shrimp, and dipped in Tabasco Butter Sauce (see page 166).

FLASH-FRIED WHOLE LIONFISH
WITH VIETNAMESE FLAVORS

SERVES 4 AS A MAIN DISH

Frying a whole fish is an ambitious undertaking for the home cook because of the amount of oil and size of the pot required. This is something I'd recommend doing outside, especially if you're doing more than a couple. Deep-frying, even with the relatively small amount of oil called for in most of the frying recipes, causes tiny droplets of oil to become airborne and they settle all over the kitchen, particularly on anything absorbent. A turkey fryer is common in Louisiana, and if you have one of those they're perfect for large-scale outdoor use. Carports and garages burn down here every year because some oblivious person adds a semi-frozen turkey to 350-degree F grease which then overflows and ignites. Be careful! Have a fire extinguisher handy. And seriously, watch a video of what happens when you try to put out a grease fire with water! A propane grill can be a good heat source for the outside pot if you don't have said fryer.

Cutting a series of slices all the way to the bone on your whole fish allows more seasoning on the meat and makes it cook faster. It also makes eating easier because you can break off those slices when done, leaving the bones on the skeleton.

For some Asian flavor, drizzle the fish with the pungent caramel syrup I love to pair with all sorts of crunchy things called Nuoc Mau Plus, page 160. Garnish with crushed peanuts and pair it with Vietnamese Apple-Carrot Salad (page 188) or Mirliton Slaw (page 185). And if you're going to the trouble of heating a large amount of oil for a whole fish, by all means make Brabant Potatoes (page 176) and Buttermilk Hush Puppies (page 113) to go with it.

2 to 4 dressed whole lionfish (see Note) (Alternatives are small snappers, branzino, or trout)

Paul Prudhomme's Magic Seasoning Blend Shrimp Magic or Home Creole Seasoning (see page 24), to taste

2 to 3 quarts vegetable oil for deep-fat frying

1 cup cornstarch

1 recipe Tempura Batter (page 118), kept chilled in the refrigerator or on ice

½ cup Nuoc Mau Plus (page 160)

1 cup chopped, roasted peanuts, optional

1 cup torn leaves of fresh herbs (cilantro, basil, dill, mint—any or all)

Cilantro Purée (page 166), optional

Cut 3 or 4 diagonal slices on each side of the whole fish all the way to the bone. Season the dressed fish liberally with Shrimp Magic on both sides and between the slices. (Slicing the fish makes for faster cooking.) Refrigerate until ready to use.

Pour oil into a turkey fryer or large pot and heat to 375 degrees F. Line a tray with paper towels and set near the fryer.

Remove the fish from the refrigerator. Dust the fish with cornstarch and shake off the excess. Stir the batter (the cornstarch has a tendency to settle to the bottom). Holding each fish by the tail, dip it into the batter, making sure the slices are coated. Hold over the batter to drain the excess and lower it, still holding by the tail, into the hot oil, waving it back and forth for a few seconds before releasing it.

Cook for 4 to 5 minutes, depending on the size of the fish, until crispy and golden brown.

Use a slotted spoon to transfer the fish to the paper towel–lined tray to drain. To serve, drizzle with the Nouc Mau Plus and sprinkle with chopped peanuts, if using, and the torn herbs. Garnish plate with drizzle of cilantro purée if you wish.

SUGGESTED WINE PAIRING: *Serve with Tablas Creek Côtes de Tablas Blanc (Paso Robles, California). You'll need a wine with more than one grape to access the many different flavors in this dish, and this Viognier-based blend of several Rhône grapes fits the bill.*

Note: A lionfish has fourteen venomous spines, so if you want to dress one yourself, be careful, otherwise have your fishmonger do it for you. I've never stuck myself with a live one, but I'm told it feels like getting stung by a hornet and hit with a hammer. Although some people cut the spines off at the body, I like a wilder presentation so I leave most of them intact—I might clip an inch or so off each spine. Scale the fish under running water—most will be removed just by the force of the sprayer, but you may need to scrape a bit with a spoon. Then proceed with the recipe. Heat denatures the venom, so don't be afraid to eat one prepared this way!

SPOTLIGHT ON SOFT-SHELL CRABS

Soft-shell crabs are the true harbinger of spring here in Louisiana, along with the first Creole tomatoes, prized for their bright flavor and lasting only barely a month before the heat takes over. When I was a chef in Atlanta, we were taught to accept only lively soft-shells, which were well on their way to becoming hard again. The more fragile "velvets" available in New Orleans—which usually die when shedding—are the ones I prefer. These super-soft delicacies are the freshest crab taste there is and, once they're cleaned, you eat every bit—feet and all. I'm totally convinced deep-frying is the best way to prepare them.

To clean, cut off its face right behind the eyes and, using the tip of your knife, reach inside the cavity created and scrape out the small, fluid-filled sand sack. Cut off the apron on the other side of the shell—wide for girls, narrow for jimmies. Lift the pointed edges of the top shell to expose the gills and either pinch out with your fingers or cut with scissors.

SOFT-SHELL CRAB BLT

MAKES 4 SANDWICHES

Like practically every Southerner, I highly esteem fresh homegrown tomatoes on white bread with mayonnaise. It's not far to go to turn this into a great BLT, and this recipe guilds the lily even more. Soft-shell crab and Creole tomatoes—our early-season local variety—hit at about the same time here. Pure ambrosia to eat!

Make these only if you have incredibly fresh crab and perfectly ripe tomatoes. If you don't have good fresh tomatoes, use green tomatoes, breaded and fried following the instructions for frying the crab. Fried dill pickle chips are good as an accompaniment.

1 to 1 ½ cups all-purpose flour

4 tablespoons Chef Paul Prudhomme's Magic Seasoning Blends Shrimp Magic or other Creole seasoning

1 cup milk

4 small to medium fresh soft-shell crabs, cleaned (see Spotlight on Soft-Shell Crabs)

Kosher salt and freshly ground black pepper

8 slices best-quality thick bacon

1 ripe avocado

1 large, ripe tomato

Lettuce cups from 1 head Bibb lettuce, flattened with the palm of your hand

About 8 cups vegetable oil for deep-fat frying

4 Sally Lunn rolls (page 175) or other sandwich rolls of choice

2 tablespoons mayonnaise mixed with 1 teaspoon Tabasco Sauce

Preheat oven to 350 degrees F.

Pour the flour into a shallow dish and stir in the Shrimp Magic. Pour the milk into another shallow dish. Season the crabs on both sides with salt and pepper. Dust in flour, dip into milk wash for 1 minute, and dredge again in the flour. Set on a tray and set aside.

Place the bacon slices on a baking sheet with a rim and cook in oven for about 15 minutes until crisp. Drain on paper towels.

Slice the avocado and tomato and arrange on top of the flattened lettuce cups.

Heat 2 medium saucepans with about 4 cups of oil each to 350 degrees F. Add 2 crabs to each pot and fry on both sides until golden brown, turning once, 5 to 6 minutes total. Drain on paper towels.

Heat the Sally Lunn rolls in a warm oven for a few minutes and cut them almost in half, leaving a hinge on one side. Spread with the seasoned mayonnaise.

Place the avocado, tomato, and lettuce stacks on the bottom of the split buns. Add 2 slices of bacon to each. Wedge the fried crab in there somewhere—it's definitely overstuffed, so you might want to secure it with a skewer.

SUGGESTED WINE PAIRING: *Serve with Ferrari Chardonnay (Sonoma, California), a smooth, complex white wine that stands up to the richness of this dish.*

FRIED OYSTER SLAW DOG

SERVES 4 AS A MAIN DISH

Anything fried is great with slaw. Tossing that anything in hot sauce butter and combining it with slaw on a homemade Sally Lunn roll shaped like a hot dog bun is ambrosial, especially if it's made with salty Gulf oysters. (If you don't want to make your own buns, there's always Bunny Bread . . .)

4 Sally Lunn Hot Dog Buns (page 175) or hot dog buns of choice

1 egg

1 cup milk

½ cup all-purpose flour

1 cup corn flour

¼ cup cornmeal

1 tablespoon Chef Paul Prudhomme's Magic Seasoning Blends Shrimp Magic or Home Creole Seasoning (page 24)

2 or 3 cups vegetable oil for deep-fat frying

12 to 16 fresh oysters

Tabasco Butter Sauce, (page 166), warm

1 recipe Mom's Coleslaw (page 184)

Preheat the oven to 200 degrees F. Warm the buns for 5 minutes while you fry the oysters.

Set three wide bowls near the stovetop. Beat the egg with the milk in one, place the flour in another, and the corn flour, cornmeal, and Shrimp Magic in the third.

Pour oil into Dutch oven or deep-fat fryer and heat to 350 degrees F. Line a tray with paper towels and set near the fryer.

Drain the oysters well, dredge first in flour, then soak in egg wash a minute or so until the flour is sticky. Then gently roll in the cornmeal mix.

Add oysters to the hot oil, a few at a time (don't crowd the pan), and fry until crispy on all sides, a minute or two. Remove and drain on paper towels. (If you want to prebread them and leave them in the meal refrigerated ahead of time, that's fine.)

Transfer oysters to a mixing bowl. Toss in the Tabasco Butter Sauce, open the buns, and place 3 or 4 oysters inside each one. Top liberally with slaw. Eat with lots of napkins handy.

SUGGESTED WINE PAIRING: Serve with Cooper Mountain Pinot Gris (Beaverton, Oregon), 2016. Crisp and minerally, with hints of pear, this white will work as a nice counterbalance to the fried oysters and slaw.

CHICKEN-FRIED ALLIGATOR WITH MASHED POTATOES AND CHICKEN SKIN CRACKLING "GRAVY"

SERVES 4 AS A MAIN DISH

Alligator may be a reptile, but it's officially classified as a seafood here in Louisiana. The hunting and trapping season is tightly controlled and the population is healthy, and you'll find various preparations of it on menus all over the state. The tail meat of farm-raised alligator has been mechanically tenderized and tastes a lot like dark-meat chicken. For maximum tenderness, I like to give it a few good whacks with the heel of a French knife before dredging and skillet-frying into a down-home dinner with mashed potatoes and plenty of creamy butter sauce shot through with bits of seasoned fried chicken skin. It's also good simmered in Sauce Piquant (page 133), but for that I skip the dredging to avoid a floury taste.

Mashed Potatoes with Chicken Skin Crackling "Gravy" (page 177)

2 cups milk

2 cups all-purpose flour, seasoned with 2 tablespoons salt and 1 tablespoon black pepper

1 to 1 ½ pounds farm-raised alligator meat, cut into 2-inch pieces

Chef Paul Prudhomme's Magic Seasoning Blends Shrimp Magic or Home Creole Seasoning (page 24)

1 cup vegetable oil or lard for shallow-fat frying

Make the mashed potatoes and gravy, folding half the chicken skins into the sauce. Keep warm.

Line a pan with paper towels and set near the stove. Pour milk into one shallow bowl and seasoned flour into another.

Spank the alligator pieces flat with the heel of a French knife to about a ¼-inch thickness. Season the pieces liberally with Shrimp Magic, then dust them with seasoned flour, and dip them in milk (leaving them in for a couple of minutes to allow the flour to get sticky). Drop them back into the flour to coat.

Heat oil in a large cast iron skillet over medium-high heat to 350 degrees F. Drop the pieces into the hot oil, a few at a time, and fry a couple of minutes on each side until crispy and golden. Drain on the paper towels. Serve on hot plates, with mashed potatoes and ladle the "gravy" over both. Garnish with more of the crumbled chicken skins.

SUGGESTED WINE PAIRING: Serve with Saldo Zinfandel (Napa Valley, California), a rich, smooth red with hints of black pepper and chocolate that elevates this meat-and-potatoes dish.

SIMMERED AND STEWED

I may get slammed for this, not being a native Louisianan. But many of New Orleans' most famous dishes are actually variations on one cooking method. Some have more tomato, or include okra or have less stock, but the foundation of each dish is the same: dark roux made of flour slowly caramelized in hot oil; the Cajun/Creole holy trinity of onions, bell peppers, and celery; aromatics and spices; tomatoes (unless you're from Lafayette or points west of there where tomatoes are heresy), and a good, rich stock. I still remember the "aha" moment the first time I tasted this combination. I was at the Culinary Institute of America in Hyde Park, New York, in the 1980s and had a part-time job in a place called Spanky's Cajun Restaurant in Poughkeepsie. The source for all their recipes was the 1984 edition of *Chef Paul Prudhomme's Louisiana Kitchen*, the first cookbook by the New Orleans icon, and one of the first American chefs recognized by the popular media. It was a big thrill for me later in life when I moved to New Orleans and got to work with him on some seasoning blends. His influence on me as a chef is evident in how I make my roux and stocks, the key components in the soups and other spicy, slow-simmered dishes for which New Orleans cuisine is renowned. In this chapter, I will tell you how I make mine, and how you can incorporate them into your own dishes and make them your own. Once you master those, you're well on your way to shrimp Creole. From there, it is a slight adjustment to sauce piquant, Cajun court bouillon, jambalaya, and pretty darn close to gumbo.

Each roux and stock involves multiple steps that build taste, and the more frequently you make them, the more adept you become at tasting the flavors you're after at each stage of development.

A well-made broth can be the catalyst for a multitude of other great meals built on a foundation of fresh seafood and stock, and in this chapter I will share some of those as well. Though more time-consuming than other cooking methods, these dishes require far less coordination and last-minute juggling, allowing you to cook at a more relaxed pace and take in the wonderful spice-filled aromas that fill your kitchen as you stir.

ROUXS

A basic roux consists of flour and fat. The trick is cooking these two ingredients to the right color. For most of these recipes, the desired shade is the color of dark brown sugar. If you've ever caramelized sugar, you may have noticed that it takes some time to get any color, but when it does it goes from light amber to dark brown very quickly. Roux acts in a similar fashion, and it's important to have your vegetables cut and ready to mix in when the right color is achieved. This cools it off and stops the browning while it cooks the vegetables. The classical rule about adding cold stock to hot roux—or vice versa—to prevent lumping doesn't apply here because the vegetables have that same cooling effect. At this stage, the color will advance one shade so don't be concerned about that. Like caramel, roux is hot and will stick to your skin, so be very careful not to splash yourself while stirring it. For a relatively small amount of roux, as for Creole sauce, I cook on the stove. For a larger amount, as for gumbo, I find it easier to brown in the oven.

BASIC FISH STOCK

1 GALLON

This is the stock I use for my gumbos and risottos. The first step to making top-quality fish stock is to get LOTS of bones. If your foundation is weak, your dish won't have the layered flavor you're trying to achieve. For a gallon of finished stock, I fill a 3- to 4-gallon pot with at least five pounds of bones from fresh, relatively lean fish that have all traces of viscera removed and have been rinsed in cold water until the water runs clean. Gumbo crabs are frozen bodies with the middles (the part with the lump meat) removed, and sold as a frozen product. Fresh blue crabs are good as well. Any shrimp shells that you may have saved in the freezer can go in. Fish heads are fine, too, if fresh and well-rinsed. This is a light stock that should have a clean, fresh flavor. It will reduce while making the soup and become more concentrated.

1 onion, rough chopped	3 to 4 sprigs fresh thyme	2 cups frozen shrimp shells or heads (or whatever you have)
2 stalks celery (no leaves), chopped	5 pounds bones from very fresh, relatively lean fish, cleaned	1 cup white wine
2 bay leaves	1 pound whole live blue crabs or frozen gumbo crabs	Water to cover (about 1 ½ gallons)
10 peppercorns		

Place onion, celery, bay leaves, peppercorns, and thyme in a very large stockpot.

Place the fish bones, crabs, and shrimp shells on top of the vegetables, add the wine, and pour in enough water to cover the bones and vegetables. Bring slowly to a simmer and cook for 20 minutes, skimming off foam as needed. Turn off the heat, cover, and let sit for one hour. Strain and reserve.

STRONG SHRIMP STOCK

MAKES 1 QUART

Sacrificing a pound of whole shrimp to grind into the stock is essential to getting great flavor. For an even richer stock, add fish stock in place of the water if you have some.

2 tablespoons canola or olive oil

2 tablespoons diced onion

2 tablespoons diced carrot

1 tablespoon diced celery

2 cloves garlic, rough chopped

Shells (and heads if available) from 2 pounds of wild-caught American shrimp

1 pound unpeeled wild-caught American shrimp, rough chopped, including shells (this is an extra expense, but it's necessary for flavor)

½ cup white wine

½ cup canned tomatoes, mashed up a bit

1 bay leaf

6 cups water

Heat a large saucepan to medium; add the oil, onion, carrot, celery, and garlic and cook for a couple of minutes, and then add the shrimp shells and chopped shrimp. Cook on high, stirring often, for 3 minutes.

Add the wine and reduce to almost dry, and then add the tomatoes with any juice along with the bay leaf.

Add the water and bring to a boil. Reduce the heat to a simmer and cook until the volume is reduced to a little over 4 cups, about 30 minutes. You may need to raise the heat or add more liquid if it's cooking too slowly or too fast, but 30 minutes is a bare minimum for flavor extraction with this quantity of shrimp.

Remove the bay leaf and purée the mixture well with an immersion blender. Or use a regular blender and put a clean towel over the top, allowing for expansion of the hot liquid, and cover loosely with the lid.

Force this puréed mixture through a fine strainer or sieve, mashing it to get all the juice. This can be done well ahead of time and refrigerated or frozen.

QUICK MULTIPURPOSE SEAFOOD STOCK VARIATION: For a lighter stock that can be used in place of fish stock, follow this recipe, omitting adding the whole shrimp, and skip the purée. Just strain it after it has simmered for 30 minutes.

SHRIMP CREOLE AND ITS COUSINS

CREOLE MOTHER SAUCE

1 QUART

Creole sauce is a hallmark of New Orleans cooking and takes time and a bit of technique to get right. It's usually mixed with shrimp and served over rice for shrimp Creole, but it can be used to braise anything from green beans to wild game. A good homemade stock and well-made brown roux are essential. Okra isn't traditional, but I like to add a cupful in with the sautéed vegetables for flavor and thickening. The good news is, except for the final step of sautéing the protein or vegetables, it can be made ahead of time and refrigerated for up to a week or frozen. Once you have this base, you can go in infinite directions.

¼ cup canola oil

2 tablespoons all-purpose flour

1 cup diced green bell pepper

1 cup diced onion

½ cup diced celery

1 cup sliced okra

1 tablespoon minced fresh garlic

1 small bay leaf

1 (28-ounce) can whole peeled tomatoes

1 quart Strong Shrimp Stock (page 129)

1 tablespoon Chef Paul Prudhomme's Magic Seasoning Blends Shrimp Magic or Home Creole Seasoning (page 24)

1 teaspoon kosher salt

To make the roux, heat the oil on high in a large, heavy-bottom pot. Whisk the flour into the hot oil and continue to whisk constantly. Use a large spoon to scrape the corners of the skillet the whisk won't reach so that it cooks evenly.

When the color is approaching that of dark brown sugar, which should be 2 or 3 minutes, remove the pan from the heat and stir in the bell pepper, onion, celery, okra, garlic, and bay leaf. The roux color will advance one shade. Cover and cook on very low heat for 15 minutes.

Add the tomatoes with juice, mashing them up with your hands into small pieces, and then add the stock. Scrape the bottom of the pan with a ladle or spoon to release any crusted bits. Season with the Shrimp Magic and salt.

Bring this to a simmer and cook on low boil for about an hour to reduce by about 40 percent. Skim off the fat by tilting the pan and allowing the grease to collect along the sides so it can easily be removed with a large spoon. Remove the bay leaf.

This can be made several days in advance and refrigerated, or several months ahead and frozen.

This spicy tomato-based sauce can used in so many ways with so many different proteins, and can paired with a wide variety of wines, red or white.

COLORFUL CHARACTERS AND CRITTERS OF NEW ORLEANS

One of the things I love about New Orleans is the high regard in which we hold our "characters," and Mac Rebennack, the musical icon better known as Dr. John, is certainly one of them. I got to know him several years ago when a friend of his who happens to be my shrimp supplier, Roy Todd, brought him into the restaurant for dinner. Having spent five years of my life hiring rock 'n' roll bands back in Georgia, I probably have a better idea of the general idiosyncrasies of musicians than most folks. To say his diet is special is an understatement. He believes "wild food" is healthier than anything else and has recruited me to cook some of his favorites for him (since I couldn't put them on my menus even if I wanted to): ducks, pouldeau, deer neck, nutria, numerous raccoons, and the only possum I ever prepared.

When he was a judge on Top Chef here, I was called to bring him a dish to pair with a hot sauce tasting. Since I wasn't given any lead time to source anything more exotic, I made him the wildest thing I could come up with on short notice: alligator sauce piquant. Another time after a show here, I delivered frog legs, also in sauce piquant—he likes that—in Japanese Bento boxes. When I asked if I could get the boxes back, I was told he liked them so much he placed them on his Voodoo altar.

Actually sauce piquant is a good way to prepare all sorts of small game critters. Season the animal well, and then brown and simmer in the sauce until tender. I recently served a combo raccoon and bobcat sauce piquant to a very tony crowd at a gallery opening in my neighborhood as one of several unusual items requested by the artist and it was very well received.

CLASSIC SHRIMP CREOLE

SERVES 4 AS A MAIN DISH

With a quart of Creole Mother Sauce in the refrigerator, a company-worthy dinner is only minutes away. Heat up the sauce while you cook the rice, toss a salad, and heat a loaf of bread. You can simply drop the shrimp into the simmering sauce, but I like to season the shrimp separately and give them a quick sauté to add a little more caramelization.

1 quart Creole Mother Sauce (page 130)

¼ cup chopped green onions

2 pounds 16–20 wild-caught American shrimp, peeled and deveined

1 teaspoon Chef Paul Prudhomme's Magic Seasoning Blend Shrimp Magic or Home Creole Seasoning (page 24)

1 tablespoon vegetable oil

3 cups cooked rice

Chopped fresh parsley

Reheat the sauce base over medium heat, if necessary. Stir in the green onions, lower the heat a little, and continue cooking for 4 or 5 more minutes.

Season the peeled shrimp with Shrimp Magic. Heat oil in a large skillet on high. Then add the shrimp and sauté for a few seconds on each side, and ladle the sauce into the pan. Bring the mixture to a boil, turn the heat off, and set aside.

To serve, put a big scoop of rice in the center of a large warmed soup bowl. Ladle about 1 cup of the Shrimp Creole over the rice and sprinkle with chopped parsley.

SUGGESTED WINE PAIRING: Serve with Etude Pinot Noir (Carneros, California), a silky, lush, medium-bodied red that has complex flavors of cherry and pomegranate and notes of earth and baking spice.

FROG LEGS IN SAUCE PIQUANT

SERVES 4 AS A MAIN DISH

"Piquant" is derived from the French verb, "piquer," meaning "to prick," or "to sting." Sauce Piquant is a spicier version of Creole sauce and it is meant to do just that to your tongue with hot spices. It's great with shrimp and fatty fish, such as mackerel, cobia, redfish, or just about any fish trimmings.

And it's also an excellent way to prepare alligator (page 125), chicken, and all sorts of small game critters. Frog legs are accessible, and very popular here. I like to fry only the smaller frog legs, but the bigger ones are good prepared this way and, if you like chicken, you could become a convert.

4 pairs large (the size of your thumb or larger) domestic fresh frog legs

Kosher salt and freshly ground black pepper

All-purpose flour for dusting

2 tablespoons vegetable oil

1 tablespoon butter

1 Thai chile, split

2 cups Creole Mother Sauce (page 130)

Hot cooked rice for serving

Season the frog legs liberally with salt and pepper and dust in flour. Heat a skillet on medium-to-high heat and add the oil and then the butter. Brown the frog legs quickly (if really fresh, they will kick a bit) on both sides and add the chile and the sauce. Reduce the heat, cover and simmer until tender—about 5 minutes, depending on the frog legs' size. Serve over hot cooked rice.

SUGGESTED WINE PAIRING: Serve with Groth Chardonnay (Oakville, California), a balanced, full-bodied wine with layers of tropical fruit and caramel.

CAJUN COURT BOUILLON

SERVES 4 AS A MAIN DISH

Pronounced "koo-be-yon," this brothy bayou classic is a thinner version of sauce piquant, made with fish. I think of this as a method of cooking rather than as a hard and fast recipe. This can be done using fillets from larger fish such as redfish or drum or practically anything you have, just be careful of cook time with smaller leaner fish. I like it best with fuller flavored fish like mackerel. Or if you're not afraid of a few bones, it's a great way to cook collars from fat fish like cobia or swordfish.

The method of seasoning and browning before adding the sauce, then covering and simmering until done and garnishing with freshly chopped herbs, is identical to sauce piquant, but with a little added stock to thin to the desired consistency.

1 pound redfish fillets, cut in pan-size pieces

Kosher salt and freshly ground black pepper

All-purpose flour for dusting

2 tablespoons vegetable oil

1 tablespoon butter

1 Thai chile, split (or Fresno or jalapeño)

2 cups Creole Mother Sauce (page 130)

1 cup (more or less) Basic Fish (page 128) or Shrimp Stock (page 129)

Chopped fines herbes (page 25), fresh parsley, or green onion for garnish

Hot cooked rice for serving

Season the fish liberally with salt and pepper and dust in flour.

Heat a skillet on medium-to-high heat and add the oil and then the butter. Brown the fish quickly on both sides and add the split chile, sauce, stock and fines herbes. Reduce the heat, cover, and simmer until cooked through —about 5 minutes. Serve over hot cooked rice.

SUGGESTED WINE PAIRING: Serve with Chalone Pinot Noir (Monterey, California), a silky red with flavors of raspberry, plum, and baking spices to match the complexity of the Creole flavors.

TRADITIONAL JAMBALAYA

SERVES 4 AS A MAIN DISH

This is a quick and foolproof way of preparing this dish that allows you to add whatever ingredients you like by cooking them ahead and then adding them to the sauce base. Use chicken, sausage, shrimp, crabmeat, oysters, whatever you have on hand. I like to season bone-in chicken thighs and bake them in the oven (and add sliced sausage to the pan during the last 10 minutes), and then pick the chicken meat from the bones before adding it to the jambalaya mixture.

4 cups Creole Mother Sauce (page 130)

2 or 3 cups cooked chicken, sausage, shrimp, crabmeat, oysters— whatever you have on hand

1 cup water or stock

3 cups cooked white rice

Freshly chopped parsley or green onion

Heat the sauce in a large saucepan and add the cooked chicken and/or other proteins. Add the water or stock, cover, and simmer for a few minutes, until hot. Fold in the rice. Garnish with plenty of freshly chopped parsley or green onion.

SUGGESTED WINE PAIRING: Serve with Mara Zinfandel (2006 Mara Reserve Zinfandel Library Selection), (Russian River Valley, California), a rich wine with dark fruit flavors and hints of black walnut and chocolate that complement the big, spicy flavors in this dish.

SEAFOOD GUMBO

SERVES 8 TO 12 AS A MAIN DISH

Once you're confident in your roux-making and are ready to give this a shot, get a head start on the Fish Stock (page 128). This recipe calls for enough stock for at least an hour of simmering to reduce it to the proper soup consistency. Once you make the roux and add the vegetables and aromatics, you can stop there and refrigerate before proceeding. By all means don't skimp on the seafood additions. If you're lucky enough to have some fresh-diced fish trim, toss that in. Fresh crawfish fat or crab fat are also great additions. This is designed for a big crowd, but can easily be cut in half if you are so inclined. But since the Gumbo Base freezes well, I highly recommend making the full recipe (without the added seafood) and saving a batch for another occasion. Add the seafood just before serving.

OVEN ROUX

½ cup canola oil

¾ cup all-purpose flour

OVEN ROUX Remove the top rack from the oven if necessary to accommodate a large vessel. Preheat the oven to 400 degrees. On the stovetop, heat the oil in a Dutch oven or a heavy, 3-quart ovenproof pan on medium-to-high heat and whisk in the flour until blended. Place in the hot oven and stir every 15 minutes. Be extremely careful not to splash yourself with the hot roux!

After about 45 minutes to an hour, the roux should be approaching the color of dark brown sugar. Color is the most important part of the procedure—if it's too light your gumbo could be gummy. You'll notice the mixture gets thinner as it browns.

A GUMBO FOR EVERY OCCASION

There's something magical about a rich, brown gumbo: the (seemingly) simple technique of browning flour in hot oil to make a roux, adding fairly pedestrian vegetables and seasonings, tomatoes (if you're in the eastern part of the state—Breaux Bridge and Lafayette would protest), a good homemade stock, and a long, slow cook time meld this preparation into a base that can support practically any protein whether it be chicken, duck, sausage, or seafood. Small game in particular is wonderful braised this way, and by adding a bit more roux and making more rice or potato salad a little meat can feed a lot of people. Like its other brown roux-based cousins, this is a cooking method that gets the most out of whatever animal(s) you have.

Seafood gumbo tends to be more expensive and involved than other versions and, if you live a distance from the ocean, is mostly reserved for special occasions. But if you know what you're doing, the flavor payoff will be huge. If you've never made gumbo before, I would highly recommend honing your roux technique with a gumbo using a simpler stock and more economical add-on ingredients.

Chicken-Sausage Gumbo is one of the most popular variations here, and can be made by simply following the technique for Seafood Gumbo, using an unsalted, preferably homemade, chicken stock in place of the fish stock and diced, cooked chicken and andouille or other smoked sausage instead of seafood. The day after Thanksgiving, it's common for folks around here to make a broth with the turkey carcass.

Our executive chef, Mike Nelson, has even made a surprisingly tasty vegan version using a mushroom stock (see page 180).

I know it may sound funny if you're not from Louisiana, but a big scoop of potato salad (see page 191) in the middle of your gumbo bowl instead of rice is the bomb. Either way, garnish with plenty of sliced green onions and serve with hot French bread.

GUMBO BASE

1 ½ cups diced onions

1 ½ cups diced green bell peppers

½ cup chopped celery

1 cup chopped canned tomatoes

1 tablespoon Paul Prudhomme's Magic Seasoning Blend Shrimp Magic or Home Creole Seasoning (page 24)

1 ½ teaspoons onion powder

1 ½ teaspoons garlic powder

1 ½ teaspoons kosher salt

½ teaspoon ground black pepper

⅛ teaspoon dried thyme

⅛ teaspoon cayenne pepper

½ cup sliced fresh or frozen okra

1 gallon Basic Fish Stock (page 128)

SEAFOOD

1 pound fresh Louisiana crawfish tails

1 pound picked claw crabmeat

1 cup fresh oysters, rough chopped

1 pound wild-caught American shrimp (preferably 16–20 or 21–25), peeled and rough-chopped

Hot cooked rice or Zydeque Potato Salad (page 191) for serving

GUMBO BASE While the roux is in the oven, mix together the onions, bell peppers, and celery in a bowl. Place the tomatoes with all the dried seasonings in a blender or food processor and purée.

When the dark brown sugar color of the roux is achieved, remove the pan from the oven and add the chopped vegetables and the okra, carefully stirring to coat them with the hot roux. Your roux color will advance one shade when you do this. Stir in the tomato and seasoning mixture, and transfer to a large stockpot.

Whisk the stock vigorously into the roux and vegetable-tomato mixture until all the roux is incorporated.

Bring to a boil and then reduce to a simmer. Slide the pot a little off the heat so the fat and scum will gather on the cooler side to be easily removed with a ladle or big spoon. Have a container handy for this. It takes some practice to skim the fat that collects without losing too much of the stock—slow and easy does it.

This not only cleans up the mixture by allowing you to remove fat, but also concentrates the flavor of the stock. Simmer until reduced by half, at least an hour. Beware of too vigorous a boil because this will semi-emulsify the fat and you'll end up with a greasy gumbo.

When this process is complete, the mixture will be at a medium-thick soup consistency. The vegetables will have almost disappeared and it will have a pleasant and balanced flavor. At this point, your gumbo base is complete. If desired, pour into a storage container and refrigerate for up to 4 days or freeze for 6 months.

SEAFOOD When ready to serve, bring base to a simmer over medium heat. When hot, add the seafood all at once and simmer for 10 to 15 minutes, long enough to heat through. Be careful not to overcook the seafood. Serve with rice or potato salad.

SUGGESTED WINE PAIRING: Serve with Elouan Winery Pinot Noir (Oregon Coast). It is easy to overpower delicate seafood flavors. This red, with its red fruit flavors, soft tannins, and hints of tobacco and smoke, complements the dark flavors of the roux as well as the seafood.

CRAWFISH ÉTOUFFÉE

SERVES 4 AS A MAIN DISH

Étouffée is a Louisiana seafood stew that differs from gumbos and Creole sauce-based dishes in that it's traditionally made with a light or "blond" roux cooked only until it reaches the peanut butter–color stage. My untraditional method bypasses the roux altogether. Onions and bell peppers cook slowly in lots of butter and Creole seasoning until they are meltingly tender and sweet. Then I stir in a cornstarch and water slurry, which magically brings the melted and broken butter back together into a luxuriously rich and creamy sauce. Because there is no other seasoning, I am more insistent on seeking out Shrimp Magic, my favorite blend, than in other recipes. Though not essential, it's also worth sourcing Jazzman rice (Jazzmen is the brand name), a Louisiana-grown aromatic rice with a discernible taste that can be appreciated in this simple dish.

Shrimp stock can be substituted for water in the recipe, but that's not necessary if you just want to make this with a pound package of fresh domestic crawfish tail meat.

¾ pound (3 sticks) salted butter

2 cups diced onions

½ cup diced red (and/or green or yellow) bell pepper

2 tablespoons Chef Paul Prudhomme's Magic Seasoning Blends Shrimp Magic or Home Creole Seasoning (page 24)

½ cup water or Strong Shrimp Stock (page 129)

1 tablespoon cornstarch dissolved in 2 tablespoons water

1 (1-pound) package domestic peeled and cleaned crawfish tails

1 bunch green onions, chopped

Hot cooked Jazzman rice (page 26) or jasmine rice

Melt the butter in a large saucepan over medium heat and add the onions. Cover and cook on low to medium heat to "sweat" the onions until soft but without coloring, about 30 minutes. Add the diced peppers and the Shrimp Magic, cover, and continue cooking an additional 15 minutes. Add the water or stock, bring to a boil, and whisk in the cornstarch and water slurry. Simmer for a few minutes and turn off the heat. The mixture will be broken and oily at first, but you will be able to whisk it together as it cools.

If serving right away, stir in the crawfish tails and green onion and return it to a simmer for a couple of minutes. If the sauce "breaks," just continue whisking until it comes back together.

Serve in warmed pasta bowls over hot rice.

If you plan to use it later, don't add the crawfish tails or green onion. It can be refrigerated up to 1 week. To serve, reheat slowly, whisking all the while, and add the crawfish tails and green onion.

SUGGESTED WINE PAIRING: *Serve with Rombauer Vineyard Chardonnay (Carneros, California). Smooth and medium-bodied, with aromas of apples and peaches and a hint of minerality, this Chardonnay is a great fit for a Creole-seasoned buttery-rich stew.*

CREAMY OYSTER STEW

SERVES 4 AS A MAIN DISH, 6 AS A FIRST COURSE

This is a slight variation of a classic oyster stew that's been my family's tradition for Christmas Eve supper for the last seventy years or so. My father's family settled in central North Carolina when they migrated from the western mountains for work in the textile mills, and the story is that Christmas week in December was the first time it was reliably cold enough for wagons to travel from the coast with shell oysters packed in hay. This is a quick one- or two-pot soup and if you add Oyster Butter Sauce as a garnish, it's a real show stopper. Finely diced cooked country ham can be added at the end instead of bacon if you prefer, or pork can be omitted entirely. Fresh oysters are paramount. If you shuck them yourself be sure to save all the oyster liquor, which stands in for the stock.

2 quarts water

1 tablespoon plus 2 teaspoons kosher salt, divided

2 large Idaho potatoes, peeled and cut into ½-inch cubes

4 slices thick-cut bacon, finely diced

4 tablespoons salted butter, divided

1 small white or yellow onion, cut in ½-inch dice

1 quart half-and-half

2 teaspoons kosher salt

½ teaspoon freshly ground black pepper

1 teaspoon Worcestershire sauce

1 pint oysters, with liquor (3 to 4 dozen fresh in the shell, shucked)

1 teaspoon Tabasco Sauce

Oyster Butter Sauce (page 163), warm

1 tablespoon freshly chopped parsley

Oyster crackers for serving

Bring water to a rolling boil in a medium saucepan. Add 1 tablespoon salt and potato cubes. Cook the potatoes until fork-tender, about 5 minutes. Drain and spread on a plate to cool.

Sauté the bacon in a heavy skillet on medium heat until crisp. Transfer the bacon to a paper towel–lined plate and drain off most of the fat (a little bacon fat is okay).

Add 2 tablespoons of the butter to the same skillet and melt over medium-low heat. Add the onion, cover, and "sweat" until soft but not browned, stirring occasionally. Mix with the bacon and potatoes in a bowl and rinse out the skillet.

Meanwhile, bring the half-and-half, 2 teaspoons salt, pepper, and the Worcestershire sauce to a low simmer over medium heat in a large saucepan and turn off the heat.

Add the potato mixture to the hot cream and turn on low heat.

Melt remaining 2 tablespoons butter in skillet on medium heat and add the pint of oysters. Cook just until the edges curl and then add all juices to the pot. Add the Tabasco. Divide into 4 warmed pasta bowls and swirl a few spoonfuls of the Oyster Butter Sauce in each. Top with chopped parsley and serve with a bowl of oyster crackers.

SUGGESTED WINE PAIRING: *Serve with Far Niente Chardonnay (Napa Valley, California). The crisp acidity and ripe fruit flavors of this oaky, creamy Chardonnay beautifully offset the richness of this dish.*

THAI COCONUT-CURRY SEAFOOD SOUP

SERVES 4 AS A MAIN COURSE

I am not much of a fan of Indian curries, and this is probably because I've had so many bad examples of what was a bastardized English version made with generic yellow curry powder. I am much fonder of the Thai-style green curry with coconut milk, ginger, and lemongrass.

I keep most of the ingredients in this recipe on hand at all times at home for the makings of a low-hassle dinner that is easily adaptable to pretty much any protein I happen to have on hand, even chicken. I find it especially good for making use of the various parts of the fish that you would normally throw away like the collar and the cheeks. In Asia, these fish parts are held in more esteem than fillets. But if you only had fillets, you could cut them up and use them in this recipe. Or try adding mussels and/or clams. And you can never go wrong with shrimp. Also try adding different vegetables, like okra.

2 tablespoons salted butter

1 stalk lemongrass, crushed and chopped

1 teaspoon diced fresh ginger

1 clove garlic, minced

2 teaspoons diced shallot

1 kaffir lime leaf

2 teaspoons green curry paste

5 sprigs basil stems and leaves, chopped

2 tablespoons chopped cilantro stems and leaves

4 cups Fish Stock (page 128) or chicken broth, divided

2 (13.5-ounce) cans coconut milk

2 tablespoons olive oil, divided

4 to 6 heads baby bok choy, trimmed and coarsely chopped

8 collars and cheeks, preferably from 4- to 6-pound fish; 1 pound meaty fish fillet, cut in chunks; or 1 pound peeled wild-caught American shrimp (with heads on, if possible)

1 tablespoon Paul Prudhomme's Magic Seasoning Blend Shrimp Magic or Home Creole Seasoning (page 24)

Kosher salt and freshly ground black pepper, to taste

1 tablespoon fish sauce

Thai basil and cilantro leaves for garnish

Hot cooked rice for serving

Melt the butter in a large, heavy saucepan over medium heat. Add the crushed lemongrass, ginger, garlic, shallot, and kaffir lime leaf; cook and stir a few minutes to soften (do not brown).

Add the curry paste, basil, and cilantro and raise the heat, stirring for a couple more minutes. Add 3 cups of the fish stock and the coconut milk. Simmer, uncovered, for 15 minutes. Purée with an immersion blender (or transfer to a regular blender and strain back into the pot).

Set a large sauté pan over medium-high heat and add 1 tablespoon olive oil. Add bok choy, quickly sear on all sides, and add to the soup.

If using fish, season with the Shrimp Magic. Add the remaining oil to the sauté pan and quickly sear the pieces in the hot pan until lightly browned, about 3 minutes. Put the pieces in the simmering broth. Or add the shrimp, if you are using it. Cook until the fish or shrimp are just cooked through, which should be about 4 minutes, depending on their size.

Thin with additional cup of fish stock, if desired. Adjust the seasoning with salt and pepper and add the fish sauce. Add the cilantro and basil garnish. Serve with hot rice, chopsticks and soup spoons.

SUGGESTED WINE PAIRING: *Serve with A to Z Wineworks Oregon Riesling (Oregon). This sweet, versatile wine with floral aromas and flavors of lime, honey, and pear is wonderful with Asian and Indian cuisines—a natural for this dish.*

BLENDED BITS AND PIECES

LOBSTER DUMPLINGS IN LOBSTER BUTTER SAUCE

CRABMEAT, COUNTRY HAM, AND CHANTERELLE POT STICKERS IN PEA SHOOT BUTTER SAUCE

SEAFOOD BOUDIN

SMOKED FISH DIP

OLD SCHOOL DEVILED CRABS

DEVILED CRAB-STUFFED SHRIMP

CRAWFISH AND CORN SPOONBREAD

STICKY RICE CAKES WITH SWEET AND SPICY COCONUT-SHRIMP TOPPING

MAQUE CHOUX WITH BACON, TASSO, AND SEAFOOD

Now that we've covered the best methods for showcasing the nuanced flavors and delicate textures of the most prized fillets in the seafood case, let's talk about what to do with the bits you may have left: an extra fillet, trimmed and cut into dice; a cupful of fresh crawfish tails, crabmeat, or shrimp; a freezer-full of catfish from a productive fishing trip.

It goes without saying that if you use substandard ingredients your finished dish won't be optimal. No magic trick can salvage seafood that's past its prime. On the other hand, there's plenty you can do with fish that may lack the flavor and texture you'd want from a fillet you plan to grill or sauté.

I often toss extra pieces of fish into a blender or food processor with egg, maybe some cream, and seasonings to use as a filling for dumplings or pot stickers, or for a sausage stuffing. Or you can roll the mixture into small dumplings without the wrappers (quenelles) and drop them into simmering soup as a garnish. Along with these methods, I offer you some more casual ways to stretch your catch—from a casserole to a dip to Thai-inspired topping for sticky rice cakes.

HEADS, COLLARS, AND OTHER FISH PARTS UNKNOWN

I have Asian friends who can't believe that collars and heads aren't held in higher esteem in the United States—they would much rather eat them than a boneless fillet. They love to roast the backbones of big fish like swordfish and mahi mahi. Chopsticks pick at the bones to make sure no morsel of meat goes to waste. "The closer to the bone, the sweeter the meat," is the saying. I'm not entirely sure that heads will ever go mainstream in the States, but at Fins, we fully embrace the no-waste philosophy and do offer them from time to time in highly flavored soups and stews, and they have been well-received.

Our executive chef, Michael Nelson, has devised many popular menu items around these underutilized parts. One is "fish wings": You hold them by the fin and eat them like a chicken wing. He also hot smokes the part of the swordfish that is striated like small ribs where the dorsal fin attaches to the body and serves it with a smoked jalapeño butter.

There are a number of more practical ways to explore these possibilities at home, using techniques found throughout this book.

HEADS While traveling in Singapore, Jakarta, and Bali, I had some amazing fish stews and soups, which were typically made with fish heads that, in order to be good, had to be right out of the water. I've since been inspired to use them more often myself, especially in exotically flavored soups and curries, such as Thai Coconut Curry Soup (page 140). By all means, throw the heads into the pot when you're making fish stock. Clean them well and give them a quick soak in salt water first.

COLLARS This is basically the clavicle of the fish, where the head meets the body. Therefore, there's only one per fish. We grill, roast, or hot smoke collars of bigger fish like swordfish or cobia, and they taste like the best barbecue you've ever had.

CHEEKS A fish cheek is literally the cheek meat. It needs to be from a fish eight pounds or larger to justify the labor, and it will give you a couple of scallops of meat that are an ounce or two each. You'll need several big fish to make this worthwhile. The texture is a little firmer than the meat from the middle of the fillet, but definitely worth saving if you have several big fish.

LOBSTER DUMPLINGS IN LOBSTER BUTTER SAUCE

SERVES 10 AS A FIRST COURSE

Forcemeat refers to an emulsified sausage mixture. Add cream and egg to puréed meat or fish, and you have mousseline. Those may sound like fancy cooking school terms, but it's a basic technique/ratio that can be used for an infinite number of preparations. At Fins, we have served millions of lobster dumplings and thousands of pot stickers.

SEAFOOD FORCEMEAT BASE

8 ounces drum or any lean white meat, very cold (place in freezer for 10 minutes)

2 tablespoons beaten egg, chilled

1 cup heavy cream, chilled

1 teaspoon vegetable oil

½ cup (about ½ bunch) trimmed and thinly sliced green onions

1 tablespoon Dijon mustard

1 ½ teaspoons tobiko, optional

1 tablespoon lobster base (see page 163)

1 teaspoon kosher salt

4 ounces fresh lobster meat (about ½ of the meat from a 1-pound Maine lobster, cut in ¼-inch dice (An alternative is crab)

DUMPLINGS

1 tablespoon cornstarch (plus a little more for dusting), mixed with ¼ cup cold water

50 gyoza wrappers

SAFFRON-FENNEL GARNISH

1 cup water

1 small fennel bulb, thinly sliced crosswise

1 small pinch of saffron threads

Lobster Butter Sauce (page 163), triple recipe, warm

Finely diced ripe tomato, peeled, seeded, and diced

Have all ingredients and tools (food processor bowl and blade, large metal bowl, rubber spatula) well chilled before you begin. Fill a container large enough to accommodate the bowl with ice.

SEAFOOD FORCEMEAT BASE Grind the well-chilled fish in the food processor fitted with the metal blade until it gathers into a ball. Blend in the egg, and then slowly add the cream in a thin stream until emulsified. The mixture should be the consistency of soft-serve ice cream. Transfer to the chilled metal bowl, set the bowl in the container of ice, and stir occasionally until it thickens while you prepare the rest of the ingredients.

Heat oil to medium in a small skillet. Add green onions and sauté until tender. Remove from heat and let cool. Fold green onions, mustard, tobiko, lobster base, and salt into the puréed mixture with a rubber spatula. Fold in the lobster. Refrigerate for 1 hour. (May be covered and refrigerated up to 2 days on ice.)

DUMPLINGS Dust a baking sheet lightly with cornstarch.

Set a gyoza wrapper on a work surface, keeping remaining wrappers covered with a dampened cloth while you work. Place about 2 teaspoons of the seafood mixture in the center. Dip a finger in the cornstarch-water mixture and run your wet finger around the edge of the wrapper to make it sticky, fold one side over the other to enclose, and pinch and crimp the edges together to seal. Place on the baking sheet so the dumplings don't touch. Repeat with the remaining wrappers and filling. Cover the baking sheet with plastic wrap and refrigerate.

SAFFRON-FENNEL GARNISH Bring water to a low boil in a small saucepan; add the fennel slices and saffron and poach until fennel slices are crisp-tender. Strain off the liquid and spread on a plate to cool.

Bring a large pot of salted water to boil on high heat. Add the dumplings all at once and cook 2 to 3 minutes, or until they are tender but still firm to the touch. Transfer to a heated pasta bowl, with a slotted spoon.

Ladle about 3 tablespoons of the Lobster Butter Sauce into each of 10 heated pasta bowls. Add 5 dumplings to each; sprinkle with diced tomato and the Saffron-Fennel Garnish.

SUGGESTED WINE PAIRING: Frank Family Vineyards Chardonnay (Carneros, California). Creamy with flavors of baked pear and lemon curd.

CRABMEAT, COUNTRY HAM, AND CHANTERELLE POT STICKERS IN PEA SHOOT BUTTER SAUCE

SERVES 10 AS A FIRST COURSE

We in south Louisiana have a long, wet spring bumper crop of chanterelles which pair wonderfully with country ham. For a real seasonal treat, I'll fold this combination in with a creamy crabmeat purée and encase them in gyoza skins for pot stickers—similar to the dumplings but shaped like a hat. Then I serve them in a pool of velvety, verdant butter sauce freshened with tender pea shoots.

1 recipe Seafood Forcemeat Base (page 145), with 4 ounces crabmeat instead of lobster; omit the tobiko

2 tablespoons vegetable oil, divided

¼ cup finely diced country ham

¼ cup finely sliced chanterelles or shiitake mushrooms

1 tablespoon cornstarch, plus extra for dusting

¼ cup cold water

80 gyoza wrappers

1 tablespoon salted butter (or more)

Pea Shoot Butter Sauce (page 165), triple recipe, warm

Pea shoots, for garnish

Prepare the seafood forcemeat as for the Lobster Dumplings; keep the mixture cold. Don't add the crabmeat until later.

Heat 1 tablespoon oil in a small skillet. Add ham and mushrooms and sauté until tender. Remove from heat and let cool completely. Fold into the forcemeat mixture with a rubber spatula, along with the crabmeat. Keep the mixture cold in a bowl of ice or in the refrigerator until ready to use.

Dust a baking sheet lightly with cornstarch. Mix cornstarch with cold water in a small bowl.

Set 2 gyoza wrappers on a work surface, keeping remaining wrappers covered with a dampened cloth while you work. Place about 2 teaspoons of the forcemeat mixture in the center of one of the wrappers. Dip a finger in the cornstarch-water mixture and run your wet finger around the edge of the wrapper to make it sticky. Top with the second wrapper, pressing along the edges to seal. Gather the edges with a thumb and forefinger as if making pleats. Curl the edges upward like a hat.

Place on the baking sheet so the dumplings don't touch. Repeat with the remaining wrappers and filling. Cover the baking sheet with plastic wrap and refrigerate.

Bring a large pot of salted water to boil on high heat. Line a baking sheet with paper towels.

Add the pot stickers all at once to the boiling water and cook for 3 to 4 minutes, or until they are tender but still firm to the touch. Lift them out with a skimmer or a slotted spoon, shake dry and place on the baking sheet. Set a sauté pan over medium heat; add remaining oil then butter and quickly brown the pot stickers on both sides, working about 6 or 8 at a time. You may have to add a bit more oil and butter as you go. Ladle 3 tablespoons of Pea Shoot Butter Sauce into each of 10 heated pasta bowls. Add 4 pot stickers to each; garnish with pea shoots.

SUGGESTED WINE PAIRING: *Serve with Hahn Winery Pinot Noir (Monterey, California). Flecks of mushrooms and ham move this dish into red-wine territory, and this pinot noir—with its soft tannins, red-fruit flavors, and clean finish—answers that call.*

SEAFOOD BOUDIN

SERVES 4 AS A MAIN COURSE OR 6 TO 8 AS A SNACK

Boudin is one of my favorite snack foods, along with cracklins and crawfish, west of Baton Rouge, where they are sold out of slow cookers on the counters of gas stations. These sausages are traditionally made with spicy pork with a good shot of pork liver for funk, sort of like dirty rice. Seafood boudin is much lighter, and is a great way to use up the last bit of Seafood Forcemeat. You can eat these immediately as is, or refrigerate and brown them later. You can use them as a garnish in green curry or seafood risotto, an addition to almost any fish dish, or on their own as a snack. Boudin is traditionally stuffed into sausage casings, but plastic wrap works just as well.

Special equipment: plastic wrap, string or kitchen twine

3 tablespoons olive or canola oil

3 tablespoons diced green bell pepper

½ cup diced onion

5 tablespoons diced celery

1 tablespoon finely chopped garlic

2 tablespoons Chef Paul Prudhomme's Magic Seasoning Blends Shrimp Magic or Home Creole Seasoning (page 24), divided

2 cups total of any or all of the following ingredients: ½ cup fresh fish trimmings, cut in ¼-inch dice; ½ cup cooked wild-caught American shrimp, cut in ¼-inch dice; ½ cup picked crabmeat; ½ cup cooked, diced domestic crawfish tails

1 cup soft, cooked rice (not crunchy)

1 cup Seafood Forcemeat Base (page 145)

Heat oil in a heavy-bottom saucepan over medium heat. Add bell pepper, onion, celery, and garlic. Cover and let sweat, without browning, for about 5 minutes until soft, stirring occasionally.

Stir in 1 tablespoon Shrimp Magic. Add the fish pieces if you're using them, and turn off the heat. Add any additional seafood, and stir in the additional tablespoon of seasoning and the cooked rice.

Let mixture come to room temperature or, if you're in a hurry, spread it on a plate and refrigerate 10 to 15 minutes.

Mix the cooled mixture with the forcemeat and stir well to incorporate all the ingredients.

Spread a 2-foot section of plastic wrap on the counter and spoon a line of the boudin mixture about 2 inches from the bottom. Fold the bottom of the wrap away from you and roll the mixture into a cylinder about 1 ½ inches in diameter. Twist the ends toward each other to remove any air pockets. Make the sausage shapes by tying every 3 or so inches with string or kitchen twine. Refrigerate and repeat until you've used all the mixture.

Fill a large pot halfway with water and bring to a simmer. Using a sharp skewer or toothpick, pierce each link 4 or 5 times to allow for expansion and immerse in the boiling water. Cover with a lid. (They'll want to float, so a lid helps equalize the temperature.) Cook until firm, about 6 to 8 minutes, depending on the thickness. Test by cutting one link open. It should be firm all the way through.

Served right out of the water, you can cool them slightly, remove the plastic wrap, and brown briefly in a little butter, or slice and add as a garnish to cioppino, green curry, or risotto. Or, chill and eat cold.

Depending on how you serve them, these mildly spicy sausages work with most Chardonnays or pinot noirs.

SMOKED FISH DIP

2 ¹/₂ CUPS

When you have literally any parts and pieces leftover from your fresh fish, this is a good use for them. Serve with crackers, toast, pita chips, tortilla chips, or any other dipper. If you don't have smoked fish, use any cooked fish and add drop or two of liquid smoke with an eye dropper. Taste after each drop—you definitely don't want to overdo it.

½ pound cream cheese

3 tablespoons ketchup

2 tablespoons lemon juice

½ teaspoon Tabasco Sauce

1 teaspoon prepared horseradish

1 teaspoon kosher salt

¼ teaspoon freshly ground black pepper

½ pound chilled Smoked Trout (page 81) or other smoked fish

¼ cup finely diced tender celery

¼ cup finely diced Vidalia or other sweet onion (if these aren't available you can rinse diced white or yellow onion and squeeze dry in a napkin)

Combine the cream cheese, ketchup, lemon juice, Tabasco, horseradish, salt, and pepper in the bowl of an electric mixer with a paddle attachment and blend until smooth. Add the fish and blend again for a couple of minutes until broken up and somewhat incorporated. Add the celery and onion and blend an additional 2 or 3 minutes. Chill before serving. The flavor will be better the second day and it will keep in the refrigerator for 4 or 5 days.

SUGGESTED WINE PAIRING: Serve with Domaine de la Fruitière Chardonnay (Loire Valley, France). The fruit and mineral flavors of this distinctive Chardonnay reflect the region's granite soil, and make it an excellent choice for serving at a cocktail party featuring creamy spreads and smoked fish.

OLD SCHOOL DEVILED CRABS

SERVES 10 AS A SIDE DISH (5 CUPS TOTAL)

I'll have to confess, I still love the old school fried seafood platter I used to eat in fish houses years ago. They usually contained fried catfish, shrimp, oysters, hush puppies, and a blue crab shell stuffed with this mixture. Fried potatoes and coleslaw completed this feast. Aluminum faux shells made in a crab shape have largely replaced the real thing (you can order them online), or you can just use a small ovenproof dish.

The amount of seafood added is up to you, and fish pieces or crawfish can be substituted for crab if you like. The ratio should be one part mix to two parts meat. The breading mixture (without seafood) can be refrigerated up to a week.

Special equipment: 10 fresh, cleaned or aluminum foil shells, or 4-ounce ramekins

½ cup (1 stick) salted butter

½ cup diced onion

¼ cup diced red and/or green bell pepper

½ cup finely diced celery

2 large eggs

6 tablespoons mayonnaise

½ cup ketchup

¼ cup yellow mustard

1 ½ teaspoons kosher salt

1 ½ teaspoons freshly ground black pepper

1 ½ teaspoons Tabasco Sauce

1 ½ teaspoons Worcestershire sauce

¾ cup panko breadcrumbs

1 pound lump blue crabmeat (Alternatives are crawfish, picked crab claw meat, or poached or flaked fish)

Vegetable oil spray

Preheat oven to 350 degrees F. Melt butter in a saucepan over medium-low heat, and add onion, bell pepper, and celery. Cover and cook, stirring occasionally, about 20 minutes until very soft but not brown. Spread on a plate to cool to room temperature on the counter or in the refrigerator. In a large mixing bowl, mix together the eggs, mayonnaise, ketchup, and mustard. Mix in the cooled vegetables, salt, pepper, Tabasco, and Worcestershire sauce. Fold in the bread crumbs then the crabmeat.

Pack into cleaned, vegetable oil–sprayed crab shells or ramekins. Bake for 15 to 20 minutes, or until golden brown.

DEVILED CRAB-STUFFED SHRIMP

SERVES 6 TO 8 AS AN ENTRÉE

The Old School Deviled Crabs mixture makes a fantastic stuffing for shrimp in the shell. It's a hearty, if somewhat messy, entrée that needs only salad and crusty bread for a full meal.

Vegetable oil spray or softened butter

2 pounds shell-on, extra-large (16–20) wild-caught American shrimp

½ recipe Old School Deviled Crabs (page 149)

2 tablespoons salted butter, melted

Paprika

Chopped fresh parsley for garnish

Lemon wedges

Preheat oven to 375 degrees F. Coat a large baking pan with vegetable oil spray or grease with softened butter.

Leaving the shells on, butterfly the shrimp by splitting them lengthwise almost completely through the back along the curve with a small, sharp knife. Open them and remove the sand vein. Warm the stuffing mixture for a minute or two in the microwave, if made ahead and refrigerated, before stuffing the shrimp since the shrimp meat can cook faster than the stuffing will heat through.

Gently press a heaping tablespoon of the stuffing into each split shrimp then place them, stuffed sides up, in the baking dish.

Drizzle with the melted butter and lightly sprinkle with paprika. Bake 15 to 20 minutes, depending on size of shrimp, or until shells turn pink.

Garnish with parsley and serve hot, with lemon wedges.

SUGGESTED WINE PAIRING: *Serve with J Vineyards & Winery Pinot Gris (Sonoma County, California). Fruit-forward and floral with a touch of minerality, this versatile white wine works especially well with buttery shellfish dishes.*

CRAWFISH AND CORN SPOONBREAD

8 GENEROUS SERVINGS

This is an old Southern recipe you may have eaten as corn pudding. It is a perfect—and gluten-free—accompaniment to almost any sautéed or grilled fish dish, and can be paired with or without corn butter. With this method the batter is made ahead of time, placed in custard cups, and refrigerated for up to 3 days. It is then finished quickly in a hot oven just before serving. You can also bake it in a pan all at once if you like. This base recipe can be fancied up once you have the hang of it with additional ingredients: crawfish, crabmeat, finely diced country ham, or roasted peppers. Just be sure any additions are cut finely so they are suspended in this light batter.

2 tablespoons softened butter or vegetable oil spray

2 ears corn

¾ cup half-and-half

5 egg yolks

4 tablespoons sugar

½ teaspoon freshly ground black pepper, optional

4 cups milk

1 ½ teaspoons kosher salt

1 cup cornmeal

1 stick (8 tablespoons) salted butter, cut in fourths

5 egg whites

1 pinch of cream of tartar

1 cup or so chopped crawfish tails or crabmeat

Preheat oven to 350 degrees F. Coat 8 (6-ounce) custard cups, a 4-quart baking dish, or a 9 x 13-inch pan with butter or vegetable oil spray. Cut the corn off the cob and scrape with the heel of the knife to release all the embedded juice. Purée the corn kernels and juice with half-and-half, egg yolks, sugar, and pepper with an immersion blender or in a conventional blender.

Bring milk and salt to a boil in a medium saucepan. Put cornmeal and butter in a large bowl. When the milk boils, whisk it quickly into the cornmeal and stir until butter is melted. Mix in the corn and half-and-half mixture well. Allow this to cool. Meanwhile, place egg whites and cream of tartar in a large mixing bowl and whip them to soft peaks. Quickly fold them into the custard, along with the crawfish.

Divide this mixture into your prepared baking cups or dish. At this point you can refrigerate, covered, for up to 3 days, until ready to use.

Bake for 20 to 30 minutes depending on size of baking dish, or until set. Loosen by running a spoon around the edge and invert onto a serving plate. If served as a side, leave it in the cup.

SUGGESTED WINE PAIRING: *Serve with Josh Cellars Sauvignon Blanc (California North Coast), a bright, crisp wine that is a great match for these delicate, summery flavors.*

STICKY RICE CAKES WITH SWEET AND SPICY COCONUT-SHRIMP TOPPING

SERVES 8 AS A SIDE DISH OR DESSERT

Scuba diving in the gulf of Thailand near Chumphon was a gas—we saw so many whale sharks we got tired of them. One of the things I remember best about the dive boat was the food. The captain's wife was the chef. She had a two-burner wok station on the top deck, and she provided a continuous buffet including whatever small fish she pulled in whenever we stopped, mangosteens (my new favorite fruit), and sticky rice cakes wrapped in banana leaves. My favorite topping was this coconut shrimp. This recipe has Thai chiles for heat, a little dried shrimp for funk, and a pandan leaf for a floral, vanilla-like flavor. I know it sounds weird, but it is a wonderful combination of savory, hot, and sweet flavors.

TOPPING

1 tablespoon dried shrimp (available in Asian markets)

3 cloves garlic

6 peppercorns, crushed

1 small Thai chile

1 tablespoon cilantro roots or stems

½ pound (16–20) peeled, wild-caught American shrimp

3 tablespoons coconut oil or canola oil

2 cups shredded coconut (sweetened or unsweetened, preferably freshly grated)

¼ teaspoon red food coloring (optional)

1 teaspoon kosher salt

1 ½ to 3 tablespoons coconut (or light brown) sugar

2 finely shredded kaffir lime leaves, middle stem removed

Banana leaves

STICKY RICE CAKES

1 (13.66-ounce) can coconut cream

1 tablespoon coconut (or light brown) sugar

1 teaspoon kosher salt

4-inch piece pandan leaf (available frozen in Asian markets)

Sticky Rice (page 184), warm

TOPPING Finely mince the dried shrimp with the garlic, peppercorns, whole chile, and the cilantro roots. Grind with a mortar and pestle if you have one (this amount is too small for a food processor). If not, just chop everything as fine as you can on a cutting board. Set aside and chop the fresh shrimp finely by hand.

Sauté or sweat the chile and cilantro root mixture in the coconut oil on medium heat until you smell the fragrance of the garlic. Stir in the coconut (sweetened will color more quickly). Stir constantly until the coconut starts to brown slightly, being careful not to let it get too dark. Stir in the diced shrimp and continue to cook for a few more minutes, stirring until the shrimp changes color.

Stir in the red coloring and mix until it is a uniform orange. Keep stirring while adding the salt and sugar (use the lesser amount if using sweetened coconut). Stir in the shredded kaffir lime leaves and remove from the heat. Place in a bowl, cover, and let stand at room temperature.

STICKY RICE CAKES Bring the coconut cream, sugar, salt, and pandan leaf to a simmer in a small saucepan. Cook, uncovered, for 5 minutes and then remove from the heat.

Remove the pandan leaf and mix the coconut cream with the hot sticky rice until it's incorporated; cover and let stand at room temperature.

To serve, scoop the warm sticky rice onto a banana leaf square and top with a spoonful of the coconut shrimp.

SUGGESTED WINE PAIRING: Serve with Josef Leitz Dragonstone Riesling (Rheingau, Germany), a sweet white wine balanced with high acidity that harmonizes with the sweet-fleshed seafood and spicy Asian flavors.

MAQUE CHOUX WITH BACON, TASSO, AND SEAFOOD

SERVES 4 AS A MAIN DISH

This sautéed corn dish said to have originated with the Native Americans is traditional to southern Louisiana, and every cook makes theirs a little differently. I like to embellish mine with bacon and tasso, and use roasted red pepper in place of the usual green bells. It's a great side dish to fish or any simple protein, and it can easily be turned into a main dish by folding in chopped andouille sausage and/or cooked shrimp, crawfish, crabmeat, or chunks of fish. It's also good over hot, cooked rice.

8 ears fresh corn

8 slices bacon, diced

1 medium onion, finely diced

3 tablespoons salted butter, divided

1 tablespoon plus 1 teaspoon Chef Paul Prudhomme's Magic Seasoning Blend Shrimp Magic or Home Creole Seasoning (page 24), divided

2 large ripe tomatoes, peeled, seeded and diced

2 tablespoons finely diced tasso or country ham

2 bunches green onions, trimmed and sliced

1 red bell pepper, roasted, peeled, seeded, and finely diced

½ cup heavy cream

1 pound cooked and peeled crawfish tails or shrimp (cooked or uncooked), halved or diced, optional

2 tablespoons chopped parsley

2 tablespoons chopped fines herbes (page 25), chervil, or 2 tablespoons chopped parsley and ½ teaspoon chopped tarragon

Kosher salt and freshly ground black pepper, to taste

Husk and clean the corn. Using a sharp knife, shave off the tops of the kernels and scrape the ears to remove the rest, leaving the woody part on the cob. Reserve.

Place the bacon in a large sauté pan and cook over medium-high heat until crispy. Remove and drain on paper towels, reserving the fat in the pan.

Place the onion in the pan with the reserved bacon fat. Add 2 tablespoons butter and sauté, covered, on medium low heat until soft and translucent.

Add the corn to the cooked onions with 2 teaspoons Shrimp Magic. Cook on medium heat uncovered, stirring and scraping the bottom of the pan often.

When the corn has cooked for about 5 minutes, add tomatoes, tasso, green onions and 2 more teaspoons Shrimp Magic. Continue cooking until the tomatoes start to break down, about 5 minutes.

Add red peppers and heavy cream. Raise the heat a bit and, if using, add the seafood. Cook for about 3 minutes, stir in remaining butter, the bacon, and chopped herbs and season to taste with salt and pepper. Serve over rice if desired.

SUGGESTED WINE PAIRING: *Serve with Château des Annereaux (Bordeaux, France), a dense, Merlot-based blend that works nicely with the addition of spicy, smoky meats.*

SAUCES AND DRESSINGS

HOUSE COCKTAIL SAUCE

CANE VINEGAR MIGNONETTE

MY FAVORITE TARTAR SAUCE

WHITE RÉMOULADE SAUCE

NUOC MAU PLUS

TOMATO FONDUE

BASIC THREE-MINUTE BUTTER SAUCE (BEURRE MONTÉ)

SWEET CORN AND RED PEPPER BUTTER SAUCE

LOBSTER BUTTER SAUCE

OYSTER BUTTER SAUCE

GINGER-SOY BUTTER SAUCE

PASSION FRUIT BUTTER SAUCE

MUSHROOM BUTTER SAUCE

PEA SHOOT BUTTER SAUCE

CHARRED ONION AND CHIPOTLE BUTTER SAUCE

TABASCO BUTTER SAUCE

CILANTRO PURÉE

CHILI HOLLANDAISE SAUCE

CITRUS CHILI OIL

HORSERADISH CREAM

QUICK VEAL JUS

SHERRY VINAIGRETTE

GREEN GODDESS DRESSING

A pristine fillet can be pretty wonderful seasoned with no more than a little salt once you've figured out the best way to cook it. The right sauce can take it over the top. Most of the seafood recipes in this book are paired with some type of sauce to complete the dish. Some are designed specifically for that particular recipe. Others are versatile enough to go with a variety of seafood (and even other protein) dishes well beyond the pages of this book.

In this chapter, I've singled out these multipurpose sauces for you to have at your fingertips whenever you're in need of a little extra something to dress up whatever you've reeled in, speared, or picked up from the market. The rules are pretty simple: lean fish with butter sauces; fatter fish with pungent Southeast Asian flavors, light salsas, infused oils, or herbal purées; fried seafood or boiled shellfish with mayonnaise-, ketchup-, or vinegar-based sauces.

HOUSE COCKTAIL SAUCE

MAKES ½ CUP

This is the most basic ketchup sauce for raw oysters or fried seafood—much like what you'll find in all the oyster bars here. Felix's Restaurant & Oyster Bar on Iberville is one of the oldest and most famous, and there they serve the components so customers can mix the sauce to their own taste. You probably already have most of the ingredients in your refrigerator, with the possible exception of a new jar of prepared horseradish. Look for one that's white—Tulkoff is a good brand—in the dairy section of the grocery store (rather than the condiment aisle). Because of the reaction of lemon juice with ketchup, this sauce does not keep very well, so it's best to make it in small quantities like this and discard any leftovers.

½ cup ketchup

1 tablespoon prepared white horseradish

½ lemon, juiced

1 teaspoon Worcestershire sauce

¼ teaspoon Tabasco Sauce

Mix ingredients together in a small bowl and refrigerate.

Used in Raw Oysters on the Half Shell (page 33). Louisiana-Style Boiled Shrimp in the Shell (page 50), Cornmeal-Crusted Catfish with Buttermilk Hush Puppies, page 113).

CANE VINEGAR MIGNONETTE

MAKES 1 CUP

Mignonette is the classic condiment for fresh-shucked oysters on the half shell, and it's what I use to season batter-fried fish instead of malt vinegar, the traditional accompaniment to English-style fish and chips. It's also great on fried potatoes. All mignonette sauces contain vinegar, shallots, and freshly diced pepper. The real differentiating factor is the vinegar. Red wine vinegar is traditional, but I like to add a subtle Louisiana flavor to mine with Steen's Cane Vinegar (see page 25).

1 cup cane vinegar

1 tablespoon finely minced shallot

1 tablespoon freshly cracked black pepper

1 tablespoon finely chopped parsley

1 teaspoon kosher salt

Combine all ingredients in a small bowl, cover, and store in the refrigerator for up to a week.

Used in Raw Oysters on the Half Shell (page 33), New Orleans Beer-Batter Fish and Brabant Potatoes, page 111).

MY FAVORITE TARTAR SAUCE

MAKES 1 ½ CUPS

Some people can't imagine eating fried fish without tartar sauce. Besides mayonnaise, usual ingredients are chopped onion and some kind of pickle seasoned with lemon juice and Worcestershire sauce. My version contains fresh herbs, capers, and bits of olive, and in my opinion, it's the best.

1 cup mayonnaise

2 tablespoons sweet or dill pickle relish

2 tablespoons finely diced sweet onion, rinsed and squeezed dry in a napkin

1 tablespoon finely diced green olives

1 tablespoon finely diced capers

2 tablespoons freshly squeezed lemon juice

1 teaspoon Worcestershire sauce

½ teaspoon Tabasco Sauce

1 tablespoon chopped fresh parsley

1 teaspoon chopped fresh tarragon

Mix all ingredients in a medium bowl; cover and store in the refrigerator for up to a week.

Used in Cornmeal-Crusted Catfish with Buttermilk Hush Puppies (page 113).

WHITE RÉMOULADE SAUCE

MAKES 1 ½ CUPS

This potent mayonnaise is great as a dipping sauce for boiled shrimp or any fried seafood. It should not be confused with the classic French version, which has morphed into American tartar sauce. Nor is it the same as New Orleans red rémoulade, which is tinted with paprika and often ketchup. This one leans heavier on the stone-ground Creole mustard we're famous for, fresh parsley, and lots of garlic.

1 cup mayonnaise

¼ cup chopped fresh parsley

1 tablespoon minced garlic

½ cup Zatarain's Creole mustard or other grainy mustard

1 ½ teaspoons Worcestershire sauce

1 ½ teaspoons fresh lemon juice

¼ teaspoon Tabasco Sauce

Place all the ingredients in a medium bowl and whisk vigorously until blended.

Used in Louisiana-Style Boiled Shrimp in the Shell (page 50).

NUOC MAU PLUS

MAKES 2 ½ CUPS

Open all the kitchen windows and turn on the fans—there is a good reason we call this 'stinky sauce' at Fins. This recipe is Fins' version of nuoc mau, a very pungent caramel syrup that adds complexity to many savory Vietnamese dishes and other fried foods. Drizzle it over any fried whole fish, fillet, or bite-size nugget for an appetizer.

1 ½ tablespoons dark sesame oil

3 tablespoons finely diced garlic

6 tablespoons finely diced shallots

6 tablespoons finely diced fresh ginger

1 ½ teaspoons coarsely ground black pepper

1 ½ teaspoons crushed red pepper flakes

1 ½ cups granulated sugar

½ cup water plus ¾ cup or more, to thin

¾ cup fish sauce

Heat the sesame oil on medium-low in a small skillet. Add garlic, shallots, ginger, and black and red peppers and sauté until tender but not brown. Set aside.

Meanwhile, make the caramel. Use a deep, heavy saucepan (at least 2 ½ to 3 quarts—it will bubble up madly.) Make sure it's very clean; the tiniest speck of anything can cause the melting sugar to crystallize.

Place the sugar and ½ cup of the water in the pan and stir to make a slurry. Turn the heat to medium and bring the mixture to a boil. Cook, without stirring, until the water has evaporated and the sugar starts to brown to a light amber. This should take about 10 to 15 minutes or longer. If the mixture crystallizes before it caramelizes, don't throw it out! Add a little more water, or cover the pot with a lid so that the steam melts it. Or, you can stir it vigorously at this point until melted.

Once the caramel darkens to a light amber shade, like iced tea, remove the pot from the heat and—standing away from the pot—slowly whisk in the fish sauce, a little at a time, being careful of the steam.

When all the fish sauce is incorporated, add the sautéed ginger and garlic mixture. Thin with about ½ cup to ¾ cup of water (it will thicken as it cools).

Let cool and cover tightly. This will keep practically forever in a covered container in the refrigerator.

Used in Flash-Fried Whole Lionfish with Vietnamese Flavors (page 120).

TOMATO FONDUE

MAKES ³/₄ CUP

If you have really good local tomatoes (or even some nice ripe grocery store plum tomatoes), you can whip up this five-minute tomato sauce that can add a little acid and color to any simple fish entrée. I often add a spoonful of this sauce along with a creamy butter sauce for contrast.

¼ cup extra-virgin olive oil

1 tablespoon minced garlic

1 tablespoon tomato paste

1 cup peeled, seeded, and chopped tomatoes

1 tablespoon chopped fresh basil

Kosher salt and freshly ground black pepper

Heat the oil in a small sauté pan over medium-low heat. Add the garlic and sauté until fragrant, about 30 seconds. Add tomato paste and continue cooking until mixture is soft and blended, about 2 minutes.

Slowly stir in chopped tomatoes, ¼ cup at a time, allowing mixture to return to a simmer with each addition. Add basil; season with salt and pepper. Keep warm until ready to serve.

Used in Sheepshead à la Française with Corn and Tomato (page 69).

A BUTTER SAUCE PRIMER

Every day at GW Fins, we go through gallons of what the French call beurre monté. This silky, delicate butter sauce is a natural for fish—lighter, faster, and more forgiving than a traditional beurre blanc, and incredibly versatile. The recipe could hardly be simpler: heat a little water to boiling, blend in cold butter until it's creamy and emulsified, add a flavoring or two, and ladle onto a plate to transform any plain piece of protein into a dazzler. Traditionally this sauce is made by heating the water in a saucepan and blending in the butter, bit by bit, with a whisk. But I have found that I can get better and more reliable results by using a blender. At Fins, we use a giant immersion blender, which we set into a deep restaurant pan of hot water and cold butter and pulse for a few seconds until creamy.

Under Basic Three-Minute Butter Sauce (page 162), you'll find three different techniques to make it. Simply choose one based on the equipment you have in your kitchen. My favorite is the first one. It relies on the carryover heat from the mug to aid in the emulsion—basically turning the butter back into cream. One caveat to bear in mind: The temperature of ingredients is crucial. The butter must be very cold before adding to the boiling water, and, once blended, the sauce must be kept relatively warm, between 140 degrees F and 190 degrees F, or it could break. If this happens, you can often reblend it (with a little heated cream to help stabilize it).

Given the small investment (a stick of butter and three minutes of your time), I highly recommend stocking up on a few extra boxes of butter and practicing these methods to find the one that suits you best. Once you get the hang of it and commit the easy recipe to memory, you will be amazed at the world of flavor possibilities now open to you.

BASIC THREE-MINUTE BUTTER SAUCE (BEURRE MONTÉ)

MAKES A SCANT ¾ CUP

¼ cup water

8 tablespoons (1 stick) cold, salted butter, cut in 8 pieces

MICROWAVE AND IMMERSION BLENDER METHOD Place water in a large, heavy ceramic coffee mug; cover with plastic wrap or a small saucer and microwave on high until it reaches a rolling boil, about 2 minutes. Add the butter and use an immersion blender to combine until emulsified.

STOVETOP AND REGULAR BLENDER METHOD Bring the water to a rolling boil in a small saucepan over high heat. Place the butter in the blender container, add the boiling water, and purée until smooth.

TRADITIONAL SAUCEPAN AND WHISK METHOD Bring the water to a rolling boil in a small saucepan over high heat. Reduce the heat to low and whisk in the butter, one piece at a time, until completely emulsified. This is trickier to stabilize than the others and may take some practice. The other two methods are much easier and more reliable.

Tips

- Whichever method you use, feel free to add more butter as desired for a creamier sauce.

- If making a larger batch, double or triple the amount of butter, boiling water, and additional ingredients and use the blender or whisk method.

- If not using the butter sauce immediately, pour it into a warm ceramic coffee cup or bowl. If necessary, set the mug or bowl in a small pot of hot water over low heat to keep warm until ready to use.

- Any additional garnishes added to the basic sauce need to be hot. Adding cold ingredients may break the sauce.

- Leftover butter can be refrigerated, gently reheated, and reblended.

How Can You Mend A Broken Sauce? Don't freak! Try whizzing it again in the blender or rewhisking in the warm saucepan. If that doesn't pull it together, pour a few tablespoons of heavy cream into a small saucepan, heat to a low simmer, and whisk in the broken butter.

SWEET CORN AND RED PEPPER BUTTER SAUCE

MAKES 1 ¼ CUPS

Fresh corn and butter go well with any kind of seafood, and bits of sautéed pepper brighten up the color and flavor. I often fall back on this sauce when I want to dress up a plain fillet.

1 tablespoon salted butter

¼ cup finely diced yellow onion

2 ears corn, kernels scraped

Basic Three-Minute Butter Sauce
(page 162), warm

¼ cup ¼-inch-diced roasted red bell
pepper (see page 191)

Melt butter in a medium saucepan over medium heat. Add onion, cover, and reduce heat to low. Sauté until soft but not browned, about 5 minutes, stirring once or twice. Add corn, cover, and continue to cook an additional 3 to 6 minutes. Set aside. Add a tablespoon of water if needed to prevent sticking and burning.

Pour half the hot corn mixture into the Three-Minute Butter Sauce and blend with an immersion blender until smooth. Or, blend the mixture in a conventional blender, then pour into the Butter Sauce.

Stir in the remaining corn and diced red peppers. Keep sauce warm.

Used in Sheepshead à la Française with Tomato and Corn (page 69).

LOBSTER BUTTER SAUCE

MAKES A SCANT ¾ CUP

For the concentrated lobster base, I use Glace de Fruits de Mer Gold by More Than Gourmet (morethangormet.com).

1 teaspoon lobster base

Basic Three-Minute Butter Sauce
(page 162)

Stir the lobster base into the butter sauce. If not using within 20 minutes or so, set the cup in a small pan of water set on the lowest heat to keep warm.

Used in Lobster Dumplings in Lobster Butter Sauce (page 145).

OYSTER BUTTER SAUCE

MAKES 1 ½ CUPS

Oysters are mostly water, so it is very easy to use them in a luxurious flavored butter sauce that I use as a garnish for all kinds of fish dishes. It is also delicious swirled into an oyster stew.

½ cup fresh-shucked Louisiana
oysters with liquor

16 tablespoons (2 sticks) cold salted
butter, cut in ½-inch chunks

Heat a small sauté pan to medium and add the oysters. When the edges begin to curl, add the butter.

After about a minute, when the mixture is simmering on the edges, but there are still chunks of butter, transfer to a blender. (Don't cover the blender tightly when blending a hot mixture. Place a clean towel over the top instead).

Purée to emulsify. (Or blend with an immersion blender while in the pan.) Set the mixture in warm water bath until ready to serve.

Used in Pompano en Papillote with Oysters, Rockefeller Spinach, and Tomato (page 104) and Creamy Oyster Stew (page 139).

GINGER-SOY BUTTER SAUCE

MAKES 1 CUP

While I prefer salted butter in virtually all my recipes, given the saltiness of the soy sauce, you may want to use unsalted for this one if you are sensitive to salt.

4 tablespoons soy sauce

1 tablespoon light brown sugar

1 teaspoon minced fresh ginger

3 tablespoons water

1 stick (8 tablespoons) cold butter, sliced in pats

Put soy sauce, brown sugar, and ginger in a small sauté pan and bring it to a boil. Reduce the liquid by half, being careful not to burn it—the sugar will caramelize quickly.

Bring water to a boil in a small saucepan. Add the boiling water to the reduced ginger-soy sauce, and then add the butter pats all at once. Immediately pour the mixture into the coffee mug and blend with an immersion blender until smooth. Or, blend the mixture in a conventional blender, then pour into the coffee mug. Set the mug in a pan of hot water to keep warm.

Used in Seared Yellowfin Tuna with Baby Bok Choy, Shiitakes, and Ginger-Soy Butter Sauce (page 73).

PASSION FRUIT BUTTER SAUCE

MAKES ³/₄ CUP

Passion fruit are small tropical fruits with a delicious tart flavor and—like so many exotic items that have a long way to travel to your market—are harvested underripe so they'll have a longer shelf life. Ideally, a fresh passion fruit should be purple and dark and wrinkled on the outside. The usable part is in the center and you'll probably be surprised at how little flesh is left after you remove the black seeds, but it doesn't take much to flavor a sauce. Passion fruit is available fresh and frozen in pulp or purée form—either will work fine in this recipe—in Asian or Latin markets, gourmet grocery stores, and in some supermarkets.

Cleaned pulp from 2 passion fruit (seeds removed) or 2 teaspoons frozen passion fruit purée, thawed

1 recipe Basic Three-Minute Butter Sauce (page 162)

Stir the passion fruit pulp or thawed purée into the butter sauce. If not using within 20 minutes or so, set the cup in a small pan of water set on the lowest heat to keep warm.

Used in Seared Scallops with Mango-Melon Salsa and Passion Fruit Butter Sauce (page 74).

MUSHROOM BUTTER SAUCE

MAKES 1 CUP

This butter sauce takes a little extra time to make, but it is well-worth the wait.

2 tablespoons dried porcini or morel mushrooms

½ cup boiling water

1 tablespoon salted butter, plus ½ cup (1 stick) salted butter, divided

½ cup sliced mushrooms (portabellas, cremini, shiitake, wild porcini, or chanterelles)

¼ cup soaking liquid from mushrooms or water

Rinse the dried mushrooms under cold water and place in a bowl. Cover with boiling water and let soak 15 to 20 minutes, until reconstituted. Taste the soaking liquid. Dried mushrooms vary quite a bit in pungency, so if it has a pleasant earthy flavor, reserve ¼ cup for the sauce. If it tastes tannic, discard it and use water instead.

Melt the 1 tablespoon of butter over medium-high in a small sauté pan. Add the fresh and reconstituted mushrooms and sauté until slightly browned, 2 or 3 minutes. Keep warm.

Make the Basic Three-Minute Butter Sauce as directed, (see page 162) using the remaining butter and the mushroom soaking liquid in place of the water, if desired. Add the hot sautéed mushrooms and purée.

If not using within 20 minutes or so, set the cup in a small pan of water set on the lowest heat to keep warm.

Used in Wood-Grilled Scallops with Sautéed Mushrooms, Mushroom Risotto, and Mushroom Butter Sauce (page 165).

PEA SHOOT BUTTER SAUCE

MAKES ¾ CUP

Tender-leaved pea shoots are a rare seasonal treat, available only for a brief period in spring. Here's an easy way to take advantage of their fresh-pea flavor.

½ cup pea shoots

1 recipe Basic Three-Minute Butter Sauce (page 162), warm

Blend the pea shoots into the butter sauce with an immersion blender or conventional blender.

If not using within 20 minutes or so, set the cup in a small pan of water set on the lowest heat to keep warm.

Used in Crabmeat, Country Ham, and Shiitake Pot Stickers in Pea Shoot Butter Sauce (page 165).

CHARRED ONION AND CHIPOTLE BUTTER SAUCE

MAKES 1 CUP

The smokey-spicy flavors of this work well with any grilled or short-smoked fish.

1 tablespoon salted butter

2 tablespoons finely diced onion

1 teaspoon finely diced canned chipotle pepper in adobo sauce

1 recipe Basic Three-Minute Butter Sauce (page 162)

Melt butter in a small sauté pan over medium heat. Add the onion; cover and cook on low to medium heat for 5 minutes, stirring occasionally, until soft. Uncover, raise the heat, and cook, stirring often, until the onion is browned. Add the chipotle pepper.

Blend the hot onion-chipotle mixture into the Basic Three-Minute Butter Sauce; keep warm.

Used in Short-Smoked Smoked Salmon Fillets with Charred Onion and Chipotle Butter Sauce (page 90).

TABASCO BUTTER SAUCE

MAKES ¾ CUP

This is a slightly more refined version of the sauce for hot chicken wings, designed for fried seafood instead.

1 tablespoon Tabasco Sauce

1 recipe Basic Three-Minute Butter Sauce (page 162), warm

Place the hot sauce in a very small skillet and bring it to a boil over high heat. Reduce to 1 teaspoon, being careful not to inhale fumes!

Stir the reduced hot pepper sauce into the butter sauce and keep warm.

Used in Fried Oyster Slaw Dog (page 124).

CILANTRO PURÉE

MAKES 1 CUP

Keep a squeeze bottle of this on hand to liven up a plain piece of fish, vegetables, or just about anything else.

1 bunch cilantro, leaves picked, stems discarded

4 large outside leaves from romaine or iceberg lettuce

1 jalapeño pepper, split and seeded

½ cup canola oil

Pinch kosher salt

Place all ingredients in blender and purée until smooth. Pour into a squeeze bottle and refrigerate for up to 1 week.

Used in Whole Grilled Branzino with Baby Squash (page 84) and Flash-Fried Whole Lionfish with Vietnamese Flavors (page 120).

CHILI HOLLANDAISE SAUCE

MAKES 1 CUP

Hollandaise is a butter sauce made richer with the addition of egg yolk. Flavored with chili seasonings, it's a wonderful complement for blackened fish. It's quick to make and quite stable if you clarify the butter (remove the milk solids), control the temperature with a thermometer, and add it very slowly to the egg mixture as you whisk.

CHILI REDUCTION

2 tablespoons salted butter

1 teaspoon minced garlic

1 teaspoon minced shallot

2 teaspoons chili powder

1 teaspoon ground cumin

HOLLANDAISE

1 cup (2 sticks) butter

1 egg yolk

1 teaspoon white vinegar

¼ teaspoon Tabasco Sauce

¼ teaspoon Worcestershire sauce

1 tablespoon water

½ teaspoon kosher salt

CHILI REDUCTION Melt the butter in a small saucepan over medium heat. Add the garlic and shallot; sauté until soft and translucent, taking care not to brown, stirring occasionally. Add the chili powder and cumin and continue cooking for another minute or two. Set aside.

HOLLANDAISE Clarify the butter by putting it in a large, clear glass measuring cup (be careful—it can boil over). Set in the microwave and melt on medium heat, watching carefully, until it separates into three layers: foam at the top, clarified butter in the middle, and water at the bottom. Allow the solids to settle to the bottom of the container. Scoop off the foam.

Meanwhile, place the egg yolk, vinegar, Tabasco, Worcestershire, and water in a metal bowl (set on a wet scrunched up towel to keep steady). Whisk until emulsified.

Check the temperature of the butter with a thermometer and either heat or cool to 150 degrees. Slowly whisk the hot melted butter into the egg mixture in a thin, steady stream, leaving behind the whey at the bottom of the measuring cup. Discard the whey.

Transfer the hollandaise to a small bowl and whisk in the salt and chili reduction. Put in a squeeze bottle for easy handling. If the sauce thickens too much before serving, whisk in a tablespoon of warm water.

Used in Blackened Swordfish with Chili Hollandaise (page 75).

CITRUS CHILE OIL

MAKES 1 CUP

This and the Cilantro Purée (Cilantro Purée, page 166) are primarily plate decorations, adding punches of intense color and flavor to any simple grilled, fried, or sautéed seafood entrée.

1 cup vegetable oil

2 tablespoons whole annatto seeds

1 lemon, zested

1 orange, zested

1 jalapeño pepper, quartered and seeded

Place all ingredients in a saucepan and bring to a simmer; remove from heat, and then allow to sit for 2 hours. Strain the chile oil into a small container, discard the solids, and then set aside and cover until ready to use, or refrigerate for up to 1 month.

Used in Whole Grilled Branzino with Baby Squash (page 84) and Flash-Fried Whole Lionfish with Vietnamese Flavors (page 120).

HORSERADISH CREAM

MAKES ABOUT 1 CUP

Everyone thinks of whipped cream as a sweet addition to desserts, but it is also a good way to add a little fat to savory dishes. Whipping by hand is easy as long as you don't try to do a lot of it. It won't last but a couple of hours, but you can make it that far ahead if need be.

½ cup heavy cream, chilled

¼ teaspoon Tabasco Sauce

¼ teaspoon Worcestershire sauce

2 teaspoons finely grated horseradish root (or white processed horseradish found in the dairy section)

Kosher salt

Pour the cold cream into a chilled bowl and whisk vigorously until it just starts to thicken. A big bowl works better than a small one for this. Add the Tabasco, Worcestershire, and horseradish and continue whisking until it's at the soft peak stage. Season to taste with salt. You can whisk again just before serving to tighten it up if you like, but it should still flow slightly. Cover and refrigerate.

Used in Smoked Rainbow Trout with Horseradish Cream (page 81).

QUICK VEAL JUS

MAKES ¾ CUP

Jus is a slight reduction of veal stock and is the foundation of classical French cooking. Though most often used in meat dishes, it goes well with full-flavored fish. This isn't a classical veal jus and isn't meant to be. I have had good luck with the More Than Gourmet commercial concentrates available in some retail stores and online.

2 tablespoons salted butter, divided

1 tablespoon diced shallot

½ cup sliced mushrooms or stems, any kind

1 sprig (about 4 stems) whole thyme

1 piece of bay leaf the size of a dime

5 parsley stems

4 crushed peppercorns

¼ cup red wine

1 ½ tablespoons (½ of a 1.5-ounce container) More Than Gourmet Classic Reduced Veal Stock (morethangourmet.com)

1 cup water

Melt 1 tablespoon of the butter in a sauté pan on medium heat; add the shallots and mushrooms and sauté for about 5 minutes. Add the thyme, bay leaf, parsley stems, and peppercorns and continue cooking for a minute longer.

Pour in wine and reduce by half. Add the veal concentrate; stir until it dissolves. Add the water and simmer gently until reduced to about ¾ of a cup.

Strain through a fine strainer, forcing all the liquid out of the vegetables. Whisk in the remaining butter. Keep warm until ready to use, or refrigerate up to 2 weeks (freeze for longer storage).

Used in Macadamia and Peppercorn-Crusted Swordfish (page 103).

SHERRY VINAIGRETTE

MAKES 1 1/2 CUPS

This is my go-to for any green salad, and many other cold dishes.

¼ cup sherry vinegar

1 tablespoon Dijon mustard

1 tablespoon sugar

1 ½ teaspoons kosher salt

A few grindings of freshly ground black pepper

1 ½ teaspoons minced fines herbes (page 25) or combination of parsley, chives, and chervil or tarragon

½ cup extra-virgin olive oil

½ cup vegetable oil

Place vinegar, mustard, sugar, salt, pepper, and fines herbes in a blender container. Turn on low speed and slowly add the oils in a thin stream so that the dressing emulsifies. (Or whisk the first 5 ingredients in a mixing bowl, then slowly whisk in the oils.) Reserve at room temperature. Cover and refrigerate for longer storage.

Used in Creole Tomato Salad with Cucumbers, Sweet Onions, and Blue Cheese (page 192), Mango, Papaya, Tomato, and Avocado Salad with Lemon-Herb Aioli (page 195), Tuna-Muffuletta-Niçoise Salad (page 49).

GREEN GODDESS DRESSING

MAKES 1 1/4 CUPS

Warren Leruth was an innovative chef whose famous restaurant, LeRuth's, was highly influential in getting New Orleans food out of the antique doldrums where it had been stuck for generations. He was also a food scientist who worked in product research and development for years, both in packaged products and dishes for chains, including signatures like the red beans for Popeyes. I met him after he had closed his restaurant and we talked food for hours. He was a nice man and got me a job consulting with Outback Steakhouse to help make ends meet while we were building Fins. We pay homage to him with our version of his Green Goddess, which he created for the Seven Seas line. Its creamy blend of anchovy, herbs, and citrus is a perfect complement to seafood.

1 cup mayonnaise

1 lemon, juiced

1 anchovy fillet, rinsed

1 pinch of citric acid, optional

1 tablespoon chopped parsley

1 tablespoon chopped basil

1 tablespoon chopped chervil

1 tablespoon chopped chives

1 tablespoon chopped tarragon

¼ teaspoon kosher salt

¼ teaspoon freshly ground black pepper

2 tablespoons buttermilk

Purée all ingredients with a blender until smooth, creamy, and uniformly green. Cover and chill in the refrigerator for up to a week.

Used in Green Goddess Chopped Salad (page 192).

GRAINS, SIDES, AND SALADS

GW FINS SIGNATURE BISCUITS

SKILLET CORNBREAD

HOT WATER CORNBREAD

GOAT CHEESE GRITS

SALLY LUNN ROLLS

BRABANT POTATOES

MASHED POTATOES WITH
CHICKEN SKIN
CRACKLING "GRAVY"

SHORTCUT SEAFOOD RISOTTO

WILD MUSHROOM RISOTTO

SWEET CORN AND
POSOLE RISOTTO

STICKY RICE

MOM'S COLESLAW

THAI-STYLE MIRLITON SALAD

SUMMER SUCCOTASH

VIETNAMESE
GREEN APPLE SALAD

ITALIAN OLIVE SALAD

SMOKED TRI-COLOR PEPPER
AND GRILLED ONION SALSA

ZYDEQUE POTATO SALAD

CREOLE TOMATO SALAD WITH
CUCUMBERS, SWEET ONIONS,
AND BLUE CHEESE

GREEN GODDESS
CHOPPED SALAD

MANGO, PAPAYA, TOMATO,
AND AVOCADO SALAD WITH
LEMON-HERB AIOLI

In this chapter, I share with you a collection of some of my favorite side dishes for serving with seafood—from childhood, the restaurant, and my travels abroad. Each is designed to go with at least one recipe from the preceding pages. They're also very adaptable. At home, you can plate them the way we do at the restaurant, or pass them around the table family-style in bowls and bread baskets to go with heaping platters of fried or grilled fish, or any other simple entrée.

GW FINS SIGNATURE BISCUITS

MAKES 2 ¹/₂-3 DOZEN BISCUITS

I had my doubts when Gary Wollerman, my business partner whose initials are in our name, suggested offering drop biscuits for our bread service. I told him "nobody wants to eat biscuits in a fine dining restaurant" or some such. Boy, was I wrong. Two decades later, we're still famous for our hot-out-of-the-oven drop biscuits and justifiably so.

They could hardly be simpler: just White Lily self-rising flour, lard, whole milk, and a little sugar. No kneading or rolling— just scoop, drop, bake, and eat fresh from the oven with whipped butter. Continuously delivered, the danger is you'll eat too many and ruin your appetite.

Vegetable oil spray

4 cups self-rising flour (I use White Lily)

¾ cup lard

¼ cup sugar

1 ½ cups whole milk

Soft salted butter for serving

Heat oven to 400 degrees F. Spray a baking sheet with vegetable oil spray. Mix flour and lard together in a large bowl with a pastry blender (or fork) until the fat is worked in and the mixture is a coarse crumb consistency. Add sugar and stir in milk to make a soft dough. Let rest for a few minutes. Drop using a small ice cream scoop onto prepared baking sheet. Bake for 15 to 18 minutes, or until lightly browned. Serve immediately with soft salted butter.

SKILLET CORNBREAD

SERVES 6 AS A SIDE DISH

If I have access to fresh shelled, dried corn, I'll go to the trouble of grinding and sifting it and making cornbread from scratch, but I do keep a bag of either White Lily or Martha White cornbread mix in the freezer. To me, these two classic brands Southerners have long sworn by have the formula down pat. Baking in a cast iron skillet greased with smoking-hot lard or bacon grease is key to its crispy crust. Long ago at my dad's restaurant in Georgia, we used this recipe to make johnnycakes, which are really just cornbread pancakes. Just spoon tablespoons of batter onto a hot greased skillet and cook like pancakes.

All baking powder-leavened breads should be eaten fresh and hot.

¼ cup plus 3 tablespoons lard or
   bacon grease, divided

1 large egg

¾ cup whole milk

¾ cup plus 2 tablespoons buttermilk

2 cups Martha White or White Lily
   cornmeal mix

Set a large cast iron skillet in the oven and heat to 450 degrees.

Melt the lard in a small saucepan on top of the stove or in a bowl in the microwave.

Beat the egg, add the milks, stir in the cornmeal mix, and then add ¼ cup plus 1 tablespoon of the melted lard.

When the oven is hot, remove the skillet, add the remaining 2 tablespoons lard (it will be smoking hot), swirl, and pour in the batter. This is what makes a crispy, delicious crust. The batter will be quite thin. Bake 20 to 25 minutes, until a skewer inserted in the center comes out clean. Don't worry if the top isn't brown. When it's done, just invert it on a cutting board. That's where the brown will be. Cut into wedges and serve while too hot to hold.

HOT WATER CORNBREAD

MAKES 30 SMALL FRITTERS

Hot water cornbread is the mother of hush puppies, and when you look at the ingredients it's a little surprising how light they are. Boiling water and freshly ground meal with a little salt, shallow fried in fat (preferably lard) sounds like it would make ammunition for a slingshot, but if you go to the trouble of sourcing fresh meal—essential for this recipe—you'll be rewarded with a wonderful-tasting part of early American history.

1 cup freshly ground cornmeal (from a
   farmers market or local mill)

2 teaspoons kosher salt

1 cup boiling water

¼ cup lard (or 1 cup if deep-frying)

Put the meal in a mixing bowl with the salt. Stir in the boiling water. Cover the bowl with plastic wrap, and set aside. Heat the lard in a heavy-bottom saucepan or skillet to 350 degrees F. If you don't have a thermometer you can test fry a small ball of the dough. It should sizzle and start to brown within a minute or two.

You can fry the cornbread in several shapes. Some like little patties—sort of a thick pancake shape, but I prefer small balls to drop in the fat off the point of a spoon that resemble baby hush puppies. There is more crunchy surface area that way. In any case, fry until golden brown and crispy. Taste for doneness; if you need to return them for a little more cook time, they are in no way fragile. If you want to try the pancake shape, you'll need to add a bit more boiling water to make the dough thinner.

GOAT CHEESE GRITS

SERVES 4 TO 6 AS A SIDE DISH

Misguided folk sometimes label exotic, coarsely ground meal as grits, and there is nothing wrong with cornmeal mush, either alone or as an ingredient in polenta, but far as I'm concerned it ain't grits. (Remember, I'm from Georgia.) Hominy grits, dried corn treated with an alkaline product to remove the hull, is the only variety I recognize. Having said that, instant or quick-cook grits are also an abomination. Buy the old-fashioned long-cook variety and spend the 20 minutes or so it takes to cook them. Jim Dandy, Aunt Jemima, and Quaker all sell these.

4 cups water

1 teaspoon kosher salt

1 cup old-fashioned grits

3 tablespoons salted butter

6 tablespoons soft goat cheese

Bring the water to a boil in a large saucepan, add the salt, and whisk in the grits. When it returns to a boil, lower the heat and cook about 20 minutes, scraping the bottom and sides of the pan from time to time. Low heat is essential for safety since this mixture is like sticky boiling lava. When all the water is absorbed, remove from the heat and stir in the butter and goat cheese until melted.

SALLY LUNN ROLLS

MAKES 12 ROLLS

Sally Lunn is an old English recipe that's similar to brioche, but somewhat lighter and less rich. This recipe makes a great roll hot out of the oven as well as a soft sandwich bun that keeps wrapped at room temperature for several days, or can be frozen for several months. They're just the right soft texture for a Southern Shrimp Roll (page 55) or Fried Oyster Slaw Dog (page 124).

1 cup whole milk

6 tablespoons salted butter

4 tablespoons honey

2 large eggs

2 teaspoons dry yeast

1 teaspoon kosher salt

3 cups bread flour (King Arthur or Hodgson Mill are superior), divided

Softened butter for greasing the pans

Vegetable oil spray

Heat the milk in a large glass measuring cup for 2 minutes in the microwave. Add butter and honey, stir to dissolve, and cool to 120 degrees (too hot and it will kill the yeast).

Pour into the bowl of a stand mixer fitted with a dough hook if you have one (if not, a paddle blade works fine) and add the eggs, yeast, salt, and 2 cups of the flour. Mix on low until everything is incorporated, and then on high for 4 minutes. Scrape down the sides at least once.

Turn off the mixer and add the rest of the flour. Turn mixer on low to incorporate. Then raise to high and continue to mix for an additional 4 minutes.

Scrape the dough into a buttered mixing bowl, cover with plastic wrap, and allow to rise at room temperature for 1 hour or until doubled.

Ease the doubled dough out onto a buttered surface, a counter, or cutting board and, using a sharp knife, slice it into 2-inch strips. Cut these strips into somewhat equal squares. If you have a scale, they should weigh 2 ounces, but don't worry if they're not exactly equal.

Form into smooth balls between your thumb and first finger by stretching the top and tucking the bottom inside. Again, don't worry if they're not perfect. What you're looking for is a smooth top.

Butter a 12-cup large muffin tin or 12 (4-ounce) soufflé cups. Place the balls, smooth side up in the cups and cover with a piece of plastic wrap coated with vegetable oil spray and proof for 1 hour and 15 minutes at room temperature.

Preheat the oven to 375 degrees F. Bake the rolls on the bottom rack for 20 minutes, or until golden brown.

HOT DOG BUNS Spray a baking sheet with vegetable oil spray. After the first rising, flatten the dough to about an inch thick and cut into 4 or 5-inch-long and 1-inch-wide strips. Using a very sharp knife or single-edge razor blade, cut a ½-inch-deep slice lengthwise on the top and place them a couple of inches apart on the baking sheet. (If they stick together, you can separate them after baking.)

Cover with plastic wrap sprayed with vegetable oil spray and let rise in a warm place until doubled.

Preheat the oven to 350 degrees F. Bake on the bottom rack for about 10 to 12 minutes, or until golden brown.

BRABANT POTATOES

SERVES 4 AS A SIDE DISH

Brabant potatoes are a New Orleans thing. No one seems to know how they got their name. They are twice-cooked potatoes, cubed and blanched in 200-degree F oil and then crisped and browned later in the same oil at 350 degrees F. This is the same method for making French fries, but besides the shape, the other distinction is that Brabants go right from the second fry into a pan with buttery sautéed shallots and garlic. The only thing that could make this better besides plenty of salt is slivered black garlic, which has made its way into well-stocked grocery stores lately and adds a wonderful umami layer to all sorts of things. The cloves are fermented until pitch-black, with a gooey, date-like consistency that can make it tricky to mince. It's easier if you chop them along with the fresh garlic and shallots. If you can't find it, the recipe without it will still be a hit.

2 large Idaho potatoes

4 cups vegetable oil

3 tablespoons salted butter

2 tablespoons minced garlic

2 tablespoons diced shallot

2 teaspoons minced black garlic (optional)

1 teaspoon kosher salt

¼ teaspoon freshly ground black pepper

Peel the potatoes and cut into ½-inch dice. Try to make the cubes about the same size for uniform cooking, but they don't need to be perfect squares. You should have about 4 cups. Place them in a container and cover with cold water.

Heat oil to 275 degrees F in a 2-quart saucepan. Drain the potatoes and add them carefully to the hot oil. The oil will drop in temperature immediately. Use the thermometer and try to keep the temperature in the neighborhood of 200 degrees F. If you're using an electric stove, sometimes the best way to quickly regulate the heat is to move the pan off the burner until it cools a bit. Cook until fork-tender, about 10 minutes, and remove with a slotted spoon or skimmer to a plate. Don't worry about draining them too much at this point because they're going back into the oil shortly. Move the pot of oil back on the burner and raise the temperature to 325 to 350 degrees F.

Heat the butter on medium-low in a small sauté pan, add the garlic and shallot, cover and cook until soft but not browned, 1 or 2 minutes, stirring a few times in between. Add the black garlic, if using, and thoroughly stir it in to incorporate it (it has a tendency to be sticky). Turn off the heat.

When the oil is hot, carefully add the blanched potatoes and cook until golden brown and crispy, for about 10 minutes. Remove with a skimmer or slotted spoon and drain on paper towels. Toss them in the pan with the butter-garlic mixture and add the salt and pepper.

MASHED POTATOES WITH CHICKEN SKIN CRACKLING "GRAVY"

SERVES 4 AS A SIDE DISH

Mashed potatoes is a natural for any fish dish. My method is all done in one pot and no mixer. Heating the cream isn't necessary if you work fast and the potatoes are still hot. Renaissance painters used to leave in imperfections so their works wouldn't be confused with the Divine, so a lump or two just means it's not Hungry Jack. They're great as they are, but even better when drenched in a ladleful of butter sauce flavored with bits of deep-fried chicken skins, basically an old-time cream gravy, but way better. Horseradish-Crusted Catfish Fillets (page 66) and Chicken-Fried Alligator (page 125) are great with this.

2 quarts water

1 tablespoon salt

2 large Idaho potatoes, peeled and cut into somewhat uniform 2-inch pieces

4 tablespoons salted butter

¾ cup half-and-half, heavy cream, or whole milk

Kosher salt and freshly ground black pepper, to taste

½ cup Chicken Skin Cracklings, divided

Basic Three-Minute Butter Sauce (page 162), warm

Bring water to a rolling boil in a large saucepan. Add the salt and potato pieces. Cook until fork-tender, about 8 minutes. Drain all the water out of the pot and let the potatoes steam dry.

Mash them in the pot with a potato masher. They should be dry and somewhat mealy. When the lumps are mashed out, add the butter and mix well. Whip in the cream vigorously with a wooden spoon. Season to taste with salt and pepper. Cover and keep warm.

Stir ¼ cup of cracklings into the Basic Three-Minute Butter Sauce to make the "gravy." Serve the potatoes with a ladle of sauce, garnished with the remaining cracklings.

CHICKEN SKIN CRACKLINGS

MAKES ABOUT 1 CUP CRUSHED CRACKLINGS

Ever wonder what they do with all that skin off those boring skinless chicken breasts? If you can get some from your butcher, they make a crunchy snack like pork rinds that are hard to stop eating, or they can be chopped up and folded into gravy or the creamy butter sauce here, mixed into cornbread batter, or ground into a zero-carb breading. You can also make a smaller batch with the skin off a package or two of chicken breasts or thighs, but if you're going to go to trouble and mess, you might as well make a whole batch. Leftovers can be frozen several months.

2 or 3 cups vegetable oil

1 pound chicken skin, separated into smaller pieces

Kosher salt

Chef Paul Prudhomme's Magic Seasoning Blend Shrimp Magic or Home Creole Seasoning (page 24)

Heat the oil in a tall, heavy-bottom saucepan to 350 degrees F. Standing back (there will be a lot of splattering and popping), add the chicken skin and fry until golden brown and crispy, about 8 to 10 minutes (less time for a smaller portion). To check for doneness, remove a piece and see if it is crispy enough to break.

Remove and drain on paper towels. When it is cooled off, season well with salt and Shrimp Magic.

SHORTCUT SEAFOOD RISOTTO

SERVES 4 AS A SIDE DISH (OR MAIN DISH WITH DOUBLE THE SEAFOOD)

A lot of home cooks are daunted by risotto, which is traditionally made with Arborio rice, a short-grain, starchy rice from Italy that requires a watchful eye and constant stirring for 40 minutes or more to achieve its characteristic creaminess. Here at the restaurant, we start the process several hours, or even days, in advance, reducing the final cooking time to about 10 or 15 minutes so we can keep the orders moving. This two-part method also works well in a home kitchen, allowing plenty of time in between to complete the rest of the meal.

Here, I cook the rice in Fish Stock and fold shellfish in at the last minute to pair with a simple fillet, but it's also great on its own as a main dish. Use this as a template to vary the stock and vegetable and protein additions for other menus.

MAKE-AHEAD RISOTTO BASE

2 cups Fish Stock (page 128) or Quick Multipurpose Seafood Stock (page 129)

1 tablespoon salted butter

2 teaspoons chopped shallot

2 teaspoons chopped garlic

1 cup Arborio rice

½ teaspoon kosher salt

Freshly ground black pepper to taste

¼ cup white wine

1 tablespoon chopped fines herbes (page 25) or parsley

SEAFOOD RISOTTO

2 cups Fish Stock (page 128) or Quick Multipurpose Seafood Stock (page 129)

1 tablespoon salted butter

1 tablespoon minced shallot

1 teaspoon minced garlic

Kosher salt and freshly ground black pepper to taste

2 teaspoons shellfish glacé (morethangourmet.com), optional

½ pound cooked seafood: lobster tail meat, peeled crawfish tails, or peeled and deveined large shrimp (cooked or uncooked)

¼ cup grated Parmesan cheese (optional)

2 tablespoons mascarpone cheese or softened butter

Chopped parsley or fines herbes (page 25) for garnish

MAKE-AHEAD RISOTTO BASE Bring stock to a simmer in a small saucepan and keep warm. Melt butter in a large saucepan over medium heat. Add shallot and garlic and sauté for 1 to 2 minutes until tender, and then stir in the rice to coat with the fat. Season with salt and a pinch of black pepper. Add the wine, stirring constantly until all the liquid is absorbed. When the pan is dry, add the hot stock, ½ cup at a time, stirring continuously until the pot is again dry before adding additional stock. When the stock is absorbed, add the herbs. Remove from the heat, spread out on a baking sheet, and refrigerate to cool about 30 minutes or so, uncovered. When completely cool, cover with plastic for up to 2 days.

SEAFOOD RISOTTO Remove the risotto base from the refrigerator. Bring the stock to a simmer in a small saucepan and keep warm. Melt butter in a large sauté pan over medium heat. Add shallot and garlic and sauté for 1 to 2 minutes until tender, and then stir in the cooled risotto base. Lightly season with salt and pepper, and begin adding the additional stock ½ cup at a time, (along with the shellfish glacé, if using), stirring and allowing the pan to dry between additions. Taste for doneness. The grains should be creamy—not mushy—and uniformly cooked if you've stirred properly.

If you're not quite ready to serve, remove it from the heat and add a bit more stock or water to reheat if needed. It is essential that the risotto is completely done before adding the seafood, cheeses, and parsley.

WILD MUSHROOM RISOTTO

SERVES 4 AS A SIDE DISH

Follow the recipe for the Make-Ahead Risotto Base (page 178) in the Shortcut Seafood Risotto, using Mushroom Stock instead of the Fish Stock. Refrigerate as directed. Meanwhile, prepare the Sautéed Wild Mushrooms and set aside. Proceed with the risotto finishing step, omitting the seafood and topping each serving with a scoop of Sautéed Wild Mushrooms, along with more fresh herbs if desired.

MUSHROOM STOCK

4 CUPS

I always save the stems from fresh mushrooms (they can be frozen) to have on hand to make an earthy-flavored home-made stock that's great for braises and soups, and also for one of my favorite risottos. Double or triple the recipe and freeze any extra.

1 tablespoon olive or canola oil

1 tablespoon salted butter

6 cups mixed mushroom stems (or white mushrooms)

2 tablespoons dried porcini or morel mushrooms

3 tablespoons finely diced shallots

¼ cup finely diced carrot

¼ cup finely diced celery

¼ cup finely diced onion

1 teaspoon chopped fresh thyme

1 small bay leaf

¼ teaspoon crushed black peppercorns

½ cup red wine

6 cups water

2 teaspoons salt

Prepare the stock by heating the oil in a heavy-bottom saucepan on high heat, and then adding the butter. When the butter foams, add the mushrooms and sauté until lightly browned.

Add the shallots, carrot, celery, onion, thyme, bay leaf, and crushed peppercorns and continue cooking on high, stirring until they are lightly browned.

Add the wine and continue to cook until almost completely evaporated.

Add the water, bring to a boil, reduce to a simmer, and cook until the volume is reduced to 4 cups, about 30 minutes. Add the salt, and then press through a strainer. Discard the solids. Cool and refrigerate the stock until ready to use or up to 4 days, or freeze for up to 6 months.

SAUTÉED WILD MUSHROOMS

ABOUT 1 CUP

Besides topping off a vegetarian risotto, this mélange of quickly sautéed fresh and dried mushrooms— the more varieties the better—makes a terrific side dish on its own for any simple protein.

2 tablespoons dried porcini or morel mushrooms (¼ cup reconstituted)

1 tablespoon olive oil

2 tablespoons salted butter, divided

1 tablespoon finely diced shallot

1 cup stemmed, thick-sliced white mushrooms

¼ cup dry white wine

½ cup quartered, stemmed fresh shiitake mushrooms

½ cup sliced fresh oyster mushrooms

½ cup fresh white or brown beech mushrooms (optional)

2 tablespoons minced fines herbes (see page 25) or parsley

Kosher salt and freshly ground pepper to taste

Rinse the dried mushrooms under cold water, removing any debris, place in a small bowl, cover with ¼ cup boiling water and let them soak for 5 minutes or so. If you're using porcinis, pinch them with your fingers to gauge tenderness, discard any stems that are too woody. Split morels lengthwise and check the inside for grit, and rinse if needed. Taste the liquid—if it's pleasant, save it; strain out any grit and reserve. Thinly slice the mushrooms and reserve.

Place a medium, heavy-bottom sauté pan on medium heat. Add the olive oil, wait a few seconds then add 1 tablespoon of the butter. When the butter foams, add the shallot and sauté, stirring, for about a minute, until tender.

Add the white mushrooms and the reconstituted dried ones and cook on high for a couple of minutes.

Pour in the white wine and add the additional shiitake, oyster, and beech mushrooms. Continue cooking on high, tossing for another 2 minutes. Stir in the remaining butter and the fines herbes, and season to taste with salt and pepper. Reserve at room temperature.

SWEET CORN AND POSOLE RISOTTO

SERVES 4

I got to spend a week in Oaxaca a couple of years ago at the same time as the Guelaguetza Festival celebrating the corn goddess. Corn was domesticated in that region 11,000 years ago and 8,000 years later the process of nixtamilization (cooking the corn in an alkali solution of limestone or water leached through wood ashes) was developed. This is the flavor in everything from tamales and tortillas to tacos and hominy grits. Huitlacoche is a black fungus that grows on the corn ears and it sort of looks like zombie corn. It's a little exotic but worth sourcing for an earthy, almost truffle-like flavor. I culturally appropriated (which I do wherever I travel) a couple of these ingredients and added fresh sweet corn for this recipe.

POSOLE AND CORN STOCK BASE

1 cup each yellow and white dry, cracked hominy corn (Goya makes a brand available in Hispanic markets and online)

1 tablespoon salt

6 ears sweet corn, kernels cut and scraped off the cobs (reserve cobs)

3 tablespoons salted butter

2 tablespoons diced shallot

4 cloves garlic, minced

1 jalapeño chile, diced

1 poblano chile, diced

1 red bell pepper, diced

2 bay leaves

10 stems fresh thyme, tied in a sachet

1 tablespoon Chef Paul Prudhomme's Magic Seasoning Blend Shrimp Magic or Home Creole Seasoning (page 24)

POSOLE AND CORN STOCK BASE Place the cracked hominy in a heavy saucepan, rinse and drain. Add 8 cups of water and salt and cook until tender on medium-low heat, stirring occasionally, approximately 2 hours. If the mixture becomes too dry, add another cup of water. The finished posole should be cooked throughout but with a little bite.

Meanwhile, make the corn stock. Place 1 ½ quarts of water in a large saucepan and add the corn cobs, cut in 2-inch pieces. Cook on medium heat until reduced to 4 cups, about 30 minutes. Set aside.

Place the butter in a large saucepan and sauté the shallot, garlic, and jalapeño, covered, on low heat for 5 minutes. Add the poblano, red pepper, bay leaves, thyme sachet, and Shrimp Magic. Raise the heat a bit and cook for an additional 5 minutes, stirring often.

Add the sweet corn and continue cooking. Add the cooked posole and lower the heat. As the mixture simmers and dries out a little, add 2 cups of the corn stock, a half a cup at a time. Cook at a simmer, stirring often for about 30 minutes. Spread out on a pan to cool and reserve. If you're serving it in an hour or two you can skip this step.

RISOTTO

1 tablespoon salted butter

1 tablespoon minced shallot

1 tablespoon minced garlic

1 cup sliced porcini, chanterelle, or shiitake mushrooms

2 cups Posole Base

1/2 cup fresh, frozen, or bottled huitlacoche (Goya makes a brand available in Hispanic markets and online)

1 ½ cups reserved Corn Stock

½ cup grated queso fresco

Kosher salt and freshly ground black pepper to taste

Mushroom Butter Sauce (page 165), optional

RISOTTO Melt the butter in a large sauté pan, add the shallot and garlic, and sauté for 1 minute. Add the sliced mushrooms and continue cooking for a few more minutes, stirring often.

Stir in the Posole Base and the huitlacoche with any liquid. Continue cooking on medium heat while adding the Corn Stock slowly, stirring often. When the liquid is absorbed, remove from the heat and fold in the cheese. Adjust seasoning with salt and pepper. Serve with Mushroom Butter Sauce.

Note: This risotto is served with a roasted grouper collar in the photo. To prepare the fish, season a collar with salt, pepper, and Creole seasoning. Place it in a roasting pan in the oven and cook at 400 degrees F for 20 minutes.

STICKY RICE

SERVES 4 AS A SIDE DISH

I make sticky rice almost as regularly as long-grain to pair with Asian-inspired fish entrées, such as Seared Yellowfin Tuna with Baby Bok Choy (page 73). Sushi chefs would be lost without this sticky, tangy-sweet rice to wrap in seaweed with raw fish and seafood for nori rolls.

2 cups short-grain or medium-grain sushi rice

2 ¼ cups water (2 ⅔ cups for medium-grain rice)

½ cup rice vinegar

¼ cup sugar

2 tablespoons kosher salt

1 (1-inch) square of kombu (dried kelp), optional

Place the rice in a large bowl and rinse with warm water until the water turns clear. Let it soak for a few minutes and drain in a colander or sieve.

Measure water into a medium, heavy pot with a tight-fitting lid. (You can make one from two pieces of foil.) Add the rice, cover, and bring to a boil. Reduce to a simmer and cook about 15 minutes until all the water is absorbed. To check absorption without removing the lid, shake the pot and listen for any sloshing liquid. When all the water seems to be absorbed, turn off the heat and let it sit, covered, for 10 minutes to steam.

Meanwhile, make a syrup by placing the rice vinegar, sugar, salt, and kombu (if using) in a small saucepan and bring to a boil and stir until sugar is dissolved.

Uncover the rice. It should be dry and have steam holes on the surface. Taste a little for doneness, fluff it with a fork and stir in enough syrup to suit your taste (about 4 or 5 tablespoons should do it). Put the lid back on until ready to serve.

MOM'S COLESLAW

SERVES 8 AS A SIDE DISH

This is the slaw recipe I always seem to fall back on. Shaving the cabbage head with a sharp knife provides the best texture and the acid balance from the cider vinegar and sugar with the bite of the celery seeds is a perfect flavor for fried seafood and hush puppies. This is the recipe I use for my Fried Oyster Slaw Dogs (page 124). Mom is ninety-five at this writing and still makes it this way, just slower. If you want a super crunchy slaw, mix the dressing with the cabbage just before eating and conversely, if you like it a bit creamier, mix ahead and refrigerate.

1 small head green cabbage

½ cup mayonnaise

1 tablespoon apple cider vinegar

1 tablespoon sugar

½ teaspoon kosher salt

¼ teaspoon celery seeds

¼ teaspoon Tabasco Sauce

Shave the cabbage as finely as you can with a very sharp knife. You should have about 6 cups.

For the dressing, whisk together the remaining ingredients in a large bowl. Add the cabbage and toss to combine.

THAI-STYLE MIRLITON SALAD

SERVES 4 AS A SIDE DISH

I spent a month in Thailand one summer working in a ball and noodle shop in Bangkok where I ate at literally hundreds of street stands. Practically every vendor had a made-to-order green papaya salad. The chiles, garlic, and dried shrimp were crushed in a big stone mortar and the rest of the ingredients mixed in just before serving. I loved the fresh pungent flavors and was quickly schooled about how to duplicate them at home.

Mirlitons, which you probably know as chayote squash, grow like crazy in Louisiana—one vine can produce hundreds—and are used in a variety of cooked preparations. They are tender and much more delicate than green papayas and really work well with a spicy dressing.

This dressing is a little scary when you taste it alone. It's hot and has a funk from the dried shrimp and fish sauce, but mixed with the vegetables it is wonderfully refreshing and great to eat with whole grilled fish, or any fatty fish.

For this recipe, I highly recommend investing in a papaya shredder available in Asian markets (or online—Kiwi is one brand) that looks like a peeler with serrations in the blade which make fine julienne cutting a breeze. It only costs a couple of dollars and is invaluable for this type of preparation.

Special equipment: papaya shredder (see headnote), mandoline, or very sharp knife

2 mirlitons (chayote squash) or 1 green papaya (1 cup shredded)

1 small carrot

1 tablespoon finely sliced red onion

1 clove garlic, minced

1 Thai chile, stemmed and chopped

1 teaspoon dried shrimp (available in Asian markets and online)

2 limes, juiced

1 tablespoon palm or coconut sugar (light brown sugar works fine as well)

1 tablespoon fish sauce

Peel and shred the mirlitons and carrot into a fine julienne with an Asian shredder, mandoline, or very sharp knife. Mix in the red onion and refrigerate until ready to serve.

Blend together the garlic, chile, dried shrimp, lime juice, sugar, and fish sauce. (This isn't much volume, so if you're using an immersion blender you'll need a small container so the blades are covered.) When the mixture is well-blended, cover and refrigerate.

Mix the vegetables with the dressing just before plating—the acid in the dressing quickly breaks down the delicate crunch of the mirliton.

SUMMER SUCCOTASH

SERVES 4 AS A SIDE DISH

I preach a lot about shopping for seafood with an open mind, focusing on what's fresh and available rather than a hard and fast list of ingredients. The same applies when browsing the produce section or farmers market. This dish is a prime example. Generally, I only make it when there are local tomatoes and okra. Summer squash and fresh shell beans and corn are something else I look for. Fava beans? Baby carrots? Wild mushrooms? Exotic peppers? If the vegetables are fresh, they will combine wonderfully in this dish. Take the cook time of each ingredient into account as some, like tomatoes, may be added at two different times so you can get different flavors and textures.

This is a great side dish for any simple sautéed or grilled fish. Here it is paired with a sautéed red snapper (see page 106).

½ cup fresh lima beans (or frozen, thawed)

6 tablespoons unsalted butter, divided

1 tablespoon diced shallot

2 teaspoons minced garlic

½ cup chopped sweet onion

½ split Thai chile (optional)

1 cup sliced fresh okra

1 cup corn kernels, freshly cut off the cob

1 cup ½-inch-diced summer squash

1 cup peeled, seeded, and diced ripe tomato

1 teaspoon kosher salt

¼ teaspoon freshly ground black pepper

1 teaspoon minced fresh parsley

1 teaspoon minced fresh basil

½ teaspoon minced fresh dill

Blanch the lima beans for 5 minutes in a small pot of boiling salted water. Drain in a colander and set aside.

Melt 4 tablespoons butter in a large skillet over medium-low heat. Allow the other 2 tablespoons butter to soften at room temperature. Add the shallot and garlic to the hot butter, cover and cook, 2 to 3 minutes, stirring occasionally, until tender but not browned. Add the blanched lima beans, onion, Thai chile (if using), and okra. Sauté on medium heat, stirring often, for 5 minutes. Add the corn and squash and continue cooking 3 or 4 minutes, or until vegetables are crisp-tender. Add the tomatoes and season with salt and pepper. Cook a minute or two more, turn off the heat, stir in the softened butter and the herbs, and serve hot.

VIETNAMESE GREEN APPLE SALAD

SERVES 4 AS A SIDE DISH

Like the mirliton salad, this dish is spicy with big flavor. It uses shrimp paste, an intensely pungent ingredient essential in the famous Vietnamese dish Bún Bò Huế and, like fish sauce, is an essential background flavor that rounds out the dish. The crab is blended and strained, and this can be refrozen for later use. When you try these combinations, I think you'll agree that they are worth the effort to source them. Otherwise, this presentation is very similar to Thai-Style Mirliton Salad and you could actually use that if you want. Hard green mangoes can be substituted for the apples for a more Southeast Asian flavor, if they're available.

Special equipment: papaya shredder (see headnote in Thai-Style Mirliton Salad, page 185), mandoline, or very sharp knife

DRESSING

2 limes, juiced

1 Thai chile, stemmed and chopped

2 tablespoons light brown sugar

1 tablespoon fish sauce

1 clove garlic

1 tablespoon Ba Khía frozen crab, blended and strained (available in Asian markets or online)

⅛ teaspoon Mắm Tôm Bắc shrimp paste (available in Asian markets or online)

SALAD

2 Granny Smith apples or hard green mangoes

2 tablespoons shredded carrot

1 tablespoon finely julienned red bell pepper

1 teaspoon each torn Thai basil leaves, mint leaves, cilantro leaves, and dill fronds

DRESSING Blend together the lime juice, Thai chile, light brown sugar, fish sauce, garlic, blended and strained crab, and shrimp paste in a blender.

The volume of the ingredients isn't much, so if using an immersion blender you'll need a small container so the blades are immersed.

SALAD Just before serving (so there's minimal browning) cut the apples, peel and all, into a fine julienne, with an Asian shredder, mandoline, or very sharp knife.

Mix the dressing with the apples, carrot, and bell pepper and top with the herb mixture.

ITALIAN OLIVE SALAD

MAKES 1 QUART

This is the type of olive salad that made the New Orleans muffuletta famous. Similar versions can be purchased in bottles at most supermarkets around here. But you can make your own very easily, which is what I like to do. In the condiments section of your supermarket get black and green olives and a jar of the Italian giardiniera relish, which consists of an array of pickled vegetables including cauliflower, carrots, celery, bell pepper, and gherkins.

1 cup pitted Kalamata olives

1 cup pitted green olives (pimento stuffed ones are ok)

1 red bell pepper, roasted, peeled, seeded, and diced (see page 191)

1 cup prepared Italian giardiniera relish, cut into bite-size pieces

6 cloves garlic, minced

2 stalks celery, finely diced

2 teaspoons finely diced Fresno or jalapeño chile (seeds and all)

2 tablespoons chopped fresh parsley

3 tablespoons cane vinegar (see page 158) or apple cider vinegar

1 cup extra-virgin olive oil

Place the olives in a large bowl and crush them with a heavy wooden spoon. Add the roasted pepper, giardiniera, garlic, celery, chile, parsley, and vinegar.

Place in a quart container, cover with olive oil, and refrigerate. For the best flavor, allow the flavors to marry for 3 or 4 days before using, but you can use it right away if you need to. The salad can be stored, covered, in the refrigerator for up to 2 weeks.

SMOKED TRI-COLOR PEPPER AND GRILLED ONION SALSA

MAKES 2 CUPS

Here is a great way to get double duty out of your grill when you're grilling fish or, for that matter, a steak or just about anything else. Roast a variety of peppers—sweet, mild, various colors—on the open flame while you're grilling the onion slices, or the conventional way (see page 191). Then cold smoke them in the same manner as for Sizzling Oysters (page 78) and Short-Smoked Salmon (page 90). Dice the pieces large or small, depending on whether you want to serve this as a condiment or a side dish. Toss in a little vinegar and Latin herbs and spices. Serve it right away, or make it several days ahead and refrigerate. Throw as many peppers as you like on the grill and serve a crowd. It's guaranteed to be a hit.

Toasting and grinding the spices adds an extra step but it really does add a depth of flavor you won't get from the powdered stuff.

Special equipment: charcoal or propane grill, charcoal, a handful of hardwood wood chips

1 red bell pepper

1 yellow bell pepper

1 poblano pepper

1 jalapeño pepper (optional)

1 large Vidalia or other sweet onion, cut into 4 or 5 thick slices

Vegetable oil spray

1 teaspoon cumin seeds

½ teaspoon coriander seeds

2 tablespoons cider vinegar or white vinegar

1 teaspoon kosher salt

¼ teaspoon freshly ground black pepper

3 tablespoons chopped cilantro leaves and stems

Light a charcoal or propane grill as directed (see GRILLING TIPS, page 80), using 20 briquettes.

Roast the peppers until all sides are black on the open flame, and peel and clean according to the instructions on page 191. Or blacken on a gas burner or under the broiler. (The peppers can be roasted a day or two ahead and refrigerated.)

Meanwhile, spray both sides of the onion with vegetable oil spray and grill on both sides until nicely browned, about 5 minutes. Set aside to cool.

After the flames have died down to a white ash, move the coals to one side of the grill.

Set a small sauté pan over medium heat and add the cumin and coriander seeds. Move the pan constantly in a back and forth motion, until you can smell the toasted aroma and they are slightly darkened. Crush the toasted seeds with a flat-bottom saucepan, rocking it back and forth, or chop them finely with a French knife. Set aside.

Put a handful of wood chips directly on the coals and close the top, leaving a small crack in the vent so the fire isn't totally extinguished from lack of oxygen. The grill will immediately start filling with smoke and you want a large amount built up.

When the grill has built up a big head of smoke, place the cleaned peppers and grilled onion slices as far away from the heat as you can, cover, and smoke for 4 minutes.

Dice the peppers and onion in roughly the same size pieces and put in a mixing bowl. (You can use the same one you covered the roasted peppers in to minimize cleanup.)

Add the vinegar, toasted and crushed cumin and coriander seeds, salt, and pepper and mix together. Taste and adjust seasoning, if needed. Mix in the cilantro and refrigerate. This will keep in a covered container in the refrigerator for up to 4 days.

ZYDEQUE POTATO SALAD

SERVES 6 TO 8 AS A SIDE DISH

This recipe is reminiscent of my childhood in my dad's restaurant, where this dish was prominently featured on the buffet table. I've tinkered with it over the years to come up with one that tastes more of New Orleans. At the barbecue restaurant I had here, Zydeque, our gumbo was a dark roux with plenty of brisket, chicken, and pork butts, and a scoop of this potato salad really set it off. It would be great in Seafood Gumbo (page 136), or on the side at a catfish fry. Be sure to fold in the potatoes while they are still warm; they'll soak up a lot more flavor that way.

2 quarts water

1 tablespoon salt

2 pounds Idaho potatoes, peeled and cut into bite-size cubes

¼ cup diced celery

¼ cup diced onion

1 tablespoon diced pimentos

3 hard-boiled eggs, peeled and diced (see page 37)

¼ cup sweet pepper relish

2 tablespoons diced green olives

½ cup mayonnaise

1 teaspoon kosher salt

½ teaspoon Chipotle Tabasco Sauce

1 tablespoon Zatarain's Creole mustard (or Dijon)

1 tablespoon yellow mustard

Bring water to a rolling boil in a large saucepan. Add the salt and potato pieces. Cook until fork-tender, about 8 minutes. Spread out on a sheet pan to cool slightly.

Meanwhile, mix the celery, onion, pimentos, eggs, relish, olives, mayonnaise, salt, Tabasco, and mustards in a large mixing bowl. Fold in the warm potatoes. Cover and chill in the refrigerator until ready to serve.

HOW TO ROAST PEPPERS

Place the peppers over the open flame of a grill or a gas stove. Or set them on a rimmed pan and place a few inches away from the broiler unit of your oven.

Roast the peppers on all sides until blackened all over. Set them on a work surface and cover them with an inverted mixing bowl to steam, or wrap in a paper bag. When the peppers have cooled enough to handle, rub the skin off with your fingers. Rinse the peppers under running water until all the black is gone.

Cut off the top and bottom of the peppers and slit them all the way down to open them up. Remove the ribs and seeds and any remaining skin. If you blacken a jalapeño, wear rubber gloves to peel. Never touch your eyes, nose, or mouth after handling hot peppers!

CREOLE TOMATO SALAD WITH CUCUMBERS, SWEET ONIONS, AND BLUE CHEESE

SERVES 4 AS A SIDE DISH

This combination of ingredients is right out of my Southern childhood. Sliced cucumbers and onions in vinegar is still a summertime table condiment when vine-ripe tomatoes are in season. It goes without saying that locally grown, ripe, never refrigerated tomatoes are essential to this recipe. Being from Georgia, I prefer Vidalia onions to Texas sweets, and they are available when good tomatoes are—which in Louisiana means for one short season in late spring before the heat sets in.

1 large sweet onion

1 cup seasoned rice vinegar

4 large, ripe tomatoes

2 cucumbers

¼ cup Sherry Vinaigrette (page 169)

4 ounces ripe blue cheese at room temperature, preferably Roquefort

Peel and slice the onion in half through the stem. Place the flat side down and cut into ½-inch slices. Soak in the seasoned vinegar for 20 minutes.

Peel the tomatoes by first coring them and slicing an X on the bottom. Give them a 10-second dip in boiling water, and then a 30-second bath in ice water. The skin will easily slip off.

The tomatoes can just be cut into thick slices, but for a nicer presentation, place them stem side down and cut them following the shape of the tomato into large slices. Then scoop out any visible seeds with your thumb. These tomato "fillets" can then be cut the same size as the rest of the ingredients.

Peel the cucumbers, cut in half lengthwise, and then scrape out the seeds with a spoon to make "canoes." Slice on the bias 2 inches thick. Put them in a bowl and pour the vinegar off the onions on to the sliced cucumbers. Let sit for 10 minutes. Remove and drain.

Toss the vegetables in a large serving bowl with the vinaigrette and dot with small pieces of the cheese. Serve family style.

GREEN GODDESS CHOPPED SALAD

SERVES . . . . 1 OR 100

For a salad of this type, you need crunch, protein, fat, some durable lettuce, and a creamy dressing. Homemade Green Goddess Dressing, with its herbal and anchovy undertones, is my dressing of choice if seafood is in the mix.

Lettuce, chopped

Roasted red pepper

Vidalia onion slices

Olives

Garbanzo beans

Crumbled feta or blue cheese

Crispy bacon, crumbled

Avocado slices

Chopped hard-boiled eggs

Ripe tomato chunks

Kimchee or other strong pickle

Boiled shrimp, lobster or crabmeat, poached salmon or tuna

Green Goddess Dressing (page 169)

Place all chosen ingredients in a mixing bowl and toss with plenty of dressing.

MANGO, PAPAYA, TOMATO, AND AVOCADO SALAD WITH LEMON-HERB AIOLI

SERVES 4 AS A SIDE DISH

Tropical fruits make an impressive composed salad that can easily become a main dish when cooked lobster (as photographed), lump crabmeat, or grilled shrimp are added to the plate. Proper slicing is key for maximum visual effect. Premium ingredients at their peak of freshness are also critical, so only attempt this in summer. Any locally grown, never-refrigerated ripe tomato works. Papayas, mangoes, and avocados are picked and shipped green, and usually take a few days to ripen at room temperature. Any mild salad green works for this recipe, but if you can find mâche or a blend, it pairs wonderfully with the other flavors. Chervil is another ingredient that's often hard to source, so tarragon or dill can be substituted.

1 ripe mango

1 ripe papaya (large ones are best)

1 ripe avocado

2 large ripe tomatoes or 1 cup pear tomatoes

1 (6-ounce) package salad greens, washed and dried

Sherry Vinaigrette (page 169)

LEMON-HERB AIOLI

¼ cup mayonnaise

1 tablespoon freshly squeezed lemon juice

1 teaspoon chopped fresh chervil (or ¼ teaspoon chopped fresh tarragon or dill)

¼ teaspoon kosher salt

To peel and slice the mango, cut off the top and bottom, stand it up on the fat end, and slice the peel off in strips to a depth of at least ¼ inch. When all the peel is removed, slice lengthwise and scoop out the pit. If unsure, watch a YouTube video.

To peel and slice the papaya, cut in half and then cut the two halves down the middle in the same direction and clean any remaining seeds or fibers in the cavity. Carefully slice away the peel and then slice each quarter on the bias about ¼ inch thick. Keeping the slices together and sliding the flat of your knife underneath, move to a plate.

To prepare the avocado, cut the avocado in half, remove the pit, and cut into quarters. Carefully remove the peel and place cut side down on another plate for slicing just before assembly.

Peel (if desired) and slice the tomatoes. If using large tomatoes, core the tomatoes and slice a bit off the top and bottom. Cut into ½-inch slices with a sharp knife. If you're using grape or pear cherry tomatoes, slice them in half through the stem end. Set the tomatoes aside on another plate.

LEMON-HERB AIOLI Mix together the mayonnaise, lemon juice, chervil, and salt.

Slice the avocado in ½-inch slices.

To assemble, place a handful of greens at the top of each plate and layer alternating slices of mango, papaya, avocado, and tomato against it. Scatter the cut pear tomatoes if using. Leave the bottom of the plate somewhat empty if you're going to plate skewers of grilled shrimp or lobster tails. Or top the salad with poached lobster meat or crabmeat. Just before serving, dress the greens with the Sherry Vinaigrette and spoon the aioli over the cut fruit.

DRINKS, DESSERTS, AND LAGNIAPPE

KAFFIR LIME-LEMONGRASS SODA

FINGRONI

LUNDI GRAS PUNCH

STARFISH COOLER

REDEMPTION

MINI APPLE PIES WITH CHEESE STRAW CRUST
Short Dough
Cheese Straw Dough

GW FINS BREAD PUDDING

PONCHATOULA STRAWBERRY SHORTCAKES

MAPLE SYRUP AND BOURBON PRALINES

FLYNN FAMILY TOM THUMB BARS

Here in Louisiana, it's customary to send our guests home with a "little extra" something we call "lagniappe" (lan-yap). Think of the recipes that follow as my lagniappe to you: a bit of extra indulgence to complete any meal inspired by these previous chapters.

New Orleans is not about austerity or counting calories. Walk the streets, have an afternoon drink, and eat with gusto. Dance to our music even if you don't do that at home. Have a drink that comes with a story, with or without the booze. And always order your own dessert (none of this sharing business!), and get a couple of pralines for later.

KAFFIR LIME-LEMONGRASS SODA

MAKES ABOUT 2 ½ CUPS SYRUP (ENOUGH FOR 10 TO 12 DRINKS)

I got drunk one time for about 11 years. I'm afraid I belong to the ten percent or so of the population that beverage alcohol affects differently, and I don't drink it anymore. That being said, this is my go-to summer drink. The lime leaf and lemongrass simple syrup provides a great background flavor for the fresh lime juice. Ginger beer (with muddled mint) can be substituted for the soda water if you like. The syrup will keep indefinitely in the refrigerator. Of course, you could add your favorite spirit in place of some or all of the soda water if you're so inclined.

SYRUP

1 ½ cups water

1 stalk lemongrass, crushed and chopped

4 kaffir lime leaves, torn

2 cups sugar

SERVING

2 limes or lemons, juiced

Crushed ice

Soda water

Fresh mint

To make the syrup, place the water, lemongrass, and lime leaves in a medium saucepan over high heat and let boil for about 3 or 4 minutes. Whisk in the sugar and continue boiling until it's all dissolved. Set aside to steep for an hour. Strain the syrup through a sieve and refrigerate.

To serve, squeeze the citrus juice into a tall glass and add 4 tablespoons of the syrup. Fill the glass halfway with crushed ice and add the soda water. Garnish with mint.

FINGRONI

MAKES 1 DRINK

This is a play on the classic Italian gin and Campari cocktail, the Negroni. We swap out the traditional vermouth for blood orange liqueur and localize it with a splash of absinthe. Absinthe, also known as the "Green Fairy," is an anise-flavored, emerald-colored spirit that was popularized by artists and writers in Paris and was quickly embraced by the bohemian crowd in New Orleans as well. In 1912 it was banned for supposedly causing hallucinations that could lead to criminal behavior. Ted Breaux, a New Orleans chemist, fought hard to get absinthe back into the States and remains one of the country's most ardent authorities in the subject.

2 ounces Hendrick's Gin

½ ounce Campari

½ ounce Solerno Blood Orange Liqueur

Splash of Lucid absinthe

Ice

Orange wedge for garnish

Pour gin, Campari, liqueur, and absinthe in an old-fashioned glass filled with ice. Stir gently and garnish glass with an orange wedge. Or combine spirits with ice in a cocktail shaker, shake, and strain into a martini glass. Garnish with an orange wedge.

LUNDI GRAS PUNCH

MAKES 1 DRINK

Lundi Gras is the Monday before Mardi Gras, and the whole city, particularly our neighborhood in the French Quarter, is building to a crescendo for the final day's carnival season blowout. For the last decade, GW Fins has hosted a gumbo and jambalaya lunch buffet for the Krewe of Elvi, usually at least fifty people. Unfortunately they don't wear their Elvis costumes for this event, so it just looks like a normal gathering of ordinary, middle-age white folks. Libations flow and we make a special punch for the occasion which has been known to include all the weird free booze that distributors push during the year. Think "hunch punch" but with many, many more types of alcohol. Our bartenders do such a good job with these liquors that we get asked for the recipe every year!

Crushed ice

1 ounce white rum

1 ounce Everclear grain alcohol

½ ounce coconut rum

½ ounce banana liqueur

3 ounces pineapple juice

3 ounces cranberry Juice

Splash grenadine

Fill a hurricane glass or other large glass with crushed ice, add all ingredients, stir, and serve with a straw.

STARFISH COOLER

MAKES 1 DRINK

This minty, high-spirited riff on Southern sweet tea took first place at the 2007 Tales of the Cocktail, an annual festival and gathering of spirits industry professionals in New Orleans.

Orange slice

Mint leaf

Ice

½ ounce simple syrup

1 ounce Moët and Chandon White Star

1 ounce limoncello

1 ounce PAMA Pomegranate Liqueur

1 ounce unsweetened iced tea

Muddle orange slice and mint leaf in a high ball Collins glass. Fill with ice; add remaining ingredients, and stir.

REDEMPTION

MAKES 1 DRINK

Our bartenders mix a lot of Sazeracs, that New Orleans classic made by coating the inside of a chilled old-fashioned glass with absinthe and filling with rye whiskey spiked with a few drops of Peychaud's bitters. For rye whiskey-drinkers thirsty for something more unique, give this one a try.

2 or 3 blackberries

Ice

2 ounces Redemption Rye Whiskey or
  your favorite rye whiskey

3 splashes orange bitters

¾ ounce agave nectar

Rosemary sprig for garnish

Muddle the blackberries in an old-fashioned glass. Fill with ice. Add whiskey, bitters, and agave and stir. Garnish with rosemary sprig.

MINI APPLE PIES WITH CHEESE STRAW CRUST

MAKES 12 MINI (3-INCH) PIES OR 10 (4-INCH) PIES

When we were recipe testing this dessert for the opening of Fins, I made cheese straws for a garnish and my business partner, Gary, asked, "Why don't you make the top crust out of that dough?" It made sense—apples and cheese are a great combo—and it's been a customer favorite ever since.

I love freshly baked pie, so we came up with this method of making personal-size pies so there are never leftovers to be reheated. The cooked and cooled filling is preshrunk so you don't get the gap between filling and crust the way you do with the conventional method, making room for more apples, and less air!

This quantity will also make 1 (9- or 10-inch) single pie, using a half recipe of the Short Dough for the bottom crust and 1 recipe of the Cheese Straw Dough for the top. Allow an extra 5 or 10 minutes baking time. Or make bite-size pies for an hors d'oeuvre. The smaller the pie, the higher the ratio of dough to filling and the more savory it will be.

Special equipment: 12-cup (3-inch) standard muffin tin or 10 individual 4-inch tins; 2 biscuit or cookie cutters—one the diameter of the tin and the other slightly larger; rolling pin; parchment paper

FILLING

½ cup sugar

½ cup packed brown sugar

2 tablespoons salted butter

6 tablespoons water, divided

¼ cup heavy cream

1 ½ teaspoons fresh lemon juice

1 ½ teaspoons ground cinnamon

½ teaspoon ground nutmeg

Dash of kosher salt

3 pounds (9 medium) Granny Smith apples, peeled and sliced

2 tablespoons all-purpose flour

CRUSTS

Short Dough (page 204) for two 10-inch single crusts

½ recipe Cheese Straw Dough (page 205)

Vegetable oil spray

All-purpose flour for rolling

1 egg, beaten with 1 tablespoon water

To make the filling, place the sugars, butter, and 2 tablespoons water in a medium, heavy-bottom pot over medium heat; cook until the temperature reaches 275 degrees F on a candy thermometer.

Stir in the cream, and then add the lemon juice, cinnamon, nutmeg, and salt. Return to a boil and add the apples. Cook until the apples are just tender, 5 to 10 minutes, then strain the mixture into a medium-size bowl. Return all the juice to the pot, and bring to a boil. Cook over high heat until reduced by half.

Whisk the flour and remaining water together until smooth, and then whisk vigorously into the boiling syrup. Strain again, if needed, to remove any lumps.

Return the apples to the mixture and transfer to a shallow pan to cool. Place in a covered container and refrigerate until ready to use, up to a week.

To assemble, remove the Short Dough and Cheese Straw Dough from the refrigerator and let soften slightly, about 20 minutes. Spray muffin tin with vegetable oil spray.

Lightly flour a clean surface and roll 2 discs of Short Dough to about ¼-inch thickness, giving the dough a turn and dusting underneath with flour as you turn. With a floured cutter slightly wider than the tins (the rim of a glass will also work), cut 6 rounds from each disc of dough. Press the crusts into the tins, overlapping the edge by at least ½ inch. Fill each crust with the cooled apple filling, mounding it up in the center; refrigerate.

Place 1 disc of Cheese Straw Dough between 2 sheets of parchment paper (or plastic wrap) and roll to ¼-inch thickness. Remove the top sheet of parchment. With a floured cutter the width of the tin, cut 12 rounds of dough, using a knife to cut the parchment or plastic wrap underneath.

Take the pies out of the refrigerator, brush the edges with egg wash, and flip one of the cheese straw rounds over the filling then peel off the parchment. Fold and roll the edges up over the top crust. Cut 4 slits in the top of each. Refrigerate until ready to bake, or wrap airtight in plastic and freeze for up to 2 months.

If pies are frozen, let thaw in the refrigerator overnight or on the counter for an hour or two. Set a rack on the bottom shelf of the oven and heat to 400 degrees F. If using individual tins, place them in a large pan.

Place the tin in the hot oven and bake until browned and bubbling, 25 to 30 minutes.

Cool completely in the pan, about 30 minutes. Carefully run a knife around the edges to loosen the pies and remove the pies from their cups. Serve warm, with ice cream.

SHORT DOUGH

MAKES ENOUGH PASTRY FOR 2 (10-INCH) SINGLE-CRUST OR 1 DOUBLE-CRUST PIE, 12 (3-INCH OR 4-INCH) PIES, OR 24 MINI (2-INCH) PIES

This may seem like an unusually wet dough, but it makes a superior flaky crust. Work quickly in a cool place and dust the board with flour often, giving the crust a turn as you roll it. If it becomes too soft or the butter starts to break out of the dough, just return it to the refrigerator for a few minutes.

3 cups minus 2 tablespoons soft all-purpose flour, plus extra flour for dusting

¼ pound (½ cup) cold lard

¼ pound (1 stick) cold salted butter, cut in ¼-inch dice

½ cup ice cold water

Place the measured flour into a large mixing bowl and cut in the lard with a pastry blender or two forks. Or crumble the bits up to make coarse crumbs with your fingers, taking care not to over-handle. When the lard is mixed in, add the butter and incorporate until the small bits are the size of peas. This is a rich mixture and you'll probably need your pastry blender or forks to blend.

Stir in the ice water. It will appear very wet, but will thicken slightly as the water is absorbed into the flour. Divide this dough into 2 equal parts and roll in flour. Wrap each ball in plastic wrap and flatten into a disk. Refrigerate for at least 6 hours before rolling. Freezes well for two months or longer. Thaw in the refrigerator before using.

CHEESE STRAW DOUGH

MAKES 1 POUND DOUGH, OR 60 TO 72 CHEESE STRAWS OR COINS

Cheese straws are a staple snack at Southern cocktail parties: rich and crunchy with just a hint of heat from the cayenne pepper. The most common shape is made with room-temperature dough piped out with a big star tip, but I like half-dollar-size rounds with a pecan half pressed into the top. It also makes a great pie crust.

⅓ cup (5 tablespoons plus 1 teaspoon) salted butter, softened

½ pound grated sharp cheddar cheese

1 ½ ounces (½ cup) grated Parmesan cheese

1 cup all-purpose flour

⅛ teaspoon kosher salt

Pinch of cayenne pepper

Place the butter in a mixing bowl fitted with a paddle attachment. Cream the butter on medium speed until smooth, and then blend in the cheeses.

Blend in the dry ingredients on low speed until a soft dough is formed. (Since it has almost no liquid to develop gluten, it can be worked more than the Short Dough.) Form into a ball and wrap in plastic wrap. Chill at least 1 hour before using, or freeze for up to 2 months. Thaw in the refrigerator before using.

To make cheese straws or coins: Preheat oven to 325 F degrees. Place room-temperature dough in a cookie press fitted with a large star tip and press out onto parchment-lined baking sheets. Break into 2- or 3-inch pieces. Or roll the dough into long ropes about 1 inch in diameter, wrap in plastic wrap and refrigerate for at least 1 hour. Slice in ¼ inch-thick pieces, and place on the parchment. If desired, press a pecan half into each. Bake until lightly browned on the bottom, about 20 to 25 minutes. They should be a little soft when removed from the oven and will harden as they cool.

GW FINS BREAD PUDDING

MAKES 12 SERVINGS

Practically every New Orleans restaurant brags about their signature bread pudding recipe, and Fins is no different. Ours stands out because it's baked in caramel-lined individual custard cups like a flan. The caramel, the dark chocolate chunks, and the toasted pecans balance the sweetness of the white chocolate custard base. We use Leidenheimer's, the locally made bread long used for the city's po' boys, but any French bread will be good.

CROUTONS
½ pound French bread

CUSTARD
2 cups heavy cream

2 cups milk

¼ pound (1 stick) salted butter

1 cup sugar, divided

8 ounces white chocolate (Lindt or Callebaut brand), cut in ¼-inch chunks

9 large eggs

1 ½ teaspoons vanilla extract

2 ½ ounces bittersweet dark chocolate, cut in ¼-inch chunks

½ cup pecan pieces, lightly toasted

CARAMEL
10 tablespoons water, divided

1 cup sugar

Vegetable oil spray

CROUTONS Preheat the oven to 200 degrees F. Slice the bread in 1-inch cubes, spread out on a baking sheet, and bake until a crouton crumbles when pressed between your thumb and forefinger—it should be completely dry. Let cool.

CUSTARD Place the cream, milk, butter, and ½ cup of the sugar in a heavy-bottom saucepan and bring to a simmer. Remove from heat and add the white chocolate. Stir until melted.

Beat together the eggs, the remaining sugar, and the vanilla extract in a large bowl. Whisk in the hot cream mixture. Place in a shallow pan and refrigerate until cold. When the custard is cooled to 45 degrees F or so, add the croutons, the dark chocolate, and toasted pecans. Refrigerate. (This can be made the day before.)

Preheat the oven to 325 degrees F.

CARAMEL Put 4 tablespoons of water in a small, heavy saucepan and bring to a boil. Add sugar all at once. Continue to cook, without stirring, on high heat until the sugar is medium brown, about 325 degrees F on a candy thermometer. Remove from heat and gradually stir in the remaining water.

Spray 12 (6- to 8-ounce) ramekins (or a 9 x 13-inch baking dish) with vegetable oil spray. Pour the caramel into the bottom of the dishes (about 2 tablespoons each for individual cups) and swirl to evenly coat. Fill to the top with the bread pudding mixture and set the dish(es) in a larger container filled with a few inches of water. Bake in a water bath in the preheated oven for about 45 minutes for individual cups, and 50 to 60 minutes for single dish, or until an interior temperature of 170 degrees is reached on a candy thermometer.

Serve warm.

PONCHATOULA STRAWBERRY SHORTCAKES

8 OR 9 SHORTCAKES

Each April since 1972, the small town of Ponchatoula, north of New Orleans near Hammond, hosts a festival that draws about 300,000 people to celebrate the homegrown strawberries they're known for. They have strawberry and jambalaya cook-offs, and serve strawberries in everything from daiquiris to beignets to shortcake. We do our own shortcake when strawberries are in season, with a buttery, sugar-crusted biscuit base with a hint of orange zest and orange blossom water, topped with mascarpone-enriched whipped cream.

SHORTCAKE

2 ½ cups self-rising flour, plus 1 tablespoon for dusting (Martha White or White Lily), sifted (measure before sifting)

4 tablespoons cold salted butter

1 ounce (¼ cup) finely chopped, toasted pecans

1 ¼ cups heavy cream

½ orange, zested

½ teaspoon orange blossom water

1 egg

1 tablespoon water

¼ cup sugar

STRAWBERRIES AND CREAM

3 pints washed and sliced strawberries

1 ¼ cups sugar, divided

2 tablespoons Grand Marnier (optional)

1 pint heavy cream

¼ cup mascarpone cheese

½ teaspoon orange blossom water

SHORTCAKE Preheat oven to 400 degrees F. Place flour in a large bowl. Cut the butter into pea-size pieces and mix it in the flour. Add the pecans. Pour the cream in a medium bowl and stir in the zest and orange blossom water. Pour the mixture all at once into the flour mixture. Stir to form a soft dough, taking care not to overmix.

Place the dough on a floured surface and pat out to a 1 ½-inch-thick rectangle. Fold over, making a single turn and shaping the dough with your hands—not a rolling pin.

Let the dough rest, covered with a cloth, for 5 minutes and then pat out again to about 1 ½-inch thickness, fold over, and give it a second turn. Pat out the dough into a 7 x 12-inch rectangle about ¾ inch thick. Cut out with a large (3-inch) biscuit cutter. Gather up scraps, gently pat out and cut, until all the dough is used.

Beat egg with water to form an egg wash. Brush the tops of each round with the wash and invert in the ¼ cup sugar. Place sugar side up on a baking sheet lined with parchment paper and score the tops with a razor blade in a crosshatch pattern. Bake for 15 to 18 minutes, or until golden.

STRAWBERRIES AND CREAM Place the berries in a bowl with 1 cup sugar and Grand Marnier, if using; stir and set aside. Place the cream and remaining sugar in a mixing bowl and beat until half-whipped. Add the mascarpone and orange blossom water and beat just until soft peaks form. (Be careful not to overbeat the mascarpone or it may break.)

To serve, place each biscuit on a plate, cut in half, spoon some of the berries and cream over bottom halves, cover with top half of biscuit and spoon on more berries and cream if desired.

MAPLE SYRUP AND BOURBON PRALINES

MAKES 42 TO 48 PRALINES

Pecan pralines (PRAW-lenes, not PRAY-lenes contrary to what some folks may tell you) are everywhere in New Orleans, but not like my mom's. She made pralines every year for Christmas, and that's the only time of year I got to eat them as a kid. She made hers with evaporated milk and a little imitation maple extract and I loved them. I never knew anything about other kinds, and when I started making candy I wanted that flavor but without the extract.

2 cups pecan halves or pieces

¾ cup heavy cream

1 cup sugar

1 cup packed brown sugar

1 cup dark maple syrup

3 tablespoons corn syrup

1 tablespoon bourbon

1 ½ teaspoons vanilla extract

Line 2 baking sheets with parchment paper. Preheat oven to 300 degrees F. Spread the pecans on a baking sheet and lightly toast in the oven about 4 minutes, or just until hot.

Put the cream, sugars, and syrups into a heavy saucepan and cook on medium-high heat until the candy gets to 242 degrees F on a candy thermometer. It should go fairly quickly with this amount of ingredients, about 10 minutes or less. (If you don't have a thermometer, put a small spoonful of the hot mixture into a bowl of ice water. If it hardens to the point that you can form a soft ball with your fingers, it is ready. If it just dissolves, it's not ready and you need to continue cooking. Visually the candy will thicken as the liquid is cooked out and this will also give you a clue.)

At soft-ball stage, turn off the heat and add the bourbon and vanilla and then stir in the still-warm pecans.

Stir about 5 minutes, until it thickens slightly. When you think they're ready, spoon a little of the mixture onto a clean surface. If it hardens enough to pick up after a couple of minutes, it's ready. If not, keep stirring.

Use the two spoons method to form pralines. Scoop with one spoon and scrape out with the other onto the parchment-lined baking sheets to form pralines about the size of a half-dollar. If the mixture hardens in the pan so much it can't be spooned out, return the pan to low heat to remelt it a bit.

When they're hardened, wrap individually in plastic wrap and try not to eat too many.

FLYNN FAMILY TOM THUMB BARS

MAKES 30 BARS

My mom still bakes a big assortment of Christmas goodies—different fudges, cookies, brownies, and pralines—but my all-time favorite since I was little are these coconut bar cookies. She sent me two pans for last Christmas. One was supposed to be for my son, but I'm afraid I ate both of them.

CRUST

½ cup lard
½ cup salted butter, softened
1 teaspoon kosher salt
1 cup packed brown sugar
2 cups all-purpose flour
1 teaspoon vanilla
Vegetable oil spray

FILLING

2 cups packed brown sugar
2 teaspoons vanilla extract
4 eggs, beaten
4 tablespoons all-purpose flour
1 teaspoon baking powder
½ teaspoon kosher salt
3 cups sweetened shredded coconut
2 cups roughly chopped pecans

CRUST Preheat oven to 350 degrees F. With a mixer, beat lard, butter, salt, and brown sugar at medium-high speed until light and fluffy. Add flour and vanilla and mix on low speed just until combined.

Spray an 11 x 17-inch baking pan with vegetable oil spray and press the crust mixture into the pan. Bake 15 minutes, until lightly browned. Cool to room temperature.

FILLING Preheat (or lower the oven heat) to 325 degrees F. In a large bowl mix brown sugar, vanilla, eggs, flour, baking powder, and salt. Stir in coconut and pecans until well-combined.

Spread the coconut mixture evenly over the cooled crust and bake until golden brown, about 20 minutes. Cool and cut into bars.

GLOSSARY OF FINFISH

Finfish identification is confusing. Besides the widespread practice of actual mislabeling, there are regional and market names. To get some idea of the sheer number of edible finfish in the world, go to fishbase.org, which lists 34,000 species by their Latin name, as well as by their country and ecosystem. There are many times that number of names for this staggering amount of species. If you buy domestically harvested fish, you'll more readily believe, as I do, that every variety is good to eat if fresh and properly prepared.

This guide includes finfish native to the Gulf, plus some widely available species from other waters that are mentioned in this book and can be used interchangeably in many of these recipes.

For more detailed profiles, as well as information related to sustainability and availability, consult the National Oceanic and Atmospheric Administration (NOAA) Fisheries' guide to sustainable seafood: https://www.fishwatch.gov./

Ahi tuna: A term that gets tossed around, which just means tuna in Hawaiian. It can refer to bigeye or yellowfin tuna. See Yellowfin Tuna.

Amberjack: A 10- to 15-pound, mild-flavored, extra-lean fish that can be delicious if cooked correctly, but dry and unappetizing if overcooked. Smaller ones are preferable. Look for thick portions that can be steak-cut and aim on cooking them just past medium. Bar jack, yellowtail jack, and rainbow runner are also in this family and cook up similarly.

Arctic char: Char is in the salmonid family and is usually farm-raised. Depending on the source and feed, it's usually medium-fat and has a flavor that falls between freshwater trout and lean salmon. It's best sautéed quickly and served with a little brown butter and lemon.

Barracuda: A firm-textured, moderately fat fish. It is widely available in the Gulf of Mexico but not usually marketed. Its raw flesh, like that of mackerel, is light gray, but turns white when cooked. I prefer both these fish just past medium and they are great braised or on the grill.

Bass, large or smallmouth: This fish varies in flavor depending on the water it's fished from. Small pond bass sometimes have a grassy flavor and those I cold smoke or grill whole. Bass from larger or faster-moving bodies of water are good sautéed or fried but I still remove the skin.

Bass, sea (aka black sea bass): A medium-fat, 1- to 3-pound fish with firm flesh and edible skin that's great grilled or roasted whole.

Bigeye Tuna: often called ahi tuna, with a fat content in between yellowfin and bluefin.

Black cod (aka Sablefish): A full-fat, cold-water fish great for smoking. Also good in a hot and sour stock.

Bluefin tuna: The largest of the tunas weighing 1,000 pounds or more, this relatively fatty fish is the most prized of the tunas and often served as sushi and sashimi. Its numbers are declining due to its popularity and availability is sporadic.

Bluefish: A full-flavored, fine-textured fish found on the Atlantic and Gulf coasts with edible skin that requires gentle handling due to its soft flesh and high fat content. Great smoked or grilled, preferably the same day it was landed.

Bonito: The smallest and strongest-flavored of the tunas, weighing 25 pounds or less.

Branzino: A medium fat fish almost always farm-raised, primarily in Greece or Cyprus. Roast or grill whole, or sauté skin-on fillets.

Bream (aka bluegill, sunfish): A small freshwater fish (one pound would be huge); probably the first one you ever caught if you fished in a pond with a bobber and a worm. Scale, pan-fry, and eat. (See Sunfish.)

Catfish: Farmed channel catfish is the variety most available. Buy American! Avoid Basa and Swai, both of which are raised under questionable conditions. If wild is available, go for that. It is versatile, but best with seasoned corn flour and deep fried.

Chilean sea bass: A deep water and slow-growing fish, this South American and Antarctic species of cod icefish was better known as Patagonian toothfish until the 1970s when a fish wholesaler thought it would sell better if this flaky, white-fleshed delicacy had a more appetizing name. The marketing strategy worked. It's been overfished by international fleets, often in unsustainable waters, and supplies are much more limited.

Cobia: A medium-fat Gulf game fish. It is firmer than swordfish, with a sweet flavor and moderate fat content. It can be sautéed, but grills or blackens wonderfully. It's also good raw. There are also some farmed varieties available that are perfectly acceptable if domestic isn't available. Ocean Blue, a deep-water farm off Costa Rica, is one.

Cod: This lean, medium-firm fish with snow-white flesh, a large flake, and mild flavor is native to the Atlantic and Pacific Oceans. Versatile and widely available, it can substitute for grouper, halibut, sea bass, red snapper, and many other fish.

Crappie: Called Sac-a-lait in South Louisiana, these members of the sunfish family are a little fuller flavored than bream and usually a lot bigger.

Daurade (aka dorade, sea bream, orate): A small, buttery, silver-skinned fish from Mediterranean and North Atlantic waters. Ideal for grilling and in fish soups.

Dorado: Another term for mahi mahi; means "golden" in Spanish. This bright color is a quality indicator when shopping. The more golden the color, the fresher the fish.

Drum, black: A versatile low-fat fish great for sautéing or crusting. The smaller fish under 6 pounds are preferred.

Drum, red: Firm, moist, and sweet, this is the famous redfish popularized by Paul Prudhomme in the 80s. Most are now farm-raised in Texas, but there are landings off the Carolina coast and Mississippi. There is no commercial redfish fishery in Louisiana. Good blackened, grilled, sautéed, or on the half shell.

Flounder: This lean, flat-shaped, Gulf fish is popular for its mild flavor and delicate, flaky texture. Great for sautéing, or scaling and stuffing whole.

Grouper: The largest of the sea bass family, with more than 100 species, ranging from 9 inches to 9 feet in size. Plentiful in the Gulf and Atlantic, most grow to 5 to 15 pounds, and are sold whole and as fillets and steaks. Its meat is lean and firm, and takes well to grilling, blackening, roasting, and frying. The skin has a strong taste and should be removed before cooking. Warsaw, red, black, scamp, yellow edge, and gag are some of the varieties we use.

Haddock: A cousin to cod, this white-fleshed, low-fat fish can be good in a variety of preparations if you live in New England where there aren't better options.

Halibut: probably the mildest tasting saltwater fish. It is landed in Alaska starting in April and off the North Atlantic coast most of the rest of the year. It is farmed in Europe, but I prefer the flavor of wild ones. In my opinion Alaskan is superior to all others. At Fins, we buy a lot of this for Chef Mike's famous Scalibut.

Hogfish: Also called hog snapper. (See snapper.)

Jolthead porgy: Abundant in the northern Gulf of Mexico, this medium-fatty Atlantic fish typically swims in clear, shallow water, feeding on crabs and mollusks. Its delicate white flesh works well in a variety of dishes from crudo to sautés.

Lionfish: This invasive species native to the Pacific were introduced to the Gulf by accidental release. Very mild and tender, low in fat, and very good to eat. They make wonderful ceviche, are good tempura-fried, and work well for a whole fried or roasted presentation.

Lookdown: A low-fat fish that schools on the Louisiana oil rigs. Delicious scaled and roasted or fried whole.

Mackerel: Both King and its often-denigrated cousin Spanish mackerel are medium-fat and grill or blacken well. Also good smoked.

Mahi mahi (aka dorado and dolphinfish): A slightly sweet, firm, medium-fat fish that can be cooked in any preparation. Similar to grouper and snapper. Peak season is May-June.

Mako: Type of shark reminiscent of swordfish and can be prepared accordingly.

Monkfish: The skinned, deboned tails benefit from searing and braising. The meat is very dense and meaty and pairs well in a dish with bacon and big flavors.

Mullet: This fish is rich with fat and good on the grill when it's impeccably fresh. It's called Biloxi bacon when it's smoked.

Ocean perch (aka rose fish): An all-purpose, mild, inexpensive fish plentiful in both the Atlantic and the Pacific. Usually sold as skin-on fillets. Good sautéed, deep-fried, and grilled. Often fished with a deep water trawl.

Orange roughy: A mild, white-fleshed, slow-growing fish from New Zealand similar to perch. Fished with a deep water trawl.

Pollack: A low to medium-fat member of the cod family that's been used to make surimi, imitation lobster and crab meat, in a variety of shapes, notably that of King crab legs.

Pompano: Gulf pompano is cream-colored and very firm, and it's loaded with sweet, delicious fat (not to be confused with African pompano which is much larger and very lean). It doesn't appear on the market often—it usually shows up in late summer and sometimes in December as well.

Porgy (aka sea bream): See Jolthead porgy.

Puppy drum: a market term for a small drum.

Redfish: See Red drum.

Sac-a-lait: See Crappie.

Salmon: A medium to fatty, cold-water fish that is anadromous, meaning they spawn in fresh water before winding up at sea. Farmed Atlantic salmon are available year-round; the Pacific wild salmon season runs June to September. Takes well to poaching, roasting, braising, and blackening. Responsibly farmed salmon can be eaten raw.

Scrod—A small cod or haddock. A marketing term.

Sea bream: See Porgy.

Shark: A vital part of the ocean ecosystem, this family of fish, which includes rays, secretes urine through the skin so freshness is extremely important. Any hint of ammonia is an indicator to avoid this one. Shark fins are prized in Asian cultures where they're dried for soup. Finning sharks and discarding the rest of the animal is an abhorrent practice and while fins are harvested here, the rest of the meat must, by law, be brought in to the dock with them. Here, the rest of the meat is often available on the domestic market, often as steaks. (See Mako.)

Sheepshead (aka baitstealer, convict): A relative of sea bream with black horizontal stripes (hence the name convict) and human-like teeth, it's one ugly fish. But with a diet of mostly shellfish, it has a sweet shellfish-like flavor and moist, firm flesh that lends itself well to sautéing, pan-frying, grilling, etc.

Snapper, American Red: A lean, sweet, tender, and firm-textured fish with a delicious, edible skin. Great for ceviche and crudo, but takes to just about any cooking technique. Mangrove, b-liner, hog, and yellowtail snapper are also great but Mangrove needs to be served right out of the water, and you should shave off the darker flesh under the skin and the bloodline.

Sole, Dover: A European flatfish with mild, buttery flavor and firm, fine texture that makes it a great choice for simple sautés with light butter sauces. Various flounders are often marketed as sole.

Spadefish: This underutilized Gulf game fish that looks like a giant angel fish feeds on jellyfish and other small marine animals and is great for eating grilled, smoked, and pan-fried. It does have darker flesh under the skin that can be shaved off after skinning if it bothers you.

Skate: A close cousin of the stingray, and is somewhat similar in appearance and certainly in flavor. Good skinned and sautéed with brown butter or cut in pieces with the bones intact and braised.

Stingray: See Skate.

Striped bass: A popular sport fish all along the Atlantic coast. Meaty and somewhat fat, stripers can be scaled and sautéed skin on, or steamed and grilled. The bloodline, which many people find objectionable in any fish, is delicious in a striped bass.

Swordfish: A meaty, moderately fat sport fish with a firmness that makes it a good steak substitute. Great for braising, roasting, grilling, and blackening.

Sunfish: A family of freshwater fish related to perch populous through the temperate United States. Includes bluegill, crappie, and bream.

Tilapia (aka St. Peter's Fish): A farm-raised, freshwater fish widely available everywhere, both fresh and frozen, and commonly used in any preparation calling for lean, mild-flavored fillets. I don't care for the way it's raised or its flavor, and therefore don't recommend it, especially since there is always something better in the case or freezer.

Tilefish: Extra-lean, firm, white meat that can be substituted for grouper or snapper.

Triggerfish: A brightly colored fish landed mainly in the Gulf states. They are notoriously hard to fillet due to their tough, thick skin, but worth the trouble. They have a dense meat that works equally well grilled or sautéed, which usually isn't the case with such a lean fish. They are also mean little bastards that can bite through a 3mm wetsuit if aggravated or not thoroughly dispatched.

Tripletail: Sweet, white, flaky meat similar to grouper. Found inshore, near-shore, off-shore.

Trout, speckled: Spotted sea trout is the favorite of most Louisiana anglers where we have generous catch limits and a large supply to fish from. It is a fine fish for a quick sauté and great deep fried if you cook it the same day you catch it.

Trout, rainbow: Delicately flavored freshwater fish. Unless you catch it yourself it is going to be farmed.

Tuna: A saltwater fish with species that range in size from 4 to over 1,500 pounds. Available fresh in better markets, and is a popular sport fish. Yellowfin is the most common here in Louisiana. The occasional bigeye and fatty bluefin (which is a tightly controlled bycatch) sometimes show up on the lines in the early spring. Though naturally red, yellowfin tuna steaks sold in grocery fish cases, sometimes in cryovac-sealed portions, often have an unnatural magenta color because they've been treated with carbon monoxide (sometimes marketed as 'colorless wood smoke') to "set" the color. The FDA says it's safe, but some countries ban the practice for fear it could be used to mask fish that's old or even spoiled. I find that tuna treated this way has a washed-out flavor and texture, and recommend seeking out all-natural tuna that has not been treated with this process. (see Ahi Tuna, Bigeye Tuna, Bluefin Tuna, Yellowfin Tuna.)

Turbot: A large, lean flatfish similar to halibut. Those caught off European coasts are superior to domestic varieties.

Wahoo: A very lean member of the mackerel family. Best prepared rare or it is unpleasantly dry.

Walleye: A freshwater member of the pike family Yankees swear by, and for good reason. It is firm and tasty, and is best sautéed. They do have a stubborn line of bones down the center of the fillet that need to be cut out to separate it.

Whitefish: A mild, fatty member of the salmon family that inhabits the eastern North Atlantic Ocean and northern Mediterranean. Commonly fried and battered for British fish and chips. Can also be poached, grilled, or roasted, and its roe is sometimes made into caviar.

Whiting: A small, lean fish. It has a flaky texture related to cod.

Yellowfin Tuna: Usually the leanest of the commercially available tunas, but in the colder months it can develop some nice fat. Our restaurant competes with New Orleans' sushi bars for "Number One" yellowfin tuna—the best of this catch. Great for searing steaks, cutting in chunks and poaching, scraping for tartare, and shaved for crudo. "Number one" is a rather loose term, depending on the market—it really is a sliding scale and just means it's the best available. And it is going to be the most expensive by far.

INDEX

METRIC CONVERSION CHART

VOLUME MEASUREMENTS		WEIGHT MEASUREMENTS		TEMPERATURE CONVERSION	
U.S.	Metric	U.S.	Metric	Fahrenheit	Celsius
1 teaspoon	5 ml	½ ounce	15 g	250	120
1 tablespoon	15 ml	1 ounce	30 g	300	150
¼ cup	60 ml	3 ounces	90 g	325	160
⅓ cup	75 ml	4 ounces	115 g	350	180
½ cup	125 ml	8 ounces	225 g	375	190
⅔ cup	150 ml	12 ounces	350 g	400	200
¾ cup	175 ml	1 pound	450 g	425	220
1 cup	250 ml	2 ¼ pounds	1 kg	450	230

ACKNOWLEDGMENTS

FROM TENNEY FLYNN TO:

Michelle Branson and the support staff at Gibbs Smith, who understood what I set out to accomplish and helped me create the book I was hoping for.

Danny Lee, for his patience and attention to detail with two weeks of photo shooting. I've known him since he started packing a camera in grade school.

Amy Hughes, our agent, for calming storms and running interference.

My co-writer, Susan Puckett, who has continually gone above and beyond, and who is now a much better fish cook.

Patrice Jinkens, for her recipe testing help, and Terrance Green, Fins' longtime manager, for his wine-matching skills.

Pano Karatassos and Paul Albrecht, who took a chance on a "country boy" and gave me the opportunity to work with great fish.

Captain C.T. Williams of the Big Fish show, for taking me fishing for the last twenty-five years; and the fishermen, shrimpers, crabbers, and wholesalers who provide us with great Gulf products to work with every day.

My Asian influences, Kiku Somen, Phuong Lan, and Thuan Vuong, who opened up a new world of flavor to me.

Debbie Rosen, our tireless publicist who has been with us since the restaurant opened.

Executive chef Mike Nelson; sous chefs Tim Lane, Nelson Chang, and Steven Fazande; and all the hardworking staff at GW Fins.

Lee Froelich, the editor who convinced me I had some stories to tell; and my diving buddy Colleen Rush, who worked with me to sit my ass down and write.

FROM SUSAN PUCKETT TO:

The aforementioned Debbie Rosen, Amy Hughes, Michelle Branson, and the Gibbs Smith team for helping us put together the bazillion moving parts and pieces of this puzzle.

My cousin Lisa Sinders, for graciously putting me up and carting me around New Orleans during the research.

My husband Ralph Ellis, for his editing, dishwashing, and counseling services; and my mom Nancy Puckett, whose moral support was always just a phone call away.

My journalist friends Deborah Geering, Jim Auchmutey, Susan Percy, and Jerry Sealy, who gave valuable feedback and recipe-testing help; and Seth Freedman and David Ellis, for lending their chef's and fisherman's perspectives respectively.

And most of all, Tenney Flynn, for bringing me along on this ride and opening my eyes to a world of seafood more fascinating and flavorful than I ever imagined.

ABOUT US

Tenney Flynn grew up cooking in his father's Georgia restaurant. Since opening GW Fins with Gary Wollerman in 2001, he has twice been named *New Orleans Magazine's* Chef of the Year. A certified diver and spear fisher, he chairs the Audubon Nature Institute's Gulf for Lasting Fisheries (G.U.L.F.) Chefs Council.

Susan Puckett, the former food editor of the *Atlanta Journal-Constitution*, has been nominated for two James Beard Foundation awards and has written or collaborated on a dozen cookbooks. Her work has also appeared in *Eating Well, National Geographic Traveler,* and *Atlanta* magazine.